introduction to MODERN microECONOMICS

introduction to MODERN microECONOMICS

by Kelvin Lancaster
Columbia University
New York City

RAND McNALLY INTERNATIONAL COMPANY • Chicago

Printed in the United States of America

Current printing   (last digit)
15   14   13   12   11   10   9   8   7   6   5   4   3   2

Preface

This book is not a rehash of the many existing books on price theory and microeconomics. It is an attempt to give a new *elementary* account of the principles of microeconomics that is consistent with the content of modern advanced microeconomics. In teaching microeconomics at all levels, from first year undergraduate to the most advanced graduate, the author has been aware that traditional elementary price theory texts are at least a generation behind advanced theory in content and approach.

As a matter of historical fact, economic analysis has become steadily more advanced in terms of the analytical techniques used. Thus the older analyses are the more "elementary" in terms of technique, and tend to be handed on from author to author in the writing of the simpler texts. The result is that these texts contain many pieces of analysis that are known to be irrelevant, trivial, and sometimes just wrong, from the viewpoint of modern advanced theory. In writing this book, the author has discarded some things that were merely excess baggage, and some that were garbage.

This does not mean that this book is particularly revolutionary, that it reaches conclusions that differ greatly from those of existing texts, or that it is, from the traditionalist's point of view, full of "sin." It means differences in analytical approach (a more "activity analysis" approach to production, for example), a more honest statement of those problems the economist has not yet solved (intertemporal choice, for example), and more emphasis on discontinuous relationships and corner solutions.

There is no attempt in this book to give an elementary account of the *methods* of modern advanced theory. These methods are, of course, mathematical—and use mathematical techniques beyond the elementary calculus that once used to be considered the sign of "mathematical" economics. The book uses only the simplest diagrammatic, arithmetical, and occasionally the most simple algebraic, methods. Some mathematical notes are given at the end for the growing number of readers who are conversant with elementary calculus, but these are in no way necessary for the main text.

Kelvin Lancaster
Columbia University

TABLE OF CONTENTS

PREFACE   v

1. Introduction   1

2. Supply and Demand   5

2.1 General observations   2.2 Factors influencing supply and demand
2.3 Supply and demand curves   2.4 Elements of supply and demand analysis   2.5 Elasticity as a descriptive tool   2.6 Boundary equilibrium
2.7 Point supply   Further reading and exercises

3. The Market   35

3.1 The market   3.2 An ideal market   3.3 Traders as a computer
3.4 Market dynamics   3.5 Arbitrage   3.6 Speculation   3.7 Related
markets

4. Production   59

4.1 What we mean by production   4.2 Production processes   4.3 Technology and technical efficiency   4.4 Production under simple conditions
4.5 Properties of isoquants   4.6 Substitution among inputs   4.7 The production function   4.8 Returns to scale   4.9 Returns to a variable input–1
4.10 Returns to a variable input–2   4.11 Indivisibilities   Exercises

5. Costs   93

5.1 The nature of costs   5.2 Production costs   5.3 Isocost curves
5.4 Optimum input proportions   5.5 "Long-run" cost curves   5.6 Costs
with a limited input   5.7 Costs with a minimum outlay   5.8 Total, marginal and average curves   5.9 U-shaped cost curves   5.10 Indivisibilities
and economies of scale   5.11 Costs of fixed capital   Further reading
and exercises

Contents

6. Firms 137

6.1 The firm and its decisions   6.2 Revenue   6.3 Cost curves   6.4 The
role of financing   6.5 The profit maximizing output   6.6 Perfect competition   6.7 Monopoly   6.8 Competition versus monopoly   6.9 Oligopoly   6.10 The firm's demand for inputs   6.11 The giant corporation
Further reading and exercises

7. Consumers 181

7.1 Who are the consumers?   7.2 Goods and consumers   7.3 Preference
and choice   7.4 Choice with a budget constraint   7.5 Utility   7.6 Income changes   7.7 Substitution   7.8 Demand theory   7.9 The labor-
leisure choice   7.10 Bargaining and exchange   7.11 New and differentiated goods

8. Incomes 223

8.1 Distribution   8.2 Wages   8.3 Other factor payments   8.4 Imperfectly competitive factor markets

9. The Economy as a System 237

9.1 Putting the pieces together   9.2 General equilibrium   9.3 Information
and decentralization   9.4 Stability and attainment of competitive equilibrium
9.5 Simplified models of the economy   9.6 The two-good two-factor
economy

10. Welfare and Public Policy 259

10.1 Welfare   10.2 Efficient allocation   10.3 The optimal composition
of output   10.4 Efficiency and competition   10.5 Interpretation and policy implications   Further reading

11. Time, Change, and Uncertainty 279

11.1 Limitations of static models   11.2 Consumers' intertemporal decisions
11.3 Intertemporal decisions by firms   11.4 Intertemporal welfare and
growth policy   11.5 Money

MATHEMATICAL NOTES 300

ANSWERS TO EXERCISES 318

INDEX 321

CHAPTER 1

INTRODUCTION

The student of economics comes early across a distinction between *microeconomics* and *macroeconomics*. Since this is a book about microeconomics, it seems desirable to discuss the relationship between these two brands of economics, and the relationship of both to economics generally.

Microeconomics is the heir of price theory (and courses and texts in this general area are often so called), which used to be simply economics. The term "macroeconomics" developed originally to describe the preoccupations of those economists concerned with working on developments of the ideas of Keynes concerning the aggregate level of activity of the economy. In terms of their Greek roots, "micro" implies a close-up look at small objects, "macro" a broader, less magnified, view over a larger field.

The distinction used to be described as that between a detailed study of the behavior of individual decision-makers in the economy (microeconomics) and the behavior of the broad aggregates ("national income," "aggregate consumption," and so on), the latter being macroeconomics. Although there remains some truth in this simple distinction, it is no longer entirely valid. Many macroeconomists consider some parts of the economy, such as the banking system and the money and securities markets, in far more detail than they are studied in microeconomics.

The economy is a highly complex system. In order to study it, some degree of simplification is necessary. The real distinction between microeconomics and macroeconomics lies in the type of simplifications that are made, and the particular aim of those simplifications.

1

Microeconomics remains primarily concerned about economies in general—it is descended from the intellectual tradition of the "principles" of economics, which are intended to be the principles underlying *all* economies *at all times*. Thus simplification in microeconomics will often be of the kind that rejects some special relationship that holds only for one time and one place, and concentrates on features common to many times and many places. Macroeconomics, on the other hand, descends directly from analysis designed to influence public policy at particular times and particular places—Keynes was concerned with unemployment in an advanced industrial country (Britain) during the thirties. Thus simplification in macroeconomics is likely to take an opposite course to simplification in microeconomics, rejecting general possibilities in favor of known behavior here and now.

The difference in outlook has made macroeconomics more empirically oriented than microeconomics. If it can be shown that consumers in the United States during the current decade behave in a certain way this is prime data for a macroeconomist interested in providing information for decisions on next year's economic policy. It may be of much less interest to a microeconomist concerned with the general principles of consumers' behavior *unless it seems to run contrary to his expectations based on his theory*. In other words, data are used in macroeconomics primarily for *predicting* the behavior of a particular economy at a particular time, in microeconomics for *testing* the generality of his theoretical apparatus. Even this distinction cannot always be made, however, since an incorrect prediction means the failure of a macroeconomic model to pass an essential test.

It should be made clear that *modern* microeconomics, like macroeconomics, is concerned with the economy *as a whole,* not just with the behavior of isolated components. Modern microeconomics is "general equilibrium" economics, as is macroeconomics. The general equilibrium approach has greatly changed the orientation of microeconomics. It is not the study of individual components (consumers, firms) *in themselves,* but of individual components *and how they fit together.* The claim of microeconomics to be an important intellectual system lies in its success in showing how individual components, each behaving in its own way, fit together into a complete system, and, further, that this system is optimal in a certain sense. The complete general equilibrium system, finally put together only in the fifties, is comparable with classical physics as an intellectual construct.

The early concern with prices in economics was heavily influenced by medieval traditions of thought which associated moral ideas with price. Even in the early twentieth century, some authors managed to attach some moral approbation to the idea that market price equated the quantity demand with the quantity supplied, especially in the case of the markets for factors. In general equilibrium economics, we examine a set of prices by investigating what would be changed in the economy as a whole if the prices were different. We may or may not reach conclusions concerning welfare.

Modern welfare economics, a direct outgrowth of general equilibrium analysis, leads to policy prescriptions. Unlike the policy prescriptions of macroeconomics, which will be typically of the kind that an increase of so many billions of dollars in government expenditure or taxes will, in the United States in a particular year, bring full employment without inflation, those of microeconomics are essentially *structural*. The typical prescription would be as to whether the whole structure of the United States economy was or was not optimal or efficient.

Since the simplifications of microeconomics are in the direction of taking the most general (or, if one prefers, abstract) view of the behavior of individual decision-makers in the economy we lose much detail. As a result, we obtain a good description of the behavior of any *individual* decision-maker (such as a particular firm) only by adding on the detail. Thus microeconomics provides only the merest skeleton on which to build a theory of the behavior of a complex firm, such as would be desired by a business economist. In spite of the name, therefore, microeconomics is not really concerned with the close-up study of *particular* components in an actual economy.

General equilibrium economics is, indeed, *equilibrium* economics. Microeconomics is primarily concerned with behavior at equilibrium (the idea of which is developed in the book), and economists have virtually no theory of how individual decision-makers behave out of equilibrium. Historically, the concentration on equilibrium behavior led economists to pretend that the economy was always in equilibrium, or would soon return there. Much of early macroeconomics was concerned with *disequilibrium*, most typically gross disequilibrium evidenced by large unemployment, and how to return to equilibrium. The serious study of *dynamic* microeconomics has barely commenced.

Another area of microeconomics that is almost undeveloped is that concerned with intertemporal decisions. The simple microeconomic model is "timeless" in the sense that choice over time is not fully integrated into the model.

Finally we should note that, although we speak of the *economy*, what we really have is a *society*. The "economy" is an abstraction from the society as a whole, in which we concentrate on certain aspects of behavior that are amenable to analysis by economists. There is much interaction between economic and other aspects of behavior, and the ultimate analysis would be able to handle these. For the time being they are mostly ignored.

Chapter 2 introduces the best known and most basic concepts and analyses in all economics.

CONTENTS

2.1 General Observations 5
2.2 Factors Influencing Supply and Demand 7
2.3 Supply and Demand Curves 11
2.4 Elements of Supply and Demand Analysis 16
2.5 Elasticity as a Descriptive Tool 20
2.6 Boundary Equilibrium 26
2.7 Point Supply 28
Further Reading and Exercises 31

CHAPTER 2

SUPPLY AND DEMAND

2.1 General Observations

If we were data collectors from the Department of Commerce and were sent to find out what happened in the market for some commodity, there are only two items of data that we could actually observe. We could note the price at which a transaction took place, and we could note the quantity of the produce involved in the transaction. Since every transaction involves both a buyer and a seller, we would necessarily conclude that the quantity bought was equal to the quantity sold.

There would be other data, not special to the particular market, that could also be noted, such as the total population, average incomes, time of year, prices in other markets. These data concerning the background against which the market operated can be referred to as the market *circumstances*.

Although the only *observable data* ("facts") of the market are its circumstances, the price, and the quantity actually changing hands, the economist's analysis of supply, demand, and the market (and thus ultimately of the whole working of the economic system) depends essentially on the following presumption concerning buyers and sellers:

Although all transactions that actually occur in the market take place under some given set of circumstances, and at some specific price, all buyers and sellers have alternative plans as to how they would act if the price and/or the market circumstances were different from those actually in effect.

5

Discovering the Plans. Since only one price and set of circumstances are in effect at any one time, only one of the alternative plans is ever observed in operation at any one time. However, if the circumstances vary enough from one market observation to another, we may be able to derive some information concerning the various alternatives, on the fundamental assumption that there is some basic consistency in the overall set of plans. In practice, the set of techniques known collectively as *econometrics*[1] may be used to make an exploration of this kind, an exploration that is more difficult and leads to more uncertain results than the reader may suppose.

To deduce something about plans from actual behavior, we normally must be sure that what people are doing is what they planned to do under these conditions. In the absence of coercion we can suppose that at least one party to a transaction is achieving his plan. We cannot always be sure that both parties are in this position. Suppose that we observe a transaction of 100 tons at $10 per ton. Can we be certain that the buyer would not have willingly taken 110 tons at that price, but that the seller planned to sell only 100 tons, and it was the seller's plan that was fulfilled? Or that the seller planned to sell 110 tons, but the buyer would take only 100? Or even that the transaction is a compromise in which neither the buyer nor the seller achieves his plan?

Market Equilibrium. In the absence of contrary evidence, economists will assume that observed behavior also represents planned behavior. We define the situation in which all parties to a market are able to behave in accordance with the plans relevant to the circumstances and the price as one of *market equilibrium.* That is, the market is in equilibrium under a given set of circumstances if, at the actual price ruling (which is the *equilibrium market price*), all buyers can buy what they plan to buy and all sellers can sell what they plan to sell.

We shall discuss problems relating to market disequilibrium later. For the time being we shall assume that all transactions *actually taking place* are equilibrium transactions.

---

[1] *Econometrics* is the study of the problems of measurement that arise in economics. These problems have some special characteristics, due to the fact that the economy is a system and all measurements are taken with the system operating as a whole. Many of these problems would not arise if parts of the economy could be isolated and experiments carried out. In principle, we could find out consumers' alternative plans by isolating them from the actual market, then seeing how they act when confronted by prices and incomes different from those actually in effect. In practice, we cannot do this. Even if we could, we might doubt whether human beings will behave the same way in experimental situations as they would do in ordinary life.

Quantities as Flows. At this stage we should note a simple but important point concerning the use of the term *quantity* in demand and supply analysis. Production and consumption of almost all commodities in economics take place continuously. To talk of the quantity produced or consumed of some commodity bought or sold in the United States is meaningless unless we specify the period of time with which we are concerned.

In some market situations, there is a definite *market period.* For example, if a market is held every week, we can refer to the quantity that buyers plan to purchase simply as so many tons or pounds, meaning that quantity for the weekly market. If there is no stated market period, as in the examples we shall discuss in the remainder of the chapter, then we should specify quantity as a *time rate,* that is, as so many tons per annum or per week.

Having made this point, we shall adopt the usual convention in economics of assuming that the length of time involved is considered to be part of the context and known to the reader and simply expresses quantities as "tons" or "units." The exception is when we use actual figures relating to the United States or some other economy, when all the relevant information, including the length of the period, needs to be specified.

2.2 Factors Influencing Supply and Demand

Much of basic microeconomic theory is at a level of simplification at which the examples used are, unfortunately but sometimes necessarily, entirely artificial. In the case of supply and demand, it would be a pity to indulge in unnecessary flight from reality, since suitable examples can be found which are based on the study of actual markets. For this reason we shall use as our example information derived from the study of the market for watermelons in the United States. The market for watermelons has no outstanding characteristics, and is of no great significance even in the farm sector of the economy, let alone in the economy as a whole. It is precisely these properties that make it a useful example.

By using the data for observed prices and quantities over many years, analysis by econometric techniques enables us to ascertain something of the way in which the plans of buyers and sellers are influenced by changes in market circumstances and market price.

The most important factors that would influence the planned behavior of buyers and sellers in the watermelon market are shown in Table 2.1. The table shows how a change in any one of three variables would affect planned behavior.

The first entry in the table shows that a 1 per cent *rise* in the farm wage rate would cause a *fall* of 0.3 per cent in the quantity farmers would

TABLE 2.1

Factors Influencing Demand and Supply
The Market for Watermelons in the United States

Variable (Only one variable is assumed to change at a time)	A 1 per cent increase in the variable given in the left-hand column would give rise to the following percentage changes in:	
	Annual quantity of watermelons farmers would plan to send to market	*Annual quantity of watermelons consumers would plan to buy at market*
Farm wage rate	—0.3	—
Average consumer income, per annum	—	1.4
Price of watermelons	0.3	—0.9

The information in this table is derived from studies of the watermelon market in the United States, over the period 1930–1951, by Suits and L'Esperance. [Suits, D. B., "An Econometric Model of the Watermelon Market," *Journal of Farm Economics,* Vol. 37, No. 2 (May 1955), pp. 237–51; and L'Esperance, W. L., "A Case Study in Prediction: the Market for Watermelons," *Econometrica,* Vol. 32, No. 1–2 (January–April 1964), pp. 163–73.]

plan to harvest and send to market, but would have no effect on the quantity consumers would plan to buy. On the other hand, a 1 per cent rise in the level of the average consumer income would cause a rise of 1.4 per cent in the quantity consumers would plan to buy, but would have no effect on the quantity farmers would plan to sell. Both the farm wage rate and the average consumer income are *circumstances* of the market. Note that, in this particular example, each of these variables affects either planned purchases or planned sales, but not both.[2]

The price of watermelons, on the other hand, does affect both sides of the market. A 1 per cent rise in price would result in a *rise* of 0.3 per cent in planned sales and a *fall* of 0.9 per cent in planned purchases. The relative directions of these movements, planned sales rising with rising price (and falling with falling price) while planned purchases fall with rising price (and rise with falling price), are presumed typical of almost all competitive market situations. In later chapters, we shall examine the reasons that lead economists to accept these directions of movement as

---

[2] This is not necessarily typical of markets generally, since such variables may affect both sides in some cases—business expectations, for example, may affect both demand and supply in the stock market.

typical, though they are not the only possibilities. For the moment, we simply note that we are concerned with an actual market.

Disequilibrium. Suppose that, under some given set of circumstances and some price, the planned supply was greater than the planned demand. This could not be an equilibrium situation since, although all of the buyers would be able to obtain the planned quantities, some of the sellers would find that they were unable to sell all that they had planned. We would describe the market as being in a state of *excess supply.* An equilibrium could exist only if the circumstances or the price were different, in such a way as to increase planned demand, reduce planned supply, or both.

The following changes would be in the appropriate direction for reaching or moving toward equilibrium:

(1) An increase in the farm wage rate, which would decrease the quantity farmers would plan to sell.

(2) An increase in average consumer incomes, which would increase the quantity consumers would plan to buy.

(3) A decrease in the price of watermelons, which would both increase the planned demand and decrease the planned supply.

Thus a market may be brought from disequilibrium into equilibrium by a change in *any* of the factors that influence planned demand or supply. In a typical market situation, however, the economist will consider the equilibrating factor to be the *price,* for good reasons.

The values of the variables that constitute the market circumstances are primarily determined *outside* the market in question. It is obvious that average consumer incomes for the United States as a whole would not be affected to any measurable extent by happenings in the watermelon market. Even farm wages would be affected to a negligible extent, if at all, by the state of the watermelon market, since watermelon production represents only about 0.0025 per cent of the total value of all farm production in the United States.

Thus it is not easy to visualize any means whereby disequilibrium in a small market, like the watermelon market, could result in changes in market circumstances which would lead toward equilibrium. Such a mechanism might be imagined for some markets, however. Suppose that consumer incomes fell to give a disequilibrium in the automobile market, a market in which planned demand is extremely sensitive to income. It is quite possible to imagine General Motors, Ford, and Chrysler bringing political pressure on the administration to bolster the economy and restore equilibrium *without* any price change taking place. If such a possibility can occur, the market is not a *competitive* market in the economist's sense. For the time being, we shall assume that we are concerned only with markets, like that of our example, in which individual buyers and sellers are powerless to affect the market circumstances.

For these reasons, the factors we have referred to as *market circumstances* are often called *exogenous* factors, using a word whose Greek roots mean "born outside of."

Price Determination. On the other hand, unless prices are laid down by government decree, there is no obvious place in which the price of watermelons could be determined except in its own market.

To the economist, price is the most "important" factor in determining market equilibrium because it is the factor that *both affects and is affected by* the state of the market. Price is said to be *endogenous,* determined within the market.

A glance at the information in Table 2.1 (page 8) will reveal that price is not necessarily the most "important" factor in the numerical sense. A 1 per cent change in average incomes, for example, causes a greater change in planned demand than a 1 per cent change in price. Even if we take demand and supply together, a 1 per cent fall in price will result in a fall of 0.3 per cent in planned sales and a rise of 0.9 per cent in planned purchases, giving a net fall of 1.2 per cent in the excess of planned sales over planned purchases—still less than the 1.4 per cent effect of a 1 per cent rise in incomes.

Partial Analysis. The distinction between exogenous and endogenous factors is not always quite so clear cut as it is in the example given here. In many cases, for example, the market circumstances may include the price of a related product. To use a standard example, the demand for butter may well depend on the price of margarine, and the demand for margarine on the price of butter. In this case, a change in the price of butter may result in a change in the price of margarine, so the market circumstances are not independent of the occurrence within the butter market itself. It is traditional in basic economics to assume specifically that all market circumstances remain unchanged during the course of a particular market analysis, an assumption usually called *ceteris paribus* ("other things the same"). The *usefulness* of the simple market analysis depends, however, on the *realism* of assuming unchanged market circumstances, so we emphasize here the cases in which the relatively self-contained price determination is fact rather than fiction.

Economic analysis of the kind that assumes unchanged those things that we expect in fact to be affected by the behavior under consideration is known as *partial analysis*.

2.3 Supply and Demand Curves

It has already been pointed out that it is a fundamental presumption of economic analysis that buyers and sellers possess contingent plans as to how they would behave in all market circumstances and at all prices within the range of variation that is likely to occur.

In the case of *competitive markets,* with which we are chiefly concerned at this stage, we make an additional assumption: the plans of each buyer and seller are totally independent of those of any other buyer or seller.

If we collected the information concerning plans from a typical buyer, it would give, for each set of market circumstances and each price, the quantity the buyer would plan to buy. This list represents the buyer's *complete demand schedule.*

Such a demand schedule for a particular buyer would be an *individual* demand schedule. If we chose some given market circumstance (a particular income level,[3] in the case of our example) and a given price, each individual schedule would give some number as the quantity the buyer would plan to buy under those conditions. If we searched all the individual schedules for the quantity corresponding to the *same* income level and price, and added all the quantities, we would obtain the quantity that the buyers, in the aggregate, would plan to buy under the given conditions. If we performed this addition for all other possible income levels and prices, we would have a schedule showing, for each price and income level, the quantity that all buyers together would plan to buy. This would be an *aggregate* demand schedule.

Similarly, we would have for each seller a complete *individual* supply schedule, from which we could derive an *aggregate* supply schedule by the same kind of addition.

Later in the book, when we look behind the demand and supply schedules, we shall return to the individual schedule. For the time being we are interested only in aggregate schedules. In the study of actual markets we normally observe only the aggregate level of transactions, and thus obtain information only about aggregate schedules.

In the study of a particular market, we usually take the market circumstances as given and are interested in the relationship between price,

---

[3] The income relevant to the individual's schedule is his *own* income. In aggregate schedules (as for the watermelon market) it is common to use *average per capita income.* It is possible for income to be redistributed so that some individuals are poorer, some richer, without the average being changed. This redistribution will change individual schedules, and may change the aggregate schedule. In using averages, we implicitly assume that all incomes rise with the average, and that no redistribution takes place if the average is constant.

planned purchases, and planned sales under the given circumstances. Thus we are usually interested in only part of the complete demand or supply schedule, the part corresponding to given circumstances, but in the whole range of possible prices.

Extracts from the Schedule. That part of the complete schedule which shows, for specified market circumstances, the planned quantity corresponding to each price is usually referred to simply as *the* demand or supply schedule. *It is extremely important to realize, however, that this is only*

TABLE 2.2

Representative Demand and Supply Schedules
A Watermelon Market

Price (cents per pound)	Quantity (in millions of tons per year):			
	Demanded at annual per capita income of		Supplied at daily farm wage rate of	
	$2,750 (D1)	$3,000 (D2)	$7.50 (S1)	$8.20 (S2)
1.0	2.17	2.43	1.14	1.11
—	—	—	—	—
1.5	1.50	1.69	1.29	1.26
1.6	1.42	1.60	1.32	1.29
1.7	1.35	1.51	1.35	1.32
1.8	1.28	1.43	1.37	1.34
1.9	1.21	1.37	1.39	1.36
2.0	1.17	1.31	1.41	1.38
—	—	—	—	—
2.5	0.96	1.07	1.52	1.49

These schedules have been constructed by assuming that the results obtained by L'Esperance (for reference to which see the footnote to Table 2.1) would have applied exactly to the United States in 1964 if the levels of per capita income and of farm wages had been as set out in the table. Since L'Esperance's results are *estimates*, and since they refer to *average* behavior over the period 1930–1951, the schedules should not be taken as necessarily giving the *actual* behavior in 1964.

The actual production in 1964 was 1.39 million tons, the price (as received by farmers) was 1.7¢ per pound, per capita income was $2,750, and the median daily farm wage was $7.50. Thus the schedules D1 and S1 closely approximate the 1964 *equilibrium* conditions, by design. But if per capita income had, in fact, been $3,000, as in D2, we cannot be sure the schedule would have been correct as given.

The schedules are given by the equations:

(Demand Schedule) $\ln X = -0.897 \ln P + 1.396 \ln y - 10.284$
(Supply Schedule) $\ln X = 0.324 \ln P - 0.324 \ln W + 14.597$

X = quantity, P = price, y = per capita income, W = farm wage.

an extract from a more complete schedule. It is crucial that this extract be labeled correctly as to the market circumstances for which it is relevant.

Using the results of the same studies of the watermelon market as were used in Table 2.1, we can draw up aggregate demand and supply schedules that are representative of the economist's general picture. These are given in Table 2.2. Since the only market circumstance that affects demand is the average income level, and since the only market circumstance that affects supply is the farm wage, the relevant labeling is simple.

Two extracts are given from the complete demand schedule, one for average income of $2,750, the other for average income of $3,000. Two extracts are also given from the complete supply schedule, corresponding to daily farm wage rates of $7.70 and $8.20.

Note that we can make a variety of different extracts from the complete schedule. We could, for example, hold price constant in the complete demand schedule and examine the relationship between planned quantity and income. If, instead of taking planned quantity, we took planned expenditure (price times quantity), and then a curve showing its relationship to income, we would have an *Engel curve.* Such curves are discussed in Chapter 7.

The Curves. It is traditional to depict the extracts from the complete demand and supply schedules in graphical form. This is done in Figure 2.1, in which (a) gives the overall picture and (b) gives a magnified view of part of (a). Price is measured on the vertical axis, quantity on the horizontal axis. The choice of vertical axis for price is simply a convention, but

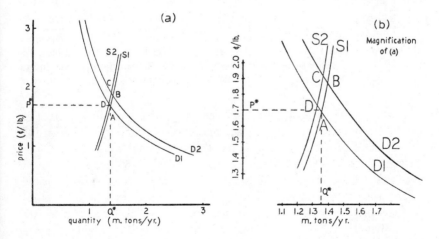

Figure 2.1

it is a very firmly established convention that is broken only on rare occasions and only for compelling reasons.

It might be noted that the convention is actually inappropriate. In the economist's analysis of the competitive market, *price* is taken as the independent variable for the buyers and sellers (that is, they accept price as given and their own actions are concerned with adjusting quantity), while the mathematical convention is that the independent variable is measured along the *horizontal* axis. The diagram must have been drawn by economists or students of economics some millions of times with price vertical, so we shall honor a tradition so well established!

There are two *demand curves* drawn in the figure, *D1* corresponding to a per capita income of $2,750 and *D2* to a per capita income of $3,000, and two *supply curves,* corresponding to a farm wage of $7.50 (*S1*) and $8.20 (*S2*).

The type of diagram shown in Figure 2.1 is so standard that it is quite common to speak of demand and supply *curves,* even when we are referring to the schedules rather than the graph.

Although we have drawn only two demand and two supply curves, there is an individual curve corresponding to every extract from the complete schedule. In the example, there is a demand curve corresponding to every income level and a supply curve corresponding to every farm wage rate.

Once we are given the market circumstances, we can pick out the appropriate curve, but not otherwise. *There is no such thing as "the" demand curve for watermelons, only a demand curve for a particular group of consumers (in this case, the whole United States population) in particular market circumstances (such as income level $2,750 for* D1*).* Of course, if the market circumstances have already been specified explicitly or by context we may speak of "the" demand curve, but we must be careful. The same considerations apply to supply curves. In later chapters we shall often speak simply of "the" demand curve, implicitly assuming that relevant circumstances are given.

Computation of the Equilibrium. Given the market circumstances, it is easy to determine the price at which market equilibrium will occur, using the schedules or the curves. Suppose the market circumstances are per capita income $2,750, farm wage $7.50. Then *D1, S1* are the relevant schedules (or curves). *D1* shows planned purchases at various prices under those circumstances, while *S1* shows planned sales. Market equilibrium will be at a price at which planned purchases and planned sales are equal. Glancing down the schedules in Table 2.2 (page 12), we can see that at a price of 1.7 cents per pound consumers plan to purchase 1.35

million tons per year while farmers plan to market 1.35 million tons per year, the figures boxed in the table. Thus 1.7 cents per pound is the *equilibrium price* at income levels of $2,750 and farm wages of $7.50. In Figure 2.1, the equilibrium price can be read off at the intersection of demand curve *D1* and supply curve *S1*, corresponding to the point *A*. The quantity changing hands (1.35 million tons) at the equilibrium price is the *equilibrium quantity*, the distance OQ^* in the diagram. The equilibrium price is the distance OP^*.

Note that both demand curves in Figure 2.1 slope downward to the right, and both supply curves slope upward to the right. In terms of the particular example, these slopes are a consequence of the property of the watermelon market, shown in Table 2.1, that a rise in price causes a fall in planned purchases but a rise in planned sales. As has already been suggested, and will be explored later, these are the *typical* slopes of demand and supply curves.

Other features of the diagram are not necessarily to be regarded as typical of market curves generally. The particular bend in the demand curves (they are convex toward the origin) was imposed on the curves by the particular econometric techniques employed in examining the data for the watermelon market; technically, the demand curves have *constant elasticity*, a term we shall examine later.

Change in Equilibrium. Returning to the analysis of market equilibrium, we can see that *different market circumstances would lead, generally, to a different equilibrium*. Suppose that the average income level had been $3,000 instead of $2,750. Then the relevant extract from the complete demand schedule would have been *D2*, and the relevant demand curve in Figure 2.1 would have been *D2*. At 1.7 cents per pound, the equilibrium price when the demand curve was *D1*, planned purchases would have been 1.51 million tons. Assuming the farm wage was still $7.50, so that *S1* was still the relevant supply curve, planned sales at this price would have been 1.35 million tons (as before). Thus planned purchases would exceed planned sales by 0.16 million tons (we say there would be an *excess demand* of 0.16 million tons at a price of 1.7 cents per pound), so that we cannot have equilibrium at this price.

Looking down schedules *D2* and *S1* in Table 2.2, we see that at a price of 1.9 cents per pound planned demand would be 1.37 million tons and planned supply would be 1.39 million tons. These are the closest pair of quantity figures that we can find in the schedules. By looking at the way the figures vary with price we see that, if the price were a fraction lower than 1.9 cents per pound, planned demand would be a fraction higher than 1.37 million tons and planned supply would be a fraction lower than 1.39

million tons. Thus the equilibrium price corresponding to an income level of $3,000 and a farm wage of $7.50 would be a shade under 1.9 cents per pound, and the equilibrium quantity would be somewhere between 1.39 and 1.38 million tons (the exact figures are 1.385 million tons at 1.875 cents per pound). This equilibrium is given by the point *B*, the inter-section of *D2* and *S1* in Figure 2.1.

With two different demand curves and two different supply curves there are four possible intersections, *A, B, C, D,* in Figure 2.1, each giving an equilibrium corresponding to a given set of market circumstances.

2.4 *Elements of Supply and Demand Analysis*

The most familiar diagram in all of economics is that which consists of a single demand and a single supply curve, with the point of intersection marked as showing the price and quantity associated with the equilibrium in that market, under the particular circumstances for which the chosen pair of curves is relevant. Such a diagram is shown in Figure 2.2. The

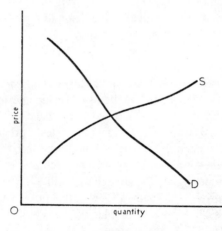

Figure 2.2

curves have been drawn with some irregularities to emphasize the point that only the general downward slope of the demand curve and the gen-eral upward slope of the supply curve are to be considered as standard features of the type of market being considered.

If the equilibrium point under a particular set of market circum-stances were all that interested us, this diagram would be a waste of time. The equilibrium point is, after all, only a *point,* so the parts of the two curves away from the intersection have no relevance. It is easy to see that, if the downward sloping curve in Figure 2.2 had been labeled as the supply curve and the upward sloping curve as the demand curve, the equilibrium point would be exactly the same as before.

The reason we, as economists, are interested at all in the supply and demand curves is precisely because we are interested in more than the equilibrium under a single set of market circumstances. We are interested in two kinds of things:

(1) What happens to the market *equilibrium* when the market circumstances change.

(2) What happens when a market is *not* in equilibrium.

The type of problem in (1) can be stated more precisely as follows. Suppose there exists a certain set of market circumstances, under which a market equilibrium prevails. Now let the circumstances change. In what way is the new market equilibrium related to the old? In particular, is the equilibrium price higher or lower, and is the equilibrium quantity higher or lower?

Analysis of this kind, involving the comparison of equilibrium points under different circumstances, is called *comparative statics*. Until quite recently, almost all of economic analysis was concerned either with description of equilibrium situations or with comparative static propositions.

More recent developments have included analysis of the *path* by which the market (or other part of the economic system) moves from one equilibrium position to another, or of the path toward equilibrium from a nonequilibrium situation. This type of analysis is *dynamics*. It concerns behavior out of equilibrium, and is taken up in the next chapter.

Change in Demand. An illustration of comparative static supply and demand analysis is given in Figure 2.3. It is assumed that some set of market circumstances makes S and $D1$ the appropriate supply and demand curves for some typical market. The market circumstances now change so that the relevant demand curve is $D2$, but the supply curve is unaffected. This would be the case if the average income level, but not the farm wage rate, were to change in the watermelon-market example given earlier in the chapter.

Under the first circumstances the equilibrium point on the diagram is X_1, corresponding to an equilibrium price P_1 and quantity Q_1. Under the later circumstances the equilibrium point is X_2, corresponding to price P_2 and quantity Q_2.

The particular change in circumstances that we have supposed is one in which the new demand curve $D2$ lies to the *right* of $D1$. With demand curves so related, $D2$ is usually said to represent an *increase in de-*

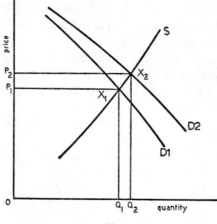

Figure 2.3

mand relative to *D1*, since the planned quantity demanded is greater *at every price* on *D2* than on *D1*. The phrase "increase in demand" always refers to a comparison between *two different demand curves*. It is not to be used to refer to an increase in quantity as we move along a single demand curve.

We see from the diagram that an increase in demand results in a higher equilibrium price and a greater equilibrium quantity, provided the supply curve is unaffected. We can also see that the price would change more and the quantity less if the *supply curve* had a steeper slope. The slope of the *demand curve* does not affect the change.

Change in Supply. There might be a change in market circumstances that would affect the supply curve but not the demand curve (such as a change in the farm wage rate in the watermelon-market example). Figure 2.4 shows the supply curve changing from *S1* to *S2* as a consequence of a change of this kind. Since planned supply is greater on *S2* than on *S1* at every price, we would refer to the change as an *increase in supply*, with the same caution about the use of the term as in the case of demand.

An increase in supply with unchanged demand results in a decrease in the equilibrium price (opposite to the effect of an increase in demand with unchanged supply) but an increase in the equilibrium quantity (as in the demand case). As in the previous case, the flatter the slope of the unchanged curve (in this case the *demand curve*), the greater the change in quantity relative to price.

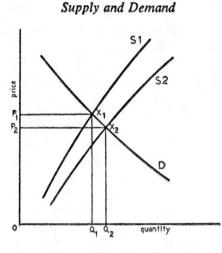

Figure 2.4

Change in Both Demand and Supply. What if demand and supply increase at the same time? Since an increase in demand and an increase in supply both tend to result in an increase in the equilibrium quantity, we certainly expect this to increase. But the effects on the equilibrium price are in opposite directions and the net result depends on the relative tendencies from the demand and supply sides. Figure 2.5 shows two cases in which both demand and supply increase, one leading to a fall in the equilibrium price, the other to a rise, but both to an increase in the equilibrium quantity.

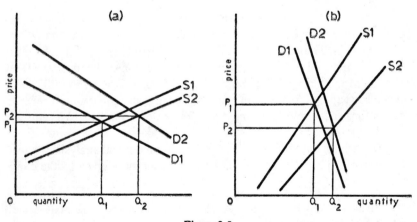

Figure 2.5

Although we may speak of the demand curve "changing" or "shifting" from *D1* to *D2,* or the supply curve "shifting" from *S1* to *S2,* it is important to realize that this is a description of what the economist is doing in drawing the diagram, not of what is happening in the market itself. The demand curve does not *shift* from *D1* to *D2*: both curves are based on extracts from the complete demand schedule. What happens is that *D1* is relevant to one set of market circumstances, *D2* to another set. When the circumstances change we remove the irrelevant curve and *replace* it by the relevant one. In looking at the relationship between two demand or two supply curves, we compare them in a right-left sense, the rightward curve representing an increase in demand and/or supply as the case may be. The two curves should not be compared in a vertical sense, since an increase in supply shifts the supply curve *down.*

Such information as the fact that a curve slopes up or down, unqualified by any information about the degree of steepness of the slope, is referred to as *qualitative* information, and statements concerning the *direction* of change of variables in which we are interested are known as *qualitative statements*. In some cases qualitative information enables us to make complete qualitative statements, as when only the demand or the supply curve shifts. In other cases, as when the supply and demand shift together, we can make a qualitative statement concerning one variable (quantity, in Figure 2.5) but not the other (price). If we could state that quantity would not only increase under some change, but increase by two tons, or by 5 per cent, we could make a *quantitative* statement.

2.5 *Elasticity as a Descriptive Tool*[4]

If we possess complete quantitative information concerning a competitive market, as we did for the watermelon market earlier in the chapter, then we can give numerical predictions for the results of any change. From Table 2.2 and Figure 2.1 we saw that an increase in demand from *D1* to *D2* (due to an increase in per capita income from $2,750 to $3,000), with unchanged supply (*S1*), would result in a change in equilibrium from 1.35 million tons at 1.7 cents per pound to 1.385 million tons at 1.875 cents per pound.

Sometimes in practice, and very often in theoretical analysis, we need to describe a market in more detailed terms than those given by the quali-

---

[4] The calculus-trained reader should supplement this section with the Mathematical Note on Section 2.5, given at the end of the book.

tative information (that a given curve slopes up or down), but do not want and probably do not have, the complete quantitative information such as that given for the watermelon market.

As we saw in the preceding section, we sometimes find it useful to be able to describe the degree of "steepness" or "flatness" of the demand or supply curve at some point. And we can do this in a straightforward way by giving the actual numerical slope of the curve at some point. For example, in Table 2.2, demand curve *D1* shows a change in quantity from 1.35 to 1.28 million tons when the price rises from 1.7 to 1.8 cents per pound, and we could actually describe the slope as -0.7 million watermelons per tenth of a cent or -700 million watermelons per dollar, or, for that matter, -70 million watermelons per dime. The disadvantage of giving slopes as they stand is that both the quantity and the money units must be clearly stated. Simply to give the slope as 0.18, for example, is as meaningless as it would be in the example to give the slope of the watermelon demand curve as -0.7.

Not only must the units in which slopes are measured be given; it is difficult to compare the significance of slopes measured in the entirely different unit. Suppose that we are told that the slope of the watermelon demand curve in the United States is -700 million watermelons per dollar and that the slope of the demand for watermelons in Latamerica is -1.47 thousand kilos per peso. Which demand curve would result in the greater change of price relative to quantity for some equal percentage change in the supply in both markets? We cannot answer a question like this without enough further information to relate the four separate units (two quantity units, two money units) to each other.

For these reasons, economists make extensive use of descriptive terms, called *elasticities,* which are independent of the units of measurement.

Definition of Elasticity. An elasticity is the ratio of the *proportional* change in one variable (that is, the change in the variable divided by its original value) to the *proportional* change in the other. In Table 2.1 the effects of the various factors influencing demand and supply are expressed as the percentage change in quantity resulting from a 1 per cent change in the factor. The percentage changes in quantities, prices, and incomes are all independent of the units in which these are measured, so the ratio of the percentage changes is also independent of the units. The numbers given in Table 2.1 are, in fact, *elasticities.* If we are told that the elasticity is -2.0, we do not need to know in what units either price or quantity is measured.

Elasticity is no more than a useful descriptive summary of the characteristics of a relationship between two variables. We can discuss the elasticity of any relationship, and economists use the term quite extensively, but it is most used in describing demand and supply curves. Since we think of a demand or supply curve as expressing the planned quantity (the dependent variable) as a function of market price (the independent variable), elasticity of demand or supply is expressed as a proportional (or percentage) change in quantity divided by the proportional (or percentage) change in price.

Choice of the term "elasticity" was made because it is a measure of the responsiveness of quantity changes to price changes, or, more generally, of effective variables to causal variables. If the quantity supply curve changes by a large proportion for a relatively small proportional change in price, the value of the elasticity is high, and there is no upper numerical limit to the possible value of an elasticity. The relationship may have infinite elasticity, and this will be the case if the quantity varies with no change in price. An infinite elasticity for demand and supply curves corresponds to a *horizontal* curve in the conventional diagram; we speak of such a curve as being "perfectly elastic."

If the proportional change in quantity is small compared with the proportional change in price, demand or supply relationship exhibits low responsiveness to price changes and has a low elasticity. The lower limit, numerically, for an elasticity is zero, when the quantity is completely unaffected by price changes. This corresponds to a *vertical* demand or supply curve.

Sign Conventions. Although elasticity is an extremely useful descriptive term, there are some aspects of its use which can result in confusion unless care is taken. The first, easily cleared up, applies to the elasticity of *demand.* Since the normal demand curve is downward sloping, an increase in price results in a decrease in quantity. In accordance with the usual algebraic convention, a positive price change will be associated with a negative quantity change and vice versa, so that the ratio between the proportional changes will be negative. Thus the demand elasticity ought to be negative (unless the demand curve has an upward slope), and we have used the negative sign with demand elasticities. Sometimes, however, we are discussing the *numerical value* of the demand elasticity and we may drop the minus sign, taking it for granted. When an actual numerical value for elasticity is given (such as -0.37), it is better to give the minus sign, and this is almost always done in tabulating actual empirically determined elasticities. Even economists who are consistent in their use of the sign in such tabulations will, however, speak of -2.13 as a "higher elasticity" than -0.82, meaning numerically greater, and we shall do the same thing throughout this book.

Changes Should Be Small. A second confusing aspect of elasticity measurements, less easy to clear up than the conventions with respect to sign of demand elasticity, is that the rigorous definition of an elasticity is as the *limit of the ratio* of the proportional quantity change to the proportional price change as the latter becomes very small. If the changes are not sufficiently small, the value of the elasticity is different for movement in one direction of the curve as compared with movement in the opposite direction. Suppose that the quantity, on a supply curve, changed from 100 units to 110 units when the price changed from 1 to 2. This would be a 10 per cent increase in the quantity for a 100 per cent increase in price, giving an elasticity of 0.10. But if now the price fell from 2 back to 1, and the quantity from 110 to 100, this would be a 9.09 per cent decrease in quantity for a 50 per cent decrease in price, giving an elasticity of about 0.18 between exactly the same two points on the supply curve as before. If we took a smaller change, so that the quantity rose from 100 to 101 when the price rose from 1 to 1.1, the elasticity would now be 0.10 computed from the price rise, approximately 0.11 from the price fall; and if the price change was only from 1 to 1.01, the computed value of the elasticity would be the same to two decimal places.

A distinction used to be made between "arc elasticities," measured between points on the curve some distance apart and therefore having this asymmetry property, and "point elasticities," defined above. In modern usage, only point elasticities are given when numerical values are implied. For descriptive work, when we are interested only in knowing whether elasticities are high or low and not in exact numerical values, the distinction is less important. There are two cases in which no confusion can arise:

The completely vertical curve always has zero elasticity at all points over all ranges and a completely horizontal curve has infinite elasticity (positive for a supply curve, negative for a demand curve), however measured.

Straight-Line Demand and Supply. The third possible confusion is already nearly cleared up by the above discussion. The elasticity is a measure of the properties of the curve at a given point and may differ at other points. A simple example is a straight-line demand curve, *D*, shown in Figure 2.6. A movement from X to X', at the top of the curve, represents an infinite proportional change in quantity (a finite actual change, divided by zero), so the elasticity at X is infinite. A movement from Y to Y', at the bottom of the curve, represents a small finite change in quantity for an

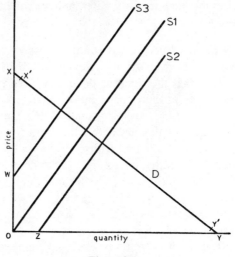

Figure 2.6

infinite proportional change in price and thus a negligible proportional quantity change for a *small* proportional price change, so the elasticity is zero at Y. It is easy to see that the elasticity rises continuously in numerical value from Y to X, so that all numerical values of elasticity are represented somewhere along the line.

A straight-line supply curve does not necessarily show the same variation of elasticity, however. The supply curve $S1$ in Figure 2.6, which passes through the origin, has a constant elasticity equal to 1, since the proportional change in quantity is always equal to the proportional change in price. Supply curve $S2$, which does not pass through the origin, can be shown to have zero elasticity at the bottom end, Z, increasing continuously to approach 1 as we move along it, while supply curve $S3$, cutting the price axis rather than the quantity axis, has infinite elasticity at W, decreasing continuously to approach 1 as we move out along the curve.

Constant Elasticity Curves. A curve *may*, of course, have constant elasticity, and the demand and supply curves of the watermelon market depicted in Figure 2.1 have this property. This happens to be the case because the investigators *assumed* constant elasticity in examining the watermelon market in the United States, and set out to determine the set of constant elasticity curves that best fitted the data.

Empirical investigations of actual markets are often made under the assumption of constant elasticity in order to simplify the problem enough to allow the investigators to arrive at some numerical estimates.

Other Elasticities. The elasticity of a price-quantity relationship is only the most common use of elasticity concept. Almost as common is the relationship between the proportional change in quantity demanded and the proportional change in income *(income elasticity)*, or the proportional change in quantity of one good and the proportional change in the price of another, usually called a *cross price elasticity.* Elasticities are also used as descriptive terms for relationships other than demand and supply.

Use of Elasticities. The usefulness of ordinary price elasticities as descriptive terms may be illustrated by referring back to the discussions of the effect of a shift in supply or demand curve on market equilibrium. For a *small* shift in the supply curve, the two market equilibria have points close together on the demand curve, so that the relationship between the proportional quantity change and the proportional price change resulting from the shift in the supply curve is nothing other than the elasticity of the *demand* curve. The higher the elasticity of the demand at the original equilibrium point, the more a small shift in supply would change quantity compared with price and vice versa. Similarly, for a small shift in demand, the higher the elasticity of supply, the more the shift will result in quantity changes rather than price changes.

Elasticities are used more often as broad descriptions ("highly elastic," "low elasticity," and so on) than as exact numbers, even when these may have been estimated. For the *price elasticity of demand,* however, the numerical value 1 ("unit elasticity") has a special significance in relationship to total expenditure.

Expenditure and Elasticity. Consider a given demand curve, and then consider the effect on total *expenditure,* not just quantity, of, say, a 1 per cent fall in price. Insofar as price has fallen by 1 per cent, expenditure would fall by 1 per cent if the original quantity were still purchased. But insofar as the quantity increases with a fall in price, so does expenditure. The percentage increase in quantity is $|\eta|$,[5] the numerical value of the demand elasticity. Thus expenditure will tend to fall 1 per cent from the price change, and to rise $|\eta|$ per cent from the quantity change.

If $|\eta| > 1$ (in which case we say the curve is "elastic"), the rise outweighs the fall, and expenditure *increases* with a fall in price. If $|\eta| < 1$ ("inelastic"), expenditure *decreases* with a fall in price. If $|\eta| = 1$ ("unit elasticity"), expenditure is unchanged with change in price.

---

[5] The Greek letter η is commonly used for demand elasticities. It is read "eta." The symbol $|\eta|$ means the absolute or numerical value of η (the number without its negative sign) and should be read "mod eta."

This kind of effect does not occur with a regular supply curve, since price and quantity change in the *same* direction. Whether the numerical value of an elasticity is greater than or less than unity becomes important primarily in cases in which two variables change in opposite directions.

2.6 Boundary Equilibrium

The traditional demand and supply curve diagram always shows the two curves crossing neatly to give a position of equilibrium, but it does not necessarily follow that we can always find a price or any set of market circumstances at which quantity demanded and quantity supplied are equal. Look at Figure 2.7 (a). This shows a supply curve that intersects

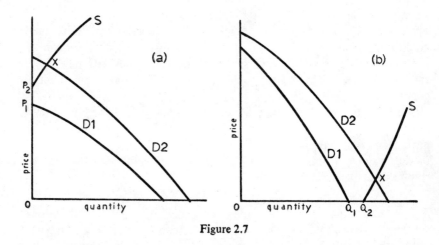

Figure 2.7

the vertical axis some distance above the origin, implying that a certain minimum price is necessary even to obtain a very small quantity of the good, a type of supply curve that might apply to many goods. We may suppose this market to be that for solid gold Cadillacs.

The only thing unusual about this market is that the demand curve *D1* intersects the vertical axis *below* the minimum price at which any will be supplied. The demand curve for solid gold Cadillacs is such that even the most willing potential buyer is not willing enough to pay the least price for which such an object will be produced. The curves *S* and *D1* do not intersect. In the geometric sense they will intersect somewhere off to the left of the diagram, but this is irrelevant since we consider prices and quantities to be essentially positive quantities. The supply and demand curves are defined only in the positive quadrant.

What is the equilibrium in this market? It is obvious that, under these circumstances, no solid gold Cadillacs will either be bought or sold and it would seem reasonable to give the equilibrium quantity as zero. The equilibrium price is not quite without meaning, for if the price were announced to be above P_2, production of solid gold Cadillacs would commence, while if it were stated to be below P_1, orders for them would start coming in. Since an equilibrium in the simple sense of an intersection of the demand and supply curves does not exist here, we preserve the spirit of the idea as closely as possible by defining the equilibrium in this case as quantity zero, price indefinite but in the range P_1 to P_2.

We would refer to such an equilibrium as a *boundary* equilibrium (sometimes a *corner solution*) since the level of one of the variables (here the quantity) is determined by the boundary of permissible values. An equilibrium of the ordinary kind is an *interior* equilibrium.

Shift Between Interior and Boundary. A market may have a boundary equilibrium under some circumstances and an ordinary interior equilibrium under others. Suppose, in the example given above, that there was a considerable rise in income, or a redistribution of income that made the rich very rich indeed. Then the demand for gold Cadillacs would be expected to increase. If it increased to $D2$, we would have an interior equilibrium at X.

Boundary equilibria of the above kind, where the quantity is zero, are of little interest so long as the nature of the equilibrium does not change. The good is simply not produced and its possible existence is not particularly interesting. However, a market may have a boundary equilibrium under some circumstances, but ordinary equilibrium under others. A technological discovery that lowers costs, or an increase in incomes, may cause the market to reach an interior equilibrium. In the example given, a large rise in the incomes of the very rich might shift the demand for solid gold Cadillacs to $D2$, giving an interior equilibrium at X.

In the case of a technological discovery that dramatically lowers costs, we may refer to the appearance of a supply curve capable of giving an interior equilibrium as the marketing of a "new" product. The product may not really be new in the technological sense; what is new is the ability to produce it at a price that is low enough to attract some buyers. Some inventors (including Edison) had a genius for taking something that might be technically feasible and making it *economically* feasible in this way.

Figure 2.7(b) depicts a situation in which some non-zero but limited quantity of a good is available at zero price, but further quantities are available only at some positive price. A case of this kind might be the supply of pure water to a certain locality. A certain quantity may be freely available from a river or a spring, but larger quantities require the digging of a well, water purification processes, or the transport of water from a distance. So long as the demand curve is like *D1*, intersecting the horizontal axis to the left of a point at which it is intersected by *S*, there is no intersection of demand and supply curves.

We would characterize the market situation formed by *S* and *D1* as a boundary equilibrium at zero price and quantity Q_1.

Free Goods. A good for which the market circumstances correspond to a boundary equilibrium at zero price is commonly referred to as a *free good*.[6] It is important to realize that the property of "freeness" is not inherent in the good, in spite of the phraseology, but in the market circumstances. If demand shifted sufficiently, say from *D1* to *D2* in the diagram, there would now be an interior equilibrium at *X* and the free good would no longer be free. Many things that were once free goods, such as pure water, clean air, and outdoor campsites, have ceased to be so, often because of a shift in the supply curve as well as in the demand curve. In some cases the price of such goods may still not be paid directly by the consumer but through taxes, which may make them appear still free to the ordinary consumer. The economist reserves the term "free good" for those goods (the air we breathe, for example) which have a zero price to society as a whole.

2.7 Point Supply

A supply *curve* implies intention by the supplier or suppliers to sell over a range of prices, or to sell different quantities (or both), leaving the equilibrium to be determined in the market. This is the situation characteristic of the ordinary competitive market situation.

There are, however, situations in which the supplier plans to sell some one fixed quantity at some one price, so that supply is represented by a single point rather than by a curve. For example, as we shall see later, a monopolist or any imperfectly competitive firm will plan to produce a certain quantity and to sell it at a specific price, eliminating the supply *curve* from that market. A planned economy will often have the same type of supply conditions, the plan setting both the amount to be supplied and the price to be charged.

Because of the extent to which demand and supply analysis pervades

---

[6] Economics can be considered to be about *scarcity*. A good which will remain a free good under all conceivable circumstances for the economy in question is not "scarce." A good which, although a free good, could cease to be so with a possible change in the economy will be considered *scarce* in the economist's sense.

so much economic thinking, it is important to build a bridge to these situations by considering demand and supply analysis with point supply.

Point supply implies that the conditions for a competitive market do
not exist on the supply side. There are no longer a large number of suppliers, each representing a small proportion of the total, but typically a
single supplier.

Even in the planned economy, however, competitive conditions still
exist on the demand side. There remain a very large number of consumers,
each individually unable to affect the market. In a soviet-type economy,
most *consumer* goods are sold on some kind of market.

Excess Demand Situations. A case of this kind is depicted in Figure
2.8(a). The demand curve D is familiar, but the supply schedule is repre-

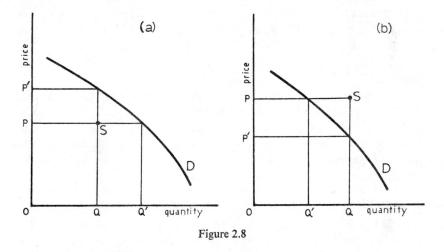

Figure 2.8

sented by a single point S. Such a point supply means simply that suppliers
offer to sell a fixed quantity Q at a fixed price P. S does not happen to lie
on D, nor does it lie on either axis, so we have neither an interior nor a
boundary equilibrium. If the price is absolutely fixed at P, then the quantity supplied is Q. The quantity demanded at this price, from the demand
curve, is Q', so that the only market situation attainable is one of *excess
demand,* and that is not equilibrium.

In an actual market with these characteristics, lucky or early buyers
would obtain the goods, unlucky or later buyers would find nothing left
on the traders' counters. The latter may still obtain the goods by offering
to buy (at a higher price) from early or lucky buyers. Individuals (ticket
scalpers, for example) may set out to profit in this way by being first in

line. Such activity has elements of both *arbitrage* and *speculation*, discussed in the next chapter.

A market situation of this kind is likely to arise in a centrally planned economy. The planners have decided that the appropriate quantity to produce is Q, the appropriate price at which to sell it is P, but they have misjudged demand conditions. A perfect plan would result in S lying somewhere along D so that there would be an equilibrium position, but perfect plans are difficult to formulate. A similar case could arise with a monopolist[7] in a real situation, since the textbook assumption of perfect knowledge concerning demand is rarely achieved.

With excess demand, market planners might choose to remain in a disequilibrium situation, the deficient supply probably going to those most willing to line up for goods. They might prefer to distribute the quantity Q in a different way, by admitting P was an inappropriate choice for the price and increasing the price to P', the price at which the quantity demanded is exactly Q. In this case we would have a market *equilibrium,* but the supply schedule would no longer be the point S but the vertical line through S. The supply curve is now an inelastic curve giving an ordinary interior equilibrium.

In a soviet-type centrally planned economy there have been, and are, ideological objections to appearing to have the price determined by market equilibrium, so the ideologically more acceptable device would be to add a tax of P' minus P per unit and continue to state the "price" to be P. In fact, the consumer price would be P' and the result would be that of ordinary market equilibrium, *given that the supply was to be fixed at* Q.

Excess Supply Situations. Recent years have seen the U.S.S.R. and other countries with soviet-type centrally planned economies make some moves in the direction of allowing the attainment of ordinary market equilibrium, a shift in policy usually referred to as "Libermanism," after the soviet economist Liberman who was a prominent public advocate of making more use of market type of influences in planning policy. The reason for this change in policy may be seen by comparing the situation just discussed with that depicted in Figure 2.8(b). In the second diagram we also have a situation in which supply is represented by S but in this case the point lies outside the demand curve rather than inside it.

When the point supply lies outside the demand curve, the quantity demanded at the given price, Q', is *less* than the quantity offered, Q, and we have a situation of *excess supply*. The market planners can react to excess supply in the same way as to excess demand, by maintaining the

---

[7] Monopoly is discussed in Chapter 6.

disequilibrium situation, or by allowing prices to vary, in this case downward. But maintaining the disequilibrium situation with excess supply means that unsold goods pile up at the points of supply and their presence is extremely obvious to the planners, who are associated with suppliers rather than with consumers.

The important factor here is that the demand curve is an outer boundary of consumers' collective choices under the given market circumstances. Although the demand curve itself represents the unfettered choice by consumers of the quantity they would buy at various prices, points within the demand curve (that is, between it and the origin) represent quantities they would accept if they could have no more. But points outside the demand curve represent quantities consumers cannot be induced to accept.

Thus, if most markets are in a state of excess demand, as was the case during the whole period of soviet development up into the fifties, then that excess demand can be ignored without too much difficulty, since all goods can be sold at the prices assigned and any problems fall on to the consumers. Once markets commence to show excess supply, however, the consumers make their presence felt by refusing to buy all that is offered, the extent of the excess supply becomes obvious (the extent of excess demand could only be discovered by some market survey that asked consumers how much they would have bought had they been able), and the maintenance of a system of disequilibrium markets becomes only too obviously inefficient.

Avoidance of disequilibrium situations requires either very skillful planning with very accurate data on consumer demand, so that planned production and prices correspond with a point on the demand curve, or the operation of some market mechanism that will enable equilibrium to be reached without prior knowledge of market conditions.

The reader should be careful to remember that the monopolistic firm in the United States can face a problem of this kind similar to that faced by a factory manager in the Soviet Union.

FURTHER READING

Supply and demand analysis is very standard material. A large number of examples of the use of this analysis are given in Chapters 11 and 12 of K. E. Boulding, *Economic Analysis, Volume I: Microeconomics,* Harper & Row, 1966.

EXERCISES

(1) Following are the individual demand schedules for four consumers, A, B, C, D, over the price range $20/ton to $25/ton. Assume that these schedules all relate to the same market circumstances, and refer to the same length of market period.

Price ($/ton)	Quantity demanded (tons), by			
	A	B	C	D
20	35	120	42	12
21	34	90	42	13
22	33	70	42	14
23	32	50	42	15
24	31	30	42	16
25	30	0	42	17

Of these four demand schedules, there is one with each of the following properties:

(i) completely inelastic.

(ii) elasticity less than unity, but greater than zero.

(iii) elasticity greater than unity.

(iv) giving a demand curve with slope opposite to normal.

(The value of the elasticity refers to the *numerical* value. The relevant property can be assumed to hold everywhere along the demand curve, since this has been designed into the figures.)

(2) Draw up the *aggregate* demand schedule for a market consisting of the four consumers in (1). Assuming that the market is competitive (in spite of the small number of buyers), find the equilibrium price and quantity if the aggregate supply schedule is as follows:

Price ($/ton)	Quantity supplied (tons)
20	0
21	29
22	89
23	139
24	179
25	229

(3) Suppose that in (1) consumer B withdrew from the market, but that it remained competitive. Draw up the new aggregate demand schedule.

(i) What is the elasticity of the aggregate demand curve?

(ii) Find the new equilibrium price and quantity with the supply schedule of (2).

Chapter 3 is concerned with the mechanism and dynamic behavior of the market.

CONTENTS

3.1 The Market   35
3.2 An Ideal Market   37
3.3 Traders as a Computer   39
3.4 Market Dynamics   43
3.5 Arbitrage   49
3.6 Speculation   51
3.7 Related Markets   55

CHAPTER 3

THE MARKET

3.1 The Market

In the previous chapter we discussed demand and supply, used the term "market" quite freely, and even defined "market equilibrium." But we did not define or describe exactly what we meant by the term "market."

The term is used by economists in several different ways, but all are derived from the same general idea. A *market transaction* is a transaction involving *voluntary exchange between different individuals*. A market is simply a context in which market transactions take place.

Most transactions in an economy such as that of the United States are market transactions, but not all are. The government does not raise revenue by market transactions, but by taxes which involve compulsion. In a peasant economy, much that is produced is consumed directly by the producer—we say that the production does not pass *through the market,* since exchange between different individuals is not involved. Even in the United States there are a large number of transactions of this kind, such as when parts made in one division of a large corporation are transferred to an assembly division. Even though accounting transfers of money may be made, the parts do not pass through the market since the divisions do not act independently and therefore are not different "individuals" in the economic sense.

Voluntary Exchange Required. A market involves voluntary exchange. Without the voluntary element, a transaction cannot be regarded as a market transaction. Exactly what constitutes a voluntary exchange is not always completely clear, however. If I am accosted in a dark street and offered the option of my money or my life, I am free to choose between the alternatives, but not free to leave the "market" completely. There are less drastic bargaining situations with similar characteristics, but we would not regard these as a market *unless the option of simply refusing to exchange were available.*

Laws can prohibit a certain market, but they cannot insure its existence. Indeed, prohibiting a market may be extremely difficult if there are sufficient individuals interested in the exchange in question, as evidenced by the persistence of "black markets" in war time or in a highly regulated economy, markets in narcotics, and so on.

"Compulsory marketing" is a contradiction in terms unless it simply means all alternative markets are prohibited and individuals exchange in the stated market or not at all. Otherwise, the transaction is seizure with compensation and is not a market transaction.

Many true markets are institutionalized and regulated. The New York Stock Exchange is an institution for regulating the market in certain stocks. Some of these regulations have been devised as voluntary constraints by those in the market, some have been imposed by the society (via the Securities and Exchange Commission). The regulation may affect the working of the market although, in the Stock Exchange case, they are chiefly concerned with characteristics of the market not contained in the economist's basic model. The essential property, of freedom to accept or reject an offer, is retained.

Neither Party Worse Off. The voluntary nature of market transactions is sufficient ground for the statement of the fundamental proposition of normative or welfare economics (that aspect of economics which attempts to rank configurations of the economic system on a "better" or "worse" criterion): *neither party to a market transaction is, to his knowledge at the time, made worse off by the transaction.*

This follows from the nature of the market transaction and an implicit assumption that the chosen action (in this case engaging in the transaction rather than doing nothing) is preferred, or at least is not worse than the alternative.

The qualification to the proposition should be noted. A market transaction may lead to a party becoming worse off, either from changes after the event or because he was not aware of the full implications of the action. A transaction may, of course, take place on less favorable terms than one party had anticipated before the event—this is what we usually mean by "losing" on a transaction—but the occurrence of the transaction, if it was possible for both parties to do nothing, is evidence of neither party losing by it.

The economist's basic description of the market, which is the subject of this chapter, should be regarded as describing a model, an idealization, or a generalization of actual markets. There is no market possessing the pristine simplicity of the economist's basic description—although there are some that approximate it—yet all markets share certain fundamental characteristics with it. Every real market has some aspects unique to it, but our task is to examine the characteristics common to all markets.

Finally, we note that the market is the place in which interaction between individuals takes place. In the simplest and most idealized models of the economy, the market is taken to be the *only* place where individuals interact with each other on economic matters.

3.2 An Ideal Market

In the basic description of market equilibrium, such as was given in the previous chapter, the determination of equilibrium is made to seem simple. We obtain the individual supply and demand schedules, we assemble them into aggregate demand and supply schedules, and we then look to see at what price the quantity demanded is equal to the quantity supplied.

Real Markets. Real markets do not usually operate like the ideal, for one very simple reason:

There is no one in a market who is in a position to assemble the information together in the manner of our example.

Indeed, in the absence of a conscious effort on the part of some statistics-gathering body, like the departments of Commerce, Labor, or Agriculture, or some special industry-organized statistics bureau, the *total quantity passing through the market would remain unknown to anyone.*

The *price* (if there is, indeed, a uniform price) is the only information which is known in the market, since this is common to every transaction. Every trader will know how much he himself has traded, but not the aggregate amount traded by everyone. This is not because of secrecy, but simply because the information is not evident—it must be collected and assembled.

An Idealized Model. We can, however, imagine the existence of a market so organized that it resembles the basic model. It is extremely helpful in understanding the behavior of actual markets to describe this imaginary ideal market, which we can suppose to be something like the following fantasy:

Each trader (buyer or seller) knows the market circumstances for the day in question, and has his set of contingent plans (his demand or supply schedule), showing how much he will buy or sell at every conceivable price. For some prices, of course, the quantity may be zero.

Since it is an essential presumption of all simple economic models of the market that the demand and supply schedules represent an absolute commitment to buy or sell the relevant quantities at those prices, whatever may happen in the process of price determination itself, we can say that there is an essential element of *predecision*. That is, the trader can write out, *in advance,* his demand and supply schedules, because his willingness to buy or sell a certain quantity at equilibrium depends only on the equilibrium price and not on any events which take place in the process of determining that price.

We can suppose the individual demand and supply schedules to be punched on IBM cards. At the opening of the market the trader (or his office boy, since all the trader's decisions are already incorporated into the schedule) hands his deck of cards in to the market management. Names of the traders need not be on the cards, since the market process is quite *anonymous* and identification of individual schedules is irrelevant.

The traders, or their deputies, now sit quietly reading newspapers while the market goes to work. The IBM cards are fed into the computer which simply adds them appropriately to obtain aggregate demand and supply schedules, then searches the aggregate schedules for a price which equates the quantity demanded with the quantity supplied.

Once the computer has located this price, a bell rings and the traders look up to see the equilibrium price displayed on the television screen. We would expect no wild scenes to take place whatever the market price, since the traders in the idealized model are passive *price takers*. They have already stated exactly what they would do at each price including the circumstances under which they would do nothing at all (zero quantity). Sellers may regret that the equilibrium price was so low, and buyers that it was so high, but they proceed to carry out their plans.

The essential market process is now over, once the equilibrium price has been established. To be sure, the commodities have to be distributed from the sellers to the buyers. The method is irrelevant, since at the equilibrium price we know that the aggregate quantity supplied will exactly balance the aggregate quantity demanded. Suppliers could simply dump their produce into a pile, being paid (at the equilibrium price, of course) by the market management, who would then parcel the produce out to the buyers on receiving payment. Or buyers and sellers could line up, the first buyer buying from the first seller (or the first several sellers, if his purchases are too large to be filled by the first seller alone), and so on down the line. *Whatever scheme was used, the market would be exactly cleared so long as all buyers and sellers adhered strictly to their announced plans.*

Although the market information can be quite anonymous in order to determine the equilibrium price, if the cards were identified the computer could be programmed to tell which sellers should sell how much to which buyers in order to minimize the number of separate transactions. The computer problem to be solved is a variant of what is known as the *warehouse problem.*[1]

The Actual Market Place. The most striking feature of this market model is how different the vision of calm passive traders awaiting the outcome of the computation is from the usual picture of a market alive with milling, shouting, sweating traders. Yet what has been described is an accurate model of the basic market, reaching equilibrium in an efficient manner.

No real market is yet organized as the one described, although it does not seem improbable that some markets will be organized this way in the future.

The work assigned to the computer in our model must, in actual markets, be done by traders themselves. In large markets, such as stock and commodity markets, the task of reaching equilibrium is carried out by specialized floor *traders* whose *clients* are the equivalent of the traders in our model, that is, it is the clients who initiate demand and supply schedules. In small markets, traders may act as their own floor traders, but the essential fact remains that:

The milling, shouting, and sweating is the consequence of humans playing the role of the computer.

3.3 Traders as a Computer

At the end of the nineteenth century, two economists, Walras[2] (a Swiss) and Edgeworth (an Englishman), devised market models which, if taken together, give a human equivalent of our computerized model.

A market manager was supposed to call out some starting price. Traders would then call out the quantities they would offer to buy or sell

---

[1] This is also known as the *transport problem* and the *optimal assignment problem.* It was one of the earliest problems to which the technique known as *linear programming* was applied.

[2] The initial letter is pronounced as *V*.

at that price. The offers were aggregated, and if they did not clear the market, a new price was tried until the appropriate equilibrium price was found. Traders were not allowed to trade at all until the equilibrium was established, after which they made their transactions (which as in the computer model, were exactly what they had declared them to be) and the market was cleared. This process was referred to by Walras as "tatonnement,"[3] a name also used in English.

The Walras model requires, like the computer model, some organization of the market. At the minimum, it requires a manager of some kind to call prices and total bids, and agreement (or enforcement) to ensure that no trade takes place except at the equilibrium price.

Actual markets do not generally have any such organization, so we are interested in how an equilibrium can be established in a completely unorganized market. Let us be quite frank about this from the beginning:

There is a variety of models of the behavior of unorganized markets, but no complete theory of such markets.

When the market consists of a very large number of buyers and sellers, the share of each of which in total demand or supply is very small, the action of the individual buyer or seller has so little effect on the totals that it can be ignored. No buyer or seller, then, has the power to decide how the market shall adjust. The "market mechanism" must be the aggregate result of individuals adjusting passively to market circumstances over which they have no individual control.

Perfect Markets. A market consisting of a sufficiently large number of buyers and sellers, no one of which buys or sells more than a very small fraction of the total, where the commodity being traded is regarded as homogeneous, where the only criterion for a transaction is that no better bargain is available elsewhere (that is, no buyers have, for example, a "loyalty" to any particular seller), and where all traders are aware of all offers available, is characterized as a *perfect market*. There probably are no markets that have ever fully satisfied these stringent conditions, although there are markets that satisfy some of them, so we prefer to regard a model of a market with all these characteristics as the *basic market model,* providing a reference for analysis of markets which can be considered to *approximate* the conditions for the perfect market.

The Basic Model. The basic market model is usually visualized as a trial and error process of equilibrium determination. A price is somehow set, possibly by a random event. Both buyers and sellers will accept this provisionally, since it cannot be to the advantage of any seller to sell below

---

[3] The process described here is an amalgam of the Walras and Edgeworth processes.

this price, provided he can sell all he has to offer (which is a very small fraction of the total being traded). Nor can it be to the advantage of the buyer to offer a higher price, provided he can find a seller at the given price. At the same time, the seller who asks a higher price or the buyer who offers a lower price will find no one with whom to trade, provided goods are traded at the given price. But suppose the price is set above the equilibrium price. With ordinary demand and supply conditions, such a price, like P_1 in Figure 3.1, will result in excess supplies. This means, as

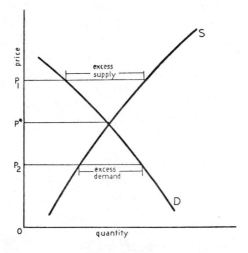

Figure 3.1

trade continues at price P_1, it will reach a stage at which buyers have made all the purchases they wish at this price while sellers still have some quantity of the good remaining. Those sellers who are going to be left with unsold goods will probably commence to offer them at lower prices before this stage is reached and buyers will probably also be aware of the impending excess supply and commence to offer a lower price.

The downward pressure on prices may lead to a new uniform price. If this is still above equilibrium, the same pressures will push it down further. Should the price be below the equilibrium price, as P_2 in Figure 3.1, excess demand and pressures of the same kind as those already described, but working in the opposite direction, would tend to push the price upward.

If the price comes to be set at P^*, the equilibrium price in Figure 3.1, there is no excess demand or supply, all buyers can find sellers at P^*, and all sellers can find buyers. There is no incentive for sellers to cut prices nor for buyers to offer higher prices while no seller can sell at a price higher than P^* nor any buyer buy at a price lower. Of course, these are the characteristics that led to the use of the term *equilibrium* to describe the situation.

Although this description of the nature of equilibrium in the basic market model is adequate, the simple mechanism by which we have supposed it to be reached is, unfortunately, not. In the description of the mechanism the word "probably" was used frequently and advisedly so, since we possess no general theory of how marketers will behave out of equilibrium. We are on safe enough ground in assuming that, if a uniform price has been set and the market is characterized by supply and demand curves with the normal directions of slope, a price above (below) equilibrium will result in behavior tending to lower (raise) the price. This effect, an instance of what we refer to as negative *feedback* (that is, divergences from equilibrium in either direction result in movements back in the general direction of equilibrium—the term has been borrowed from engineers) is not sufficient to guarantee the reaching of equilibrium, although it is a necessary condition. That negative feedback is not sufficient will be demonstrated in the next section.

Existence of a Uniform Price. In almost all discussions of the mechanism in the market, including very sophisticated dynamic models, it is assumed that somehow a uniform price comes to be set even out of equilibrium, and that the process of reaching equilibrium should not affect the supply and demand conditions at equilibrium. In many real markets there is no reason for supposing that a single price exists in the market when it is out of equilibrium. Even in the previous example it is quite likely, if the price is above the equilibrium level, that some sellers, sensing that the price was too high well before the extent of excess supply is generally apparent, will shave their prices down, sell all they have, then leave the market. Quick sales might be made at a variety of different prices. Furthermore, if sellers and buyers make deals and leave the market before the equilibrium is established, the supply and demand schedules are each changed by loss of some of the traders and equilibrium, if reached, may differ from what it would have been if no traders had left the market.

Conditions for Stability. It can be shown that,[4] if

(1) there is a uniform price in the market at all times,

(2) prices start changing instantaneously downward with excess supply *and at a rate proportional to the amount of excess supply,*

(3) prices start changing instantaneously upward with excess demand *and at a rate proportional to the amount of excess demand,*

---

[4] For the reader conversant with calculus, this is proved in the Mathematical Note on Section 3.3, page 303.

(4) if there is excess supply with price above equilibrium and excess demand with price below equilibrium (guaranteed by normal curves), then the market will converge to an equilibrium. That is, it will be *stable*. However, in an unorganized market there is no way of knowing the exact level of excess demand or supply and thus of adjusting the rate of change of prices proportionally.

Economists, possibly hypnotized by their own term "perfect market," have been unduly willing to assume that an anarchic and unorganized collection of many buyers and many sellers, each with his predecided demand or supply schedule, will automatically reach a market equilibrium among themselves. It is certainly true that there will be many tendencies in that direction, but it is an act of faith to assume the existence of a self-equilibrating market.

3.4 Market Dynamics

It is easy to see that, unless a price other than the equilibrium price results in market tendencies which push the price *towards* equilibrium (negative feedback), it is unlikely that equilibrium will be reached or that the equilibrium, if reached, will be sustained. We have seen that, if the demand and supply curves slope in the normal directions, a price above equilibrium will lead to excess supply and competitive bidding for sales will tend to push the price down, with the reverse effect of the prices below equilibrium. If the slopes of the curves were reversed, so that the supply curves sloped downward to the right and the demand curve upward, a price above equilibrium would result in excess demand and competition for goods would push the price further up, away from equilibrium. In this case, we would have *positive* feedback and no tendency, even of a rough kind, for the markets to move towards equilibrium. Negative feedback, alone, is not sufficient to guarantee that the market will always move towards equilibrium, however. The amount and timing of the price adjustment, as well as its direction, play a crucial role in the process. This is well illustrated in the relatively simple dynamic market model usually referred to (for reasons that will become obvious) as the "cobweb model."

The Cobweb Model.[5] The model was originally devised to analyze the phenomenon of the corn-hog cycle in the United States. The price of hogs

[5] The mathematics of the cobweb model is given in the Mathematical Note on Section 3.4, page 304. Algebra is required for this analysis, but *not* calculus. The original analysis by Ezekiel is reprinted in:

American Economic Association: *Readings in Business Cycle Theory*, Irwin, 1951.

before World War II showed a tendency to vary in a cyclical manner, rising to a peak, falling to a trough, then rising again, and so on. In this model, in addition to the usual assumptions of the basic market model, we make certain additional assumptions concerning the dynamic properties of the market.

(1) The market takes place at discrete intervals, which we can regard as seasons.

(2) The demand curve is to be interpreted in the ordinary way.

(3) The supply curve is given the following special interpretation: First, a point on the supply curve, like S_1 in Figure 3.2(a) expresses the fact that if the price is P_0 *this* season, suppliers will plan to produce an amount S_1 for *next* season. Second, once the supply plans are made, they are unchangeable and the quantity actually supplied will be sold for whatever it will bring.

Consider Figure 3.2(a). Suppose the price is initially at P_0 in the first

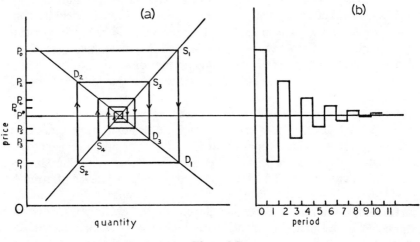

Figure 3.2

season. Producers will plan to supply a quantity S_1 in the second season. When the second season comes, the quantity S_1 will appear on the market, to be sold for what it will fetch. The price at which this quantity S_1 will all be purchased is given by the point D_1 on the demand curve corresponding to the same quantity, giving a price P_1. This is below the equilibrium price, just as P_0 was above it. At the price P_1, suppliers will plan to produce quantity S_2 for the third season. When the third season arrives, this quantity will sell for price P_2, corresponding to the point D_2 on the demand curve, a price above the equilibrium price, but closer to it than P_0 had been. This will lead to a decision to produce quantity S_3 for the fourth season, giving a price P_3, closer to the equilibrium price P^* than any of the previous prices, and so on.

If we graph the successive market prices against time, as shown in Figure 3.2(b), we see that they alternate above and below the equilibrium price, but are converging towards it. Figure 3.2(a) itself shows the reasons for the name which has been attached to the model.

Now consider Figure 3.3(a). Although it has supply and demand

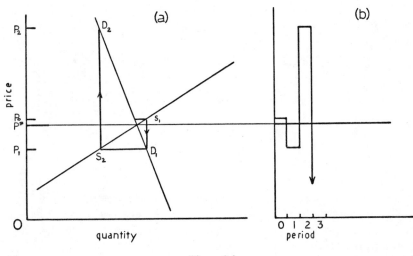

Figure 3.3

curves with the normal directions of slope, we see that, commencing with a price P_0 in the first season, the prices in successive seasons alternate about the equilibrium price, but now diverge away from it, as shown in Figure 3.3(b).

In both cases there is negative feedback. A price above equilibrium results in a fall in price. A price below equilibrium in a rise, but the amount of the price change is clearly inappropriate in the second case.

Stability of the Cobweb Model. Where is the difference between the two models? It lies, not in the directions of slope of the supply and demand curves (the same for both) but in the *relative* slopes of the curves.

In Figure 3.2, where the price converges to equilibrium (price stability) the supply curve has a slope steeper than the demand curve. In Figure

3.3, where the price diverges from equilibrium (price instability) it is the demand curve that has the steeper slope.

We can show the significance of the relative slopes in determining the stability properties quite simply. Look at Figure 3.4. A price P' will give

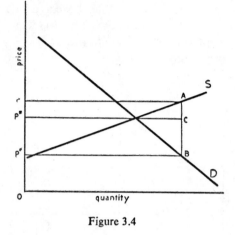

Figure 3.4

rise to planned production for the following season corresponding to the point A on the supply curve. When that season arrives, the output will fetch a price given by the point B on the demand curve vertically beneath A. If C is the point on the vertical AB which corresponds to $P*$, the equilibrium price, then an initial price P' which is above equilibrium by the amount AC will lead, in the following season, to the price P'', which is below the equilibrium by the amount CB. If AC is greater than CB, that is, the slope of the supply curve is steeper than that of the demand curve, the difference between P'' and $P*$ will be less than that between P' and $P*$ and the price will be converging towards equilibrium. If the slope of the supply curve is less than that of the demand curve, AC will be smaller than CB, and the price will diverge from the equilibrium.

If the slopes of the curves happen to be exactly equal, the price in one season will be exactly as much below equilibrium as it had been above in the previous season, and prices would alternate indefinitely without either converging to equilibrium or moving away from it. This last case was originally proposed as an explanation of the hog cycle, but an economic model whose relationship to a real phenomenon depends on exact, coincidental, and persistent relationship between two numerical parameters (here the two slopes) does not provide a very satisfactory explanation of that phenomenon.

The Market47

Lessons from the Cobweb Model. The most important aspect of cobweb example is that it is a simple dynamic model that well illustrates some of the basic determinants of stability and instability of markets generally. To read the lessons of this model, we need to interpret its strictly mathematical properties in terms of behavior. Both the stable and unstable cases show negative feedback in the sense that an above equilibrium price results in a price being lower the next season, and a below equilibrium price results in a price being higher the next season. In the ordinary cobweb example, price change represents an overshoot, since the price moves from one side of the equilibrium to the other, but it is possible to have a market model with both curves having the same direction of slope (possible, although unusual) in which the price always remains on the original side of equilibrium. In such a market, possible in principle, but not representative of the type of market to which the basic model is most applicable, the condition for stability is the same as that in the example given—the market is stable if the slope of the supply curve is steeper than than of the demand curve, whether both curves slope up or slope down.

If we consider the market mechanism involved in the cobweb case, we see that there are two adjustment processes involved. Given the price, suppliers adjust quantity to this price, but only in the following season. Given the quantity, buyers adjust price to this quantity. The steeper the supply curve, the less do suppliers change the quantity when the price changes. The steeper the demand curve, the more do buyers adjust the price when the quantity changes. Thus, if the supply curve is less steep than the demand curve, suppliers adjust quantity when the price changes, then buyers adjust the price as a result of the quantity change, but adjust it by *more* than the original change that brought about the supply adjustment. The unstable case can be likened to two players throwing a ball to each other, in which the return is faster than the original throw, so that the two players keep moving back from each other. In the stable case, the demand adjustment is less than the price change that caused the original supply adjustment, so that the price converges to equilibrium.

In this simple dynamic case, a price change sets in motion an adjustment process which results in further price change. Resulting price change is opposite in direction to the original but may be greater in numerical value, leading to instability or less, leading to stability. Thus we see that the strength, as well as the direction, of the price change which results from a previous change is an important determinant of the stability or instability of a dynamic process. In general, overresponsiveness can lead to instability. A small degree of responsiveness may lead to greater certainty of stability, but will also lead to a very slow convergence towards equilibrium.

In the simple cobweb example, if the price commences 20 per cent above equilibrium and the slope of the supply curve exceeds that of the demand curve by only 5 per cent, the price will still be over 11 per cent away from equilibrium after ten seasons. If the slope of the supply curve were double that of the demand curve, however, the price would differ from the equilibrium price by less than 1 per cent after only five seasons. Figures 3.2 and 3.3 were deliberately drawn to illustrate different rates of price change. In Figure 3.2, the numerical values of the slopes are close together, giving slow convergence. In Figure 3.3, they differ more, giving rapid divergence.

Although this model has its uses for illustrating some of the characteristics that lead to stability and instability, much of its special pattern arises from an inbuilt and unrealistic property. *The traders in the cobweb model just never learn from experience!*

The mechanism, especially in the cases in which the price does not converge rapidly to equilibrium, implies a continuous cycle of a high price followed by an increased production leading to a lower price than that at which the producers would plan to supply the quantity on offer. This results in cutting back production so that the price rises again. An observant trader might be expected to notice the pattern of alternate low and high prices, and if he is a producer, plan to supply more in the season following the low price in the expectation that the price will be high, as it has been previously. If producers would do this, the behavior of the model would change fundamentally. We shall discuss the effects of speculation, of which such behavior would be an example, in the next section.

Other Dynamic Formulations. There are many other possible types of dynamic behavior in the basic market model. A simple assumption to make would be that price falls continuously if there is excess supply and rises continuously if there is excess demand, and that the rate of change is directly proportional to the amount of excess supply or demand. If curves slope in the usual direction, such a process is always stable, as pointed out in the previous section.

The characteristics that help to make such a market stable are the continuous adjustments, a little at a time, and a diminution of these adjustments as the excess demand or supply becomes smaller, that is, as equilibrium is approached. These characteristics, especially the first, are lacking in the cobweb model. An adjustment process of the above kind is probably the most commonly used in dynamic market models. It fits in with many of the behavior characteristics we assume traders to have in the aggregate, yet it is extraordinarily difficult to relate the aggregate behavior to the behavior of individual traders. For one thing, in the absence of a centralized market management, the *amount* of excess demand or supply will remain unknown to traders, and, for another, we simply have no theory of *exactly* how a trader will behave if he cannot buy or sell at the going price.

Finally, we may note that even if a market is unstable (and there have been examples of market instability, such as stock market crashes), there may well be bounds on the extent to which prices can actually move away from equilibrium. In Figure 3.3, the unstable cobweb shows price oscillations becoming larger and larger but, in a real market, if prices became extremely low or extremely high, traders would change their behavior. The simple dynamic model should be taken, therefore, only as a representation of behavior over some "normal" price range.

3.5 Arbitrage

In discussing the basic market model so far, we have proceeded as though all transactions were made in one place. Suppose, however, that the economy covered a large area and that marketing occurred in two distinct places, east and west. Should east and west be treated as two distinct markets, perhaps reaching equilibria at quite different prices, or is there some market mechanism which will link the two markets into one?

In general, there will be mechanisms of the kind that bring the markets into a consistent relationship with each other, mechanisms generically known as *arbitrage*.

Arbitrage will occur when sufficient information concerning the happenings in the various marketplaces is available to profit-motivated traders, provided there are no sanctions against the arbitrage process. The mechanism itself is simple. If prices differ between east and west markets, a profit can be made by buying the goods in the low-priced market and reselling them in the high-priced market. Furthermore, the action of the arbitrageurs in buying in the low-priced market increases the demand in that market and tends to raise the price, assuming the local supply curve is not perfectly elastic, while reselling in the high-priced market increases the supply in that market and tends to lower the price, provided the demand is not perfectly elastic.

For markets of the ordinary kind, with upward sloping supply curves and downward sloping demand curves, arbitrage is a simple and satisfactory unifying mechanism, since it requires only knowledge of prices and profit motivation for the traders themselves, it is set in action by price differences, and the process of arbitrage itself tends to diminish those price differences.

Arbitrage is another example of a negative feedback process in which price divergence results in actions which tend to eliminate it.

Arbitrage Costs.[6] The process of arbitrage may, of course, involve some cost to the trader. The most important will be the cost of transporting the quantity in question from one market place to the other. There will be no profit in the transaction unless the price difference between the market places exceeds the cost of transporting a unit of the commodity between them, so that we could expect prices to differ between any two market places, even in equilibrium and after arbitrage, by any amount up to the cost of transport between the markets. If there are other costs of arbitrage, the difference may exceed the transport cost.

Given willing traders, the extent of possible arbitrage is determined primarily by the availability of intermarket information and the cost, chiefly of transport.

The greater the information and the lower the cost of the transactions, the more the various markets for a commodity will be unified. Thus the market in government bonds will be nationwide with a single price. The markets for standard agricultural commodities, such as a particular grade of wheat, will normally be regarded as nationwide, even worldwide, though transport costs are not negligible, because the information system works so well that the local prices differ only by the cost of transport. In a market of this kind, it is usual to take the reference price as the price of the commodity at the particular place, the same for all parts of the market, so that we can regard the market as reaching a uniform price.

There are other commodities in which the communication of information over a wide area is poor, and in which the transport costs are very large, so that the markets are localized. An extreme example is housing. Rents may vary widely over the country for equivalent accommodations.

There may be commodities for which the market fails to be unified because of inadequate transmission of information, even though transport costs may be low. Fashion goods may sell at varying prices in stores with equivalent service, even in the same city, because neither the buyers nor the sellers have available all the information concerning all prices in all stores.

Mention was made in Section 2.7 of the case in which point supply (or rationing) could lead to individuals obtaining scarce goods at the official price, then reselling at a higher price to individuals whose demand could not be satisfied on the regular market. There is a clear affinity be-

---

[6] Arbitrage is simply a special case of *production* in the economist's broad sense (See Chapter 4), and arbitrage costs a special case of *production costs* (Chapter 5).

tween this kind of activity (ticket scalping, black marketing) and arbitrage, but the constraints in the official market prevent the process reaching free market equilibrium.

Arbitrage may also occur *within* a market, if a uniform equilibrium price has not yet been reached. Arbitrageurs will buy from traders selling at low prices and resell in competition with those selling at high prices, hastening the movement towards price uniformity.

3.6 Speculation

The term speculation tends to conjure up for the layman the image of a rather dishonest market operator who either makes huge profits or is responsible for financial disasters. To the economist, speculation simply means profit-motivated responses to expected but uncertain market changes over time.

Suppose that the market for a certain commodity takes place every month and that the market circumstances are known with absolute certainty for this month and next month. Suppose also that ordinary demand and supply conditions for both months would result in a market price higher next month than this. Obviously a profit could be made by buying on this month's market, holding the commodity, then selling on next month's. Buying now would tend to raise the price now, selling next month would tend to lower the price then, so that action would tend to bring the prices in the two months closer together.

Arbitrage Over Time. Under the circumstances given, the process would be precisely analogous to arbitrage between markets separated in time instead of in space. Costs of transport in space would be replaced by costs of storage through time. There is one additional element in time arbitrage, however. Buying and holding a commodity for a month requires an *investment,* since the value of the commodity so purchased represents the use of funds which cannot be used for other purposes until the commodity is sold in the following month. Since those funds could have been lent out for interest, the trader will not make the arbitrage transaction unless the profit from it exceeds the return he could obtain for merely lending the funds for a month. Thus the time arbitrage must cover the costs of storing the commodity plus the interest that could have been earned on the funds involved, the latter being one of an important category of costs which are referred to by economists as *opportunity costs* since they are not cash outlays, but losses incurred by choosing one opportunity rather than another.

Suppose now that we have the same two markets but, in the absence of arbitrage, the price this month would be higher than next month. As before, a profit could be made by buying commodities next month at the lower price and reselling them this month at the higher price. But time, unlike space, is not symmetrical. Commodities can often be stored from the present until the future; they cannot be transferred directly from the future to the present. However, arbitrage may still be expected to operate in this case for commodities in which traders customarily maintain stocks. If the price is currently high, traders will sell now and run their stocks down below the level they would normally maintain, planning to replenish their stocks next month at the lower price. This will have the same effect as if the commodity could be transferred from the future to the present. There are no storage costs as such but there must be a cost attached to maintaining stocks below the desired level for a month, otherwise the desired level of stocks would be a meaningless concept.

If the price next month and the month after that and the future months as far ahead as anyone could consider were all known, then we would have a simple arbitrage through time analogous to arbitrage in space. But next month's price is never known with certainty during this month's market, while the price in the eastern market *can* be known with certainty in the western market. It is the difference in the information available between markets separated in time, compared with those separated in space, that makes most of the crucial difference between the two. There is also an asymmetry in the relationship between the time-separated markets that is responsible for the remainder of the difference between these and space-separated markets. The asymmetry lies in the fact that action is possible for future markets, but certain information is not available, while information is freely available for past markets but it is too late for action.

Speculation. Due to the lack of information concerning future market states, operations involving buying for later resale or selling off for later restocking, can only be based on *guesses,* some carefully formulated and others much less so, concerning the future. Such operations, based on uncertain relations between present and future markets, are *speculation.* If the future were known with certainty, these same operations would simply be arbitrage.

Unlike arbitrage, which always tends towards equalizing prices in the two markets, speculation may result in a tendency to diminish time differences in prices or in a tendency to accentuate them. Suppose that the future price would have been, as was discovered after the event, higher than the present price in the absence of any intertemporal trading. If the traders correctly guessed that this would be the case, they would tend to buy now for resale later, raising the present price and lowering the future price and bringing the present and future prices closer together.

Importance of Correct Guesses. In general, speculation based on correct guesses concerning future markets will tend to have this effect on ironing out price fluctuations and can be regarded as stabilizing speculation. If, however, traders in the above situation had incorrectly expected prices to be lower in the next period, they would have sold off in the first period, further lowering the price, then restocked in the second period, driving the price even higher. Prices in the two periods would have diverged even more as a result of speculative activity than they would have in its absence. Such activity would be regarded as destabilizing speculation.

Not all markets are suited to extensive intertemporal trading. Some commodities may be so perishable that they cannot be held from one market period to another, others may carry storage costs that are large compared to potential price differences. In some markets, traders simply may not be in the habit of thinking about potential speculative gains, although, if the gains were attractive enough, speculators experienced in other markets may discover new outlets for their activities. Almost all markets in major storable commodities do have intertemporal trading, the best known example being the stock market. This is especially suited to speculative activity, since physical storage costs are virtually zero.

The stock market in the United States has certainly seen its share of destabilizing speculation, especially notable in the 1929 crash. Before the crash, traders expected future prices to be ever higher than they were then, pushing prices further up. When their expectations were ultimately disappointed, after being fulfilled many times, they expected prices to fall even more than they would have in the absence of speculation, and the selling activities pushed them further down.

The existence of stabilizing speculation is more difficult to detect than the existence of destabilizing speculation. The U. S. stock market has many long periods of relative stability. Has this been due to stabilizing speculation, or has it just been due to the absence of too much destabilizing speculation? This is a question we cannot answer for certain in either the stock market or other markets such as foreign exchange, which have large speculative elements.

In general, destabilizing speculation requires not only inappropriate expectations concerning future prices, but a considerable consensus in the same inappropriate opinion. One of the inevitable characteristics of uncertainty concerning future prices is that people will differ in their expectations—some will think prices are going down when others think they are going up. If opinions are sufficiently dispersed, the net effect of speculation on the market may be very small. Those who think the price is going up will buy. Those who think it is going down will sell, and the two groups' activities may nearly cancel out. After the event, one of the groups will have been right, making a profit. The other will have been wrong taking a loss. Speculation will have transferred wealth from one group of speculators to the other without having affected the amount of the market very much. In a period of relative market stability it is likely that the above situation is a common one.

Stabilizing speculation is associated with correctly guessing future prices, and correctly guessing future prices with appropriate action would give the speculator a profit. The association between these two has been taken by some economists to imply that the existence of speculative profits implies that speculation is, on the whole, stabilizing. This argument does not necessarily follow, nor is it factually established that speculators as a group have made profits (as opposed to one set of speculators profiting at the expense of the others) in markets to which this opinion has been applied. The best that can be said on existing evidence is that speculation *could* be stabilized and that it might be so in fact.

Methods of Guessing. There is a very large literature of speculation, and a very large number of models of speculative markets have been discussed. The task of formal models of such markets is not to add to our knowledge of the mechanism of speculation itself (this is covered in the very simple analysis already set up), but to attempt to formulate the mechanism by which speculators make their guesses concerning the future course of prices. Since the past and the present form the only data available from which to formulate future expectations, most models of speculative markets assume that the guesses concerning future prices are based on the past history of the market, usually on the past history of prices.

A very simple model, for example, would be to suppose that traders expect prices to change from this period to the next in the same direction, and to the same amount they changed from the last period to this—a naive but simple assumption. Suppose that, in the absence of speculation, demand and supply schedules would in fact be the same in every period. Then, if nothing happened, prices would be the same in all periods, they would be expected to remain the same, and no speculation would occur. If, after a period of stable prices, an accidental and temporary price rise should occur of, say, 1 per cent, speculators would expect next period's price to be 1 per cent higher still (2 per cent above the original) and if carrying costs were zero would buy on today's market so long as the price would be lower than the expected price next period. But this buying would drive up the present price, generate expectations of next period's price being even more than 2 per cent higher than the base price, lead to more buying, rising prices, expected higher future prices and so on. Such a model would represent destabilizing speculation.

There is no end to the models of speculative behavior that can be devised, given different assumptions about the way in which speculators guess future prices on the basis of past experience, and the extent of the speculative trading that takes place. Typically, such models are stable or unstable, depending on the exact relationship between the numerical values of the various relationships assumed. The extent to which a particular model is a good representation of a particular market depends on the correspondence between the general assumption and the numerical coefficients of the model and the actual market, something that can only be established by empirical investigation of a difficult and uncertain kind.

3.7 Related Markets

We have already discussed (Section 3.5) the interaction between physically separated markets for the same good. Such markets are interconnected by simple arbitrage. We now turn to examine the interconnections between markets for different, but *related,* goods.

By related goods, we mean simply that the demand for either good depends in a significant way on the price of the other. In elasticity terms, the *cross elasticity* is not negligible. We expect, for example, that the demand for single family houses will depend on the rent of apartments as well as on the price of houses, and that the demand for automobiles will depend on the price of gasoline. We can also have goods related through the *supply* conditions, but we shall concentrate on demand only.

Substitutes and Complements. Consider two goods, A and B. If the complete demand schedule for good A includes the price of B as an important market circumstance, the goods are related, and there will be a particular demand curve for A associated with each price of B. Consider the possible relations between the demand curves for A which correspond to different prices for B. Let us look at it in the context of the direction in which the demand curve for A "shifts" when the price of B rises:

(1) If the demand curve for A shifts to the right (demand for A increases), A is said to be a *gross substitute*[7] for B.

---

[7] The substitution (or complementarity) is *gross* in the sense that it includes the effects of all relevant market factors and is based on aggregate market behavior. The gross effects are observable and measurable.

(2) If the demand curve for *A* shifts to the left (demand for *A* decreases), *A* is said to be a *gross complement* for *B*.

For a variety of reasons which will become apparent as the analysis of the book progresses, substitution is regarded as the most *typical* relationship, but complementarity may also occur (pipes and pipe tobacco would be typical complements). It can usually be assumed that the relationships are symmetric, so that *B* is a substitute for *A* if *A* is a substitute for *B*.

Equilibria in Related Markets. If two markets are related, their equilibria are inextricably connected and we cannot determine the equilibrium in either market without simultaneously determining that in the other. Suppose a change in supply conditions occurs in market *A* when both markets are in equilibrium. If the *A* market was isolated, the new equilibrium could be found as the intersection of the new supply curve with the original demand curve.

But if the intersection gives a price change, it cannot be the new equilibrium. For the price change in *A* will shift the demand curve in market *B* and change the price there. This will, in turn, shift the demand curve in market *A,* giving a new price and setting up successive changes in both markets. If the changes reach an equilibrium, the equilibrium in market *A* must be the intersection of the changed supply curve with a *new* demand curve. This must be the demand curve corresponding to the new equilibrium price in *B,* itself depending on a new demand curve which must correspond to the new equilibrium price in *A*.

Thus the equilibria must be solved simultaneously, and this cannot be done with simple supply and demand curve geometry. Because of the relatedness, any change in *either* market will give new equilibria in *both*. Because the same interrelations apply to dynamic behavior, the two markets will be stable or unstable *as a pair*.

In principle, all markets are related, as we shall see in Chapter 9. However, the relationship between one market and any *one* (or few) other may be negligible, and we can use ordinary partial analysis as an approximation. In the case we have been discussing here, the *A* and *B* markets are closely related to each other, but only remotely to other markets. We still use a partial approach, but it is the *markets as a pair* that we consider in isolation from the rest of the economy.

Chapter 4 treats the economic theory of production, drawing on modern methods of approach.

CONTENTS

4.1 What We Mean by Production   59
4.2 Production Processes   60
4.3 Technology and Technical Efficiency   61
4.4 Production Under Simple Conditions   64
4.5 Properties of Isoquants   68
4.6 Substitution Among Inputs   70
4.7 The Production Function   72
4.8 Returns to Scale   75
4.9 Returns to a Variable Input—1   79
4.10 Returns to a Variable Input—2   83
4.11 Indivisibilities   88
     Exercises   91

CHAPTER 4

PRODUCTION

4.1 What We Mean by Production

The term "production" in economics covers a much wider range of activities than in its everyday use. To the economist, production means any process which converts or transforms a commodity or commodities into a *different* commodity. Now two commodities are "different" in the economic sense if they are not viewed as completely interchangeable by all consumers.

It follows that, from this point of view, the processes below all represent production, although they may not be so called in ordinary usage.

(1) the transport of a commodity from one place to another, since an automobile in San Francisco and an identical automobile in New York are not identical commodities. Obviously a consumer in either New York or San Francisco will not regard the two as interchangeable.

(2) the storage of a commodity, since a consumer will not consider an extra orange during the harvest season as exactly equivalent to an orange during the off-season.

(3) wholesaling, breaking bulk, repackaging, and retailing, since a consumer will not consider bulk cornflakes at Battle Creek to be equivalent to a package of cornflakes at the corner store.

Furthermore, "commodities" in economics need not be physical objects, but can be services or intangible objects, so that doctors, hairdressers, and orchestras are also engaged in production.

Production, therefore, is not simply the making of physical things, but the transport, storage, and selling of these things, as well as of services and other intangibles. Modern economics does not distinguish, as some nineteenth-century economists and modern Marxists do, between "productive" and "nonproductive" labor in the economy, since production covers virtually all economic activity other than ultimate consumption. Only a small proportion of the labor force in a modern economy is *making* something in any very fundamental sense. After all, a coal miner is really just transporting coal, which is already in the mine, to the surface.

Nevertheless, activity of a manufacturing or forming kind is the *typical* production process, to economists as well as others, and most of our discussion will be in a context of this kind.

4.2 Production Processes[1]

Were we to ask a chemist, an engineer, or a cook how to make some relatively simple product, we would be given an answer in terms of raw materials or ingredients, the proportions and order in which the ingredients were to be brought together, and process times and temperatures. Since these people are clearly controlling *production processes,* or activities in which the output is different in some essential way from the inputs, it might seem that answers of this kind would provide the key to the *theory of production* in economics.

Indeed they do, but only as a beginning. The simplest *recipe,* or statement of the ingredients and their proportions, is not, from the economist's point of view, necessarily complete. First we note that ingredients do not jump out of their containers and mix themselves together—these operations require some human intervention, so the process requires some *labor* input. Second, some kind of *equipment,* even of the simplest kind, is necessary for mixing and for heating or other processing. This equipment must be provided before the process can start and will, in general, be usable for other processes, and is one type of a general category of things called *capital* by the economist. Furthermore, the process must take place somewhere and so occupies space or *land* (this is much more apparent, of course, in the case of an agricultural process such as corn growing), and the process itself takes some *time,* even if the time is mainly taken up by transporting and mixing ingredients. A process need not have a single output. An oil refinery, for example, cracks crude petroleum (combined

---

[1] The approach to production theory which is given here is derived from the modern approach known as *activity analysis.* This is closely related to *linear programming.* The two-input case given here can be studied without the use of any mathematics other than arithmetic.

with labor, capital, land, power, etc.) into several different types of refined petroleum (gasoline, diesel, fuel oil, etc.). Outputs produced together from the same process are called *joint products*.

The economist starts his analysis of production from the *complete recipe*, the statement of what inputs, including labor, capital, land and possibly other inputs, as well as ingredients or raw materials, are required to produce a specified amount of the output or outputs.

This complete recipe defines a *production process* or *productive activity*. The economist is interested in analysing such processes or activities, especially the following aspects:

(1) If we exactly double (or halve) the amount of every input, will we exactly double (or halve) the output, or will output change in a different proportion? The properties of production processes which provide the answer to such questions are *scale* properties.

(2) Is there more than one process for producing, say, one ton of corn? (Each different set of input proportions represents a different process). If there are several processes, how are the input proportions related to each other? The properties of production processes which answer these questions are properties concerning *input substitution*.

(3) If there are joint products, are there processes giving different relative amounts of the products? Can a refinery, by using different processes, vary the proportion of gasoline to fuel oil obtained from a ton of crude? These are problems of *output* or *product substitution*.

4.3 Technology and Technical Efficiency

In any given society, or part of society, at any given historical date, the recipes for a certain number of productive processes are known. The total list of all known productive processes is the *available technology* of that society of that time. Clearly the number of such processes is extremely large in the United States at the present time. It is much less in a small African country just commencing to absorb Western technology, and was much less in the United States a century ago than today.

There is no one who can be considered to know the whole technology of an advanced society, but those concerned with the production of some type of output can be presumed to be aware of that part of the whole technology which is relevant to them.

Even if we narrow down the consideration of the technology to only those processes which are relevant to the production of some particular good (cotton cloth, for example), the state of technological knowledge may not be uniform even among those actually engaged in the production of cotton cloth. Some mill managers may simply have failed to keep up with current developments and may not know certain processes which are available. Others may have, through research, developed processes which they have managed to keep secret so that these remain unknown to other firms.

As a starting point, however, the economic analysis of production assumes a general context in which there is perfect transmission of technological information, so that the available technology is assumed to be the same for all firms in the economy.

It is a matter of history that the available technology has expanded with time and presumably will continue to do so. This *technological change* is an important matter to be taken into consideration in long-run theories of economic growth, but the context of microeconomics is more typically that of a period in which the available technology is taken to be fixed. This context is less realistic in the discussion of modern industrial production with relatively rapid technological change than in the more slowly changing society in which the study of economics first commenced.

We suppose that, as new processes come to be discovered, the old ones remain known, so that the available technology is cumulative, a library of all the recipes for production that have ever been discovered.

Types of Technological Change. A new process may be related to the old in one of the following ways:

(1) It may use the same types of input, and produce the same type of output as some existing process but use a *less* quantity of some or most inputs and *no more* of the remainder, to produce a given quantity of output.

(2) It may have the same type of input and output as an existing process, but use *less* of some inputs, but *more* of others, to produce a given quantity of output.

(3) It may require inputs, or produce outputs that are of a kind not previously available at all, as for example the first production process for producing plutonium.

The third type of relationship is technologically exciting, but not easily subject to analysis at a general level so we shall be concerned with the first two.

Technical Efficiency. If, as in (1) above, the new process can produce the same output as the old but with less of some inputs and no more of others (or, equivalently, can produce more output with the same or less of all inputs), the old process has become *technically inefficient*. Note that we must take into account *all* inputs. A process that uses more raw materials is not technically inefficient if it uses less labor, or less equipment. Since there is no reason why a producer should use more inputs than he needs, it is an easy step to make our first assumption concerning the nature of production:

A process which is technically inefficient, given the available technology, will never be used.

We can use the word "never" since a technically inefficient process will remain so forever. Of course a process which is technically inefficient in 1970 might not have been so in 1870, since it may be inefficient relative only to processes discovered during the intervening century, but it will still be technically inefficient in 2070. To the extent that technological change involves the rendering of earlier processes *technically* inefficient, it can unambiguously be called *technological progress.*

Since technically inefficient processes will never be used, we do not need to consider a potential technical change which is technically inefficient with respect to the old, since it will add nothing relevant to the technology. For the same reason, technically inefficient processes are completely replaced by the more efficient process and so can be "forgotten" without diminishing the scope of the available technology.

If the new process is related to the old as in the second case given earlier, so that it uses less of some inputs but more of others, we cannot regard the old process as *technically* inefficient with respect to the new, nor the new with respect to the old. The old process will remain part of the available technology. The new process may actually be *used* in a particular economy at a particular time, in preference to the old, but we cannot assert that the old process would *never again* be found useful under any circumstances.

Consider, for example, two processes for making roads, one (the "old" process) using laborers with picks, shovels and baskets, the other (the "new" process) using workers with bulldozers and trucks. The old process clearly uses more labor, but less capital, than the new. It is not difficult to see that a society with a great deal of labor, but very short of capital equipment, might choose the old method even though it was well aware of the existence of the new. Or, taking a related but different point of view, a road contractor in a society in which wages of unskilled labor were very low, but the cost of hiring machinery was very high, might find it cost less to use the old method than the new.

Even in the United States, the old method would continue to remain part of the available technology, though it may be rarely, if ever, actually used.

Thus if two processes are so related that the first is technically inefficient relative to the second, we know without requiring any further information that the first process will not be used. But if two processes are not related in this way, we need further information before predicting which process would actually be used. The choice between processes in this case would be an *economic* choice, not a purely *technical* choice.

4.4 Production Under Simple Conditions

Let us suppose a process is known for producing something, which we shall just call the "output," and this process uses labor and equipment as inputs.

Since diagrammatic arguments have very great virtues in teaching basic economic theory, and since the page or blackboard has only two dimensions, economists traditionally simplify their basic models to two dimensions which, in this case, means two inputs. There are very few processes which do not require some raw material input as well as labor and equipment, yet most expositions of basic production theory completely ignore raw materials. For the time being, we shall follow the usual tradition but justify it by making the following assumption:

All processes use the same quantities of raw materials to produce a given level of output.

This is a very reasonable assumption. It simply amounts to assuming that the number of bricks needed to build a house is the same whether the house is built by labor with almost no equipment, or by less labor assisted by cranes, scaffolding, handcarts and other aids. The reader may wish to argue that more mechanized methods may, in fact, lead to more bricks being broken and wasted than in less mechanized methods, but we shall ignore such effects.

Once the assumption has been made, the raw material input is no longer relevant in choosing between production processes, and so may be ignored.

Output with a Single Process.[2] In terms of labor and equipment, suppose the initial process produces an output of one ton per day, using two men and one "machine," so that the inputs will be measured as two man-days

---

[2] Although we use the single process as a starting point for the analysis of production in which many processes are available, it may often be true that only one process is actually used in the economy. As will be apparent when the choice of the least cost process is discussed in the next Chapter, one process (or a specific combination of processes) will be used so long as relative input prices do not change in a major way.

The simplified models of the economy known as *Leontief* or *input-output* models are based on the use of only one process for each industry. The attraction of these models lies mainly in empirical applications. The only processes that can be *observed* are those actually being used, and so it is attractive to assume that the same processes will be used when the circumstances change. This assumption is sometimes justified, sometimes not.

and one machine Jay We suppose that the men require no supervision and that no other input such as "management" is required.

In Figure 4.1, the point P_1 represents the inputs required on this process to produce one ton of output per day.

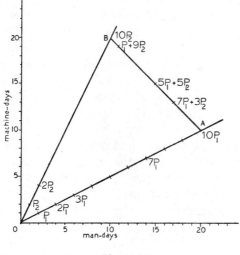

Figure 4.1

Now let us ask the question: If we took two more men, and a machine identical to the first one, and set them up in the other corner of the factory so that the two groups did not get in each other's way, why should the new group not produce exactly the same as the old?

Why not, indeed? In the absence of a specific reason to the contrary, we shall assume that the process can be duplicated. The duplication will use four man-days and two machine-days to give an output of two tons per day, represented by the point $2P_1$ on the diagram.

If the process can be exactly duplicated, it can be reproduced three, four, . . . ten, or any number of times. We shall refer to this number as the *level* at which the process is operated. Operating a process at, say seven times the unit level will use exactly seven times the amount of each input as at the unit level and produce exactly seven times the amount of output.

The inputs corresponding to operating our particular process at various levels is given by the points $3P_1$, $4P_1$, and so on in the diagram. The proportions in which the inputs are related to each other (two men per machine) are the same at all levels, so the points P_1, $2P_1$ and so on all lie on a straight line passing through the origin.

Addition of a Second Process. Now suppose a second process is added to the available technology. It might, of course, be a process that could produce one ton of output with one machine (identical with that in the first process) and only one man, in which case the first process would be technically inefficient and so discarded. The technology would still consist of a single process, but a new one. But if the second process gave one ton of output from one man and two machines (identical with the machine of the other process), neither process would be technically inefficient relative to the other, and both would remain in the technology.

In Figure 4.1, P_2 represents the inputs for operating the process at unit level. In exactly the same way as before, we can argue that operating the second process at various levels will simply multiply all inputs and the output by the level of output, giving points $2P_2$, $3P_2$, $10P_2$, and so on.

Let us concentrate on an output of 10 tons. We can now produce this by operating either P_1 (point $10P_1$ on the diagram) at a level of 10 using 20 men and 10 machines, or P_2 (point $10P_2$ on the diagram) at a level of 10, using 10 men and 20 machines. But adding the second process does more than add one new way of producing 10 tons of output, since we can combine the outputs from using one process in one corner of the factory, and the other process in the other corner.

If we operate the first process at level 5 and the second also at level 5, the combined output will be 10 tons. At these levels the first process will require 10 man-days and the second 5 man-days, a total of 15 man-days, while the combined machine inputs will be 15 machine-days. Thus we have a very important addition to the technology.

The combination $5P_1 + 5P_2$ is easily seen to be on the midpoint of the line joining points $10P_1$ and $10P_2$ in the diagram. But we can also make combinations $P_1 + 9P_2, 2P_1 + 8P_2, \ldots 9P_1 + P_2$, all of which produce 10 tons and represent input combinations also lying on the line joining $10P_1$, $10P_2$. In other words:

If the points A, B *represent, respectively, the inputs required to produce some given output by each of two processes used separately, the same output can be produced by linear combinations of the processes and the required inputs will be represented by points along the line* AB.

To obtain *all* points along AB, we need to assume that processes can be operated at fractional levels, so that we can, for example, obtain 10 tons by the combination $6.4\,P_1 + 3.6\,P_2$.

Note that there is no way of combining the processes to obtain input combinations to the left of the line through OP_2 or to the right of the line through OP_1.

Addition of a Third Process. Now let us introduce a third process into the technology, and concentrate on the problem of producing 10 tons of output per day. In Figure 4.2 points *A, B* correspond to the points $10P_1$,

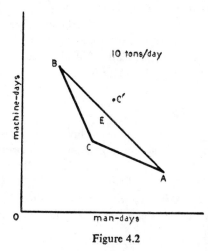

Figure 4.2

$10P_2$ in the previous diagram. If the inputs required for producing 10 tons by the third process were represented by a point like C', it is clear that C' is not technically inefficient relative to *A* or *B*, nor are *A* or *B* technically inefficient relative to C', so it might seem that such a process could be a useful addition to the technology. But we know we can produce 10 tons with any output combination along the line *AB*, and E is such a point. Compared with *E*, C' requires more of both inputs to produce 10 tons of output, and is thus inefficient. Now, in determining whether or not a point is technically inefficient, we must compare it not only with *A* and *B* but with all points along *AB*.

Thus a process corresponding to C' would not be used. But if the inputs for producing 10 tons with the new process were given by the point *C*, it would not be inefficient. Now, however, some new efficiency relationships of great importance have been introduced. *C* clearly makes *E* and some of the points on *AB* inefficient. As before, we can argue that if *A* and *C* are input combinations giving 10 tons of output, then input combinations along *AC* will also give 10 tons and, in the same way, input combinations along *BC* will give 10 tons.

Isoquants. The bent line *BCA* (drawn heavily in the diagram) therefore passes through all *efficient* processes or combinations of processes that can produce 10 tons of output, when the technology consists of 3 processes (represented at the 10-ton level by points *A, B, C*) which can be operated at any level and combined in any way.

A line like *BCA*, giving all input combinations which are *efficient* for producing some stated output level (in the example given, 10 tons), is called an *isoquant* or *isoproduct* curve—the Greek root "iso" meaning "the same." A specific isoquant is always labelled with its output (for example the "10-ton isoquant") or implicitly assumed to have such a label. From an isoquant, we can read off all the efficient ways of producing the output with which the isoquant is labelled.

4.5 *Properties of Isoquants*[3]

In the preceding section, we showed how a simple isoquant could be derived from information concerning processes that could be operated at any level without affecting each other. Here we shall develop the properties of these isoquants in more detail.

Consider Figure 4.3, in which are drawn points *A, B, C, D, E,* each representing a known process capable of producing *n* units of output. As

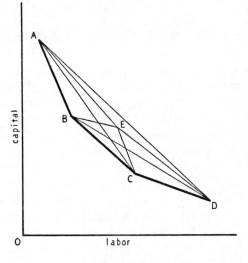

Figure 4.3

before, we assume these processes can be combined in any way with lines drawn to show the inputs for combination of all possible pairs of processes. Now the point *E* is efficient relative to combinations of *A* and *D*, but it is not efficient relative to combinations of *A* and *C*, *B* and *D*, or *B* and *C*. It

[3] For the reader trained in calculus, the properties of smooth isoquants are discussed in the Mathematical Note on this Section.

is easy to see that the only efficient processes are *A, B, C, D* and the only efficient combinations are *A* and *B, B* and *C, C* and *D*. Thus the *n*-unit isoquant is the heavily drawn bent line *ABCD*.

If we move down the isoquant from the top left-hand corner (*A*), we see that at every bend the next segment has a flatter slope than the one above and to the left of it. At every different process the isoquant bends to the right, never to the left. If we move along the route *ABEC,* the segment *EC* bends to the left relative to *BE* and consists of process combinations all of which are inefficient as compared with combinations along *BC*.

Convexity of Isoquants. Since an isoquant consists of efficient points only, we can state the two basic properties we have now shown:

(1) *Every portion of an isoquant slopes downward to the right.*

(2) *At every change of slope on an isoquant, the lower right hand portion has a flatter slope than the portion to the left and above the point at which the slope changes.*

If there are only two processes (with two inputs) the isoquant is simply a straight line sloping downward to the right, but if there are more than two processes, the general shape of the isoquant must fit property (2). This property is that *isoquants are convex to the origin.*

Note that if we take any two points on an isoquant and join them by a straight line, the part of the isoquant between the two points is either the straight line itself, or lies entirely on the origin side of the straight line, never on the side of the line away from the origin. Technically, the set of points along the isoquant and all points between this and a line joining the extreme processes forms a *convex set.*

Production with Many Processes. So far we have considered technologies consisting of only a few efficient processes. Consider Figure 4.4(a), where ten efficient processes are shown, with the isoquant made up of the nine segments A_1A_2, A_2A_3, and so on, and possessing the necessary properties. The angular shape of the earlier isoquant is already blurred, and it is easy to see that, if the number of efficient processes becomes large, the flat seg ments become very small and the isoquant is almost indistinguishable from a smooth curve, as in Figure 4.4(b).

To illustrate an important possibility in production, we have drawn A_{10} on the labor axis. This means that the process A_{10} uses only raw labor, with no capital—always a possibility. A_1, on the other hand, has been drawn somewhat away from the capital axis, to express the general fact that in spite of automation there are no known production processes that require capital but absolutely no labor at all. It must be remembered that

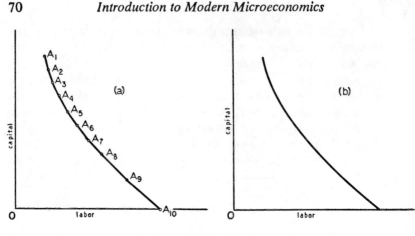

Figure 4.4

turning switches, or just being there in case of trouble, represents use of labor.

In many expositions, isoquants are drawn smoothly curved, with the shape shown in Figure 4.4(b) asserted as a so-called economic law, or simply taken as an assumption. We have chosen not to take this approach here, partly because the analysis of production in terms of individual processes is recognizable to those actually concerned with production (engineers, managers) while curved isoquants are not, and partly because many of the insights into the nature of production are lost by omitting the basic steps in the analysis.

Since production executives observe processes as discrete, rather than in a continuous array, we shall assume, in drawing a continuously curved isoquant, that we are *approximating* a many-process isoquant like that of Figure 4.4(a).[4]

4.6 Substitution Among Inputs[5]

If two processes giving the same output are both efficient, the first process must use less of one input, but more of another, when compared with the second. If this were not so, one of the processes would be in-

---

[4] We have turned a common approach upside down, treating smooth curves as approximations to large numbers of straight segments rather than straight segments as approximations to smooth curves. The old statement "nature does not make jumps" went out with the development of quantum mechanics.

Actually, neither approach is an absolute. It is sometimes convenient to treat the smooth case as an approximation to the nonsmooth (so that we can use calculus), sometimes to take things the other way round (so that we can use other methods of analysis).

[5] The calculus-oriented reader should look at the relevant Mathematical Note.

efficient. Thus if we move from one point on an isoquant to a nearby point, the amount of one input will increase while the other will decrease. We can regard such a move as that of maintaining output while *substituting* more of one input for less of the other. All movements along an isoquant necessarily involve input substitution.

Now consider Figure 4.5. This is a magnification of the part of Figure 4.4(a) near process A_5. As we change from A_4 to A_5, the amount

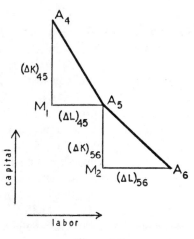

Figure 4.5

of capital used goes down, and the amount of labor used goes up. The change in the amount of capital is the vertical distance of A_4 above A_5 ($=M_1A_4$) and we shall use for this the notation $(\Delta K)_{45}$. (Δ is the capital of the Greek letter δ, delta, and is a traditional mathematical notation for a difference. The subscript 45 denotes concern with the change from process 4 to process 5. We read this expression as "delta K; 4,5.")

Similarly, we shall denote the change in labor between process 4 and process 5 by $(\Delta L)_{45}$.

Moving from A_4 to A_5, ΔK is *negative* (since capital decreases), and ΔL is positive.

The Rate of Substitution. The ratio $\dfrac{(\Delta L)_{45}}{(\Delta K)_{45}}$ is known as the *rate of substitution of labor for capital* between processes 4 and 5 along the portion of the isoquant A_4-A_5. That is, the ratio tells us how many man hours of labor we must substitute for each machine hour given up as we move between A_4 and A_5. It is sometimes referred to more loosely as the *rate of substitution between labor and capital*, a term that can equally be applied to $\Delta K/\Delta L$ (the marginal rate of substitution of capital for labor). If A_4, A_5 are "close" we speak of substitution *at the margin,* and refer to the ratio as the *marginal rate of substitution between labor and capital* at the relevant point on the isoquant.

Since $\Delta L, \Delta K$ have opposite signs, the rate of substitution is negative —a property precisely equivalent to the earlier statement that an isoquant slopes downward to the right. As in the case of the demand curve, it is convenient to take the negativity for granted and talk about the numerical value of the rate of substitution.

Changes in the Rate of Substitution. Now consider a change from process 5 to process 6. As before, we can denote the input changes by $(\Delta K)_{56}$, $(\Delta L)_{56}$. Since the slope of the portion of the isoquant $A_5 A_6$ is flatter than the portion $A_4 A_5$, it follows that the rate of substitution of labor for capital between process 5 and process 6 $(\Delta L)_{56}/(\Delta K)_{56}$ is *numerically* greater than between process 4 and process 5.

That is, as we move around the isoquant from processes requiring relatively more capital and less labor to those requiring more labor and less capital, the rate at which we must substitute labor for capital will *increase numerically* at each new process. In other words, the more we move towards processes using a high ratio of labor to capital, the less effective becomes labor as a substitute for capital, in the sense that we must substitute progressively more and more man-hours of labor for each machine-hour of capital we give up.

This property, which is exactly equivalent to the earlier statement concerning the direction in which the isoquant bends, is usually described as that of *diminishing marginal rate of substitution between inputs.*[6]

4.7 *The Production Function*[7]

In the simple production which we have been investigating, we have seen that every *efficient* combination of the two inputs gives some unique and determinate level of output, the level represented by the isoquant on which the particular input combination lies.

---

[6] The word "diminishing" can be confusing here, since we have shown the rate of substituting to be increasing in numerical terms. Rather than attempting to follow the history of the term, the reader is advised to

(i) remember the shape of an isoquant, and use this to derive any actual properties

(ii) remember that the consequence of moving around an isoquant is called "diminishing marginal rate of substitution."

[7] For a calculus approach, see the relevant Mathematical Note, page 307.

For a finite number of production processes of the kind we have been concerned with, the whole set of production possibilities can be found once we are given the inputs necessary to produce a unit level of output in each process. By operating processes at different levels, combining them, and choosing only efficient input combinations, we can discover the input combinations that will be efficient for producing any given level of output.

Sometimes we wish to describe this relationship between efficient input combinations and possible outputs in a more general way, that can be applied easily to the case where the number of different processes is so large we can consider it to be infinite.

Definition. A general statement of all outputs that can be obtained from all efficient input combinations is called the *production function.* Typically, we would write the production function for two inputs, labor and capital, as

$$X = F(K, L)$$

where X stands for output, K for capital, L for labor.

Mathematically, saying X is a *function* of K and L simply means that, if we arbitrarily choose some value for K and some value for L, the value of X is then determined. The value of X is only determined *uniquely* if we confine the production function to efficient combinations, since a given input combination can give a wide range of different outputs, of which only one (the largest output) is efficient.

Isoquant Maps. A production function involving two inputs cannot be completely depicted in two dimensions, since three quantities (X,K,L) are involved. We can, however, draw several types of two-dimensional diagram that express important properties of the production function. One way is to hold one of the three quantities constant, and graph the relationship between the other two. This is precisely what we did in drawing an isoquant—we held output (X) constant, and considered the relationships that must hold between K,L to give the chosen output. By drawing a series of isoquants, each for a different output, we obtain a useful picture of the production function, as in Figure 4.6(a) and (b). Figure 4.6(a) has been drawn with continuously curved isoquants, of the shape we have shown to be typical. The blank wedge along the K-axis expresses the fact that we have assumed that there is an upper limit to the capital to labor ratio, and that there are no *efficient* input combinations in that area. Figure 4.6(b) shows an isoquant map for a four-process technology, one process using labor only.

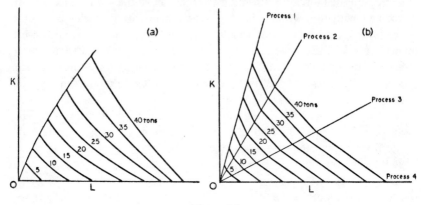

Figure 4.6

An isoquant map, like that of Figure 4.6, actually conveys all the information contained in the production function, provided we imagine the space between the isoquant lines (drawn at ten-ton intervals) to be filled in by isoquants for intermediate output levels. Given such a map, we can pick any combination of inputs, locate it on the diagram and then (provided it is in the effective domain of the production functions) read off the corresponding output by noting which isoquant passes through the point.

We might note some basic properties of isoquant maps that follow directly from our previous analysis, but which can be usefully collected together.

(1) *Isoquants are convex to the origin,* for reasons already discussed.

(2) There cannot be two different isoquants passing through the same point, since the isoquant with the lower output would then represent inefficient production. *Thus isoquants cannot meet or cross each other.*

(3) Of any two isoquants, that further from the origin must represent the higher output, otherwise the outer isoquant would represent inefficient production. Thus, *as we move outward from the origin, we cross isoquants representing successively higher production levels.*

If the reader has a good imagination for these things, he might visualize the three-dimensional graph of the production function, in which the inputs are measured in the two horizontal directions, and the output vertically, as a ridge which rises steadily away from the origin, with the height of the ridge at any point representing the level of output associated with the relevant input combination. By taking all points on the ridge which are at the same height, and looking at the line going through all these points (or contour) from vertically above, we have an isoquant. Thus an isoquant map is directly analogous to a contour map in geography.

Isoquants are, in fact, the sections of the three-dimensional production surface obtained by making a horizontal slice through the surface. Now we could choose to make other slices through the surface (particularly vertical slices of various kinds) and we will investigate the shape of these in the next section.

4.8 Returns to Scale[8]

The term "returns" occurs often in economics, in well-embedded phrases like "returns to scale," "constant returns," "diminishing returns," and "increasing returns." In principle, there should be no confusion attached to the various uses of the term, but unfortunately there is.

The idea refers to what happens when we increase inputs or some combination of inputs. Doing so will be expected to increase some kind of output—the "returns" to the increase in input. Confusions surrounding the term arise from two different sources. One is the type of variation occurring on the input side. Whereas the loose phrase "diminishing returns," which is not exact but widely used, refers typically to varying a *single* input with others fixed, "constant returns" is short for "constant returns to scale" and refers to a variation in all inputs simultaneously. Another, and deeper, source of confusion arises because "returns" is sometimes used to refer to the way in which the output varies with an increase in the *dollar value of input,* although it properly and most often refers to the effect of varying the *physical quantity of input.*

Definitions. We shall use the phrase "returns to scale" to refer *only* to the relationship between changes in the physical quantity of output and changes in the physical quantity of all inputs simultaneously and in the same proportion. The formal definitions, in their simplest form, are as follows:

If doubling or halving *all* inputs always results in *exactly doubling or halving* efficient output, the production process, production function, or production technology is said to possess *constant returns to scale.* If doubling (or halving) all inputs *more than doubles (or halves)* output, it has *increasing returns to scale,* if it *less than doubles (or halves)* output, it has *decreasing returns to scale.*

(The definition can be expressed also in terms of increasing all inputs in the same ratio, in which case we have increasing, constant, or decreasing

---

[8] There is a Mathematical Note on the material of this Section, page 308.

returns to scale if output increases by more than, the same as, or less than, that ratio. If the doubling and halving property holds for all levels of output, it is equivalent, and simpler to express and remember.)

Indivisibilities. This definition is straightforward enough, but many ambiguities still arise in general economic usage. We have previously argued that it would require some special circumstance for *exact* duplication of a production process to have any result other than doubling the output, and therefore that we should generally expect production to show constant returns to scale. We mentioned but did not then discuss "halving" a production process, for the simple reason that, while all processes can be *duplicated* (in principle, at least), it may not be possible to halve them. Whereas one man operating one machine represents a process that can be duplicated by another man and an identical machine, it simply may not be possible to devise a smaller "half-machine" that can be operated by a "half-man" (meaning half the full-time attention of a single man). This is the phenomenon of *indivisibility* that we will take up in a later section.

Input Limitations. It is also possible that, although exact duplication in principle will give double output, *in practice* it may not be possible to double all inputs. This is especially true if some input is somehow related to a state of nature. Doubling the size of the fishing fleet may not double the catch of fish, because one input, the natural availability of fish, is not changed. The purist might argue that, if one duplicated both the fleet and the fishing grounds, one would double the catch. The pragmatist would argue that, although this might well be true, we should leave the natural supply of fish out of our description of the production function for fishing, and consider only those inputs which are the control of economic agents.

Generally speaking economists will tend to omit "state of nature" inputs from consideration in extractive industries, such as mining, fishing and hunting, in which these inputs cannot be controlled. As a result, the production technology may show decreasing returns to scale for a doubling of those inputs actually under control.

It should be noted, however, that we do not necessarily treat "land" in either the agricultural or urban sense in this way since, although the total quantity of land may be fixed, the quantity used by any single producer is under his control.

We shall adopt a pragmatic approach here, by accepting that there can be circumstances under which it is not useful to consider fixed "state of nature" inputs as part of the technology and that we may have effects which can be regarded as decreasing returns to scale. Similarly, and more importantly, we shall later see that indivisibilities lead to effects which can be regarded as increasing returns to scale.

However, it should be stressed again that returns to scale is concerned with the relationship between physical quantities of inputs and physical quantities of outputs. An effect arising from an increase in price of inputs as the quantity used expands is one of *increasing cost,* not *decreasing returns to scale,* and will be discussed in the next chapter. Unfortunately, once again the simplicity and clarity of the distinction becomes muddy in practice because the data available for empirical studies is often in terms of value of output and value of inputs. Attempts to convert such data to quantity terms do not always eliminate price effects.

Constant Returns to Scale. Having considered the various possibilities that can arise, we shall make the following *Working Rule:*

A production process, production function, or production technology will be considered to show constant returns to scale everywhere except in individual cases in which there are special reasons for supposing otherwise. ("Everywhere" is introduced to eliminate special cases in which some processes may show constant returns to scale, some not.)

The isoquant map of a constant returns to scale production function has certain special properties of great importance. These are illustrated in Figure 4.7. In 4.7(a) is shown a production technology with five proc-

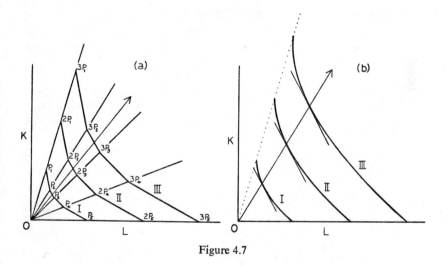

Figure 4.7

esses having constant returns to scale, of the kind we have already discussed. P_1, P_2, P_3, P_4, and P_5 represent the level of operation of each of the processes which gives some base level (say ten tons) of output. The ten-ton isoquant is then the line $P_1P_2P_3P_4P_5$. Now consider operation of the processes at double the base level, represented by the points $2P_1$, $2P_2$, $2P_3$, $2P_4$, and $2P_5$. The line joining these (*II*) is obviously the 20-ton isoquant. This isoquant obviously lies twice as far from the origin, in any direction as the 10-ton isoquant, and each segment of the 20-ton isoquant is obviously parallel to the corresponding segment of the 10-ton isoquant —that is, $2P_32P_4$, for example, is parallel to P_3P_4.

Thus for constant returns to scale we can find the 20-ton isoquant, given the 10-ton isoquant, by drawing radial lines from the origin, like the dotted line shown, and measuring twice the distance from the origin to the 10-ton isoquant. If we join all the points so found, for all radial lines in the quadrant, we have mapped out the 20-ton isoquant.

This property also holds for the 30-ton isoquant, if we measure out 3 times the radial distance to the 10-ton isoquant. The property also obviously holds if the number of processes becomes very large, and so can be applied to smoothly curved isoquants, as in 4.7(b).

Homogeneity. We can summarize these properties of the isoquant map for a constant returns to scale production function as follows:

If the production function shows constant returns to scale everywhere and we know the isoquant for some output, say X, *then we can find any other isoquant, for example that for output* bX, *by drawing radial lines from the origin, measuring a distance along each radial equal to* b *times the distance from the origin to the* X-*isoquant along the same radial, and joining the points. Furthermore, any radial will cut all isoquants at points having the same slope, that is, at which the marginal rate of substitution between inputs is the same.*

The perceptive reader might notice that it would be possible for a production function to have an isoquant map in which the curve found by joining the points all *b* times as far out along the radials as the *X*-isoquant was *an isoquant, but not the* bX-*isoquant*. The isoquants *I, II, III* in Figure 4.7(a) and (b) might, for example, represent outputs 10 tons, 40 tons, 90 tons (obviously increasing returns to scale). Such a production function is said to be *homothetic*. If the isoquant in question represents an output related to *X* by some *power* of *b*, such as b^2, $b½$ ($= \sqrt{b}$) or, more generally, b^r, the production function is said to be *homogeneous* (of degree *r*, if production corresponding to a *b*-fold increase in all inputs increases by b^r).

A *production function showing constant returns to scale everywhere is homogeneous of the first degree* (r $= 1$), *and the two terms are equivalent.*

If the production function is homogeneous of degree greater than one it shows increasing returns to scale, since if inputs are doubled, output increases by 2^r which is more than 2 if r is more than 1. Homogeneity of degree less than one implies decreasing returns to scale.

Nonconstant Returns to Scale. We cannot pursue this particular point further without becoming mathematical, but it is important for the reader to be aware of the following:

Homogeneity greater than (less than) one necessarily implies increasing (decreasing returns to scale), but increasing or decreasing returns to scale does not necessarily imply homogeneity.

In most *empirical* investigations of returns to scale, homogeneity is assumed in order to simplify the econometric work, just as we saw constant elasticity to be assumed in the empirical determinations of demand and supply curves given in Chapter 2. Homogeneity is, however, a special assumption and we should not expect it to be possessed by a general production technology that does not show constant returns to scale. Figure 4.6(a) was drawn deliberately to be non-homogeneous, which should be immediately apparent by looking at the light line marking the northwest boundary of the isoquant map. This line must obviously be straight for any homogeneous function.

Finally we can consider the relationship between returns to scale and the three-dimensional graph of the production function. In examining returns to scale, we are moving out radially from the origin (fixed input proportions) and considering the relationship between the proportionate increase in output and the proportionate increase in inputs. We can think of distances along the radial as measuring the number of fixed proportion input "doses" (where one "dose" may represent three units of capital and two of labor). Thus we are looking at a vertical slice of the production surface, taken radially through the origin, like a pie slice viewed from the side. If there are constant returns to scale, the height of the surface must double if we double the distance from the origin, so the section is that of a straight wedge, as (a) in Figure 4.8. For decreasing returns to scale, the height must rise less than in proportion to the distance from the origin, as (b) in Figure 4.8, while Figure (c) shows increasing returns to scale.

4.9 *Returns to a Variable Input—1*[9]

So far we have investigated the properties of production by considering two types of variation. In one, we kept output constant and considered

---

[9] For a calculus approach, see the Mathematical Note on this Section, page 309.

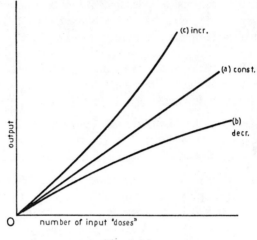

Figure 4.8

the way in which one input must vary when the other input changes, in order to maintain the output level. This type of variation gave the isoquant and the properties of input substitution. In the other, we kept the input proportions constant and considered the effect of varying all inputs in the same ratio, giving the properties of returns to scale. Considered in relation to the production surface, the isoquants corresponded to horizontal sections, the returns to scale properties corresponded to vertical sections radially through the origin.

In this section, we shall consider what happens to output when we vary one input, keeping the other fixed. The phrase "returns to a variable factor" carries the implicit idea of at least one other, nonvariable, factor. We can contrast this with the phrase "returns to scale" which implies no factors are fixed, or at least no factors that are being taken into account in the production technology.

One Fixed and One Variable Input. We shall initially examine the effect of keeping one input fixed and varying the other, in a production technology of the kind we have already analyzed in detail, that is, we assume noninteracting production processes characterized by constant returns to scale.

We shall consider the case with two inputs which we shall take, as usual, to be capital and labor. In most economic contexts it is presumed that the quantity of labor can be more readily varied than the quantity of capital, so it is traditional to assume, if one input is fixed, that it is capital.

Figure 4.9 illustrates the present case. Capital is fixed at K_o, and labor is increased steadily, so that the input combinations are those represented by the horizontal straight line through K_o. With the isoquants drawn in we can read off the output corresponding to any point on this line

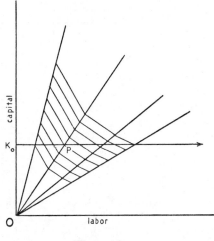

Figure 4.9

We can use the properties already established, however, to deduce some important relationships between increases in labor input and increases in output. Consider a small change in labor input near a point, like P in Figure 4.9, which corresponds to one of the production processes, and at which the slope of the isoquant changes.

Figure 4.10 concentrates on events close to P. Take some point, like M in the figure, at which the labor input is a little less than at P. Production will also be a little less than at P. We can find out how much less by drawing, through M, the line MR parallel to the isoquant (b) which passes through P. Then, since there are constant returns to scale, this must be part of the isoquant (a) through M.

From the constant returns to scale property, distances between isoquants along the line OP are proportional to actual production changes. Thus the distance RP is proportional to the change in production between isoquants (a) and (b). We shall label this change as $(\Delta Q)_{12}$ and we shall also label the change in labor between M and P (given by the distance MP) as $(\Delta L)_{12}$.

Marginal Product of an Input. The ratio $(\Delta Q)_{12}/(\Delta L)_{12}$, the ratio of the change in output to the change in labor, is a ratio of great importance.

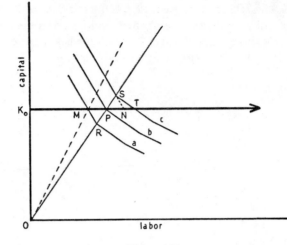

Figure 4.10

Since we are concerned with small changes, we shall label the ratio as "marginal," and since it represents the product obtained by increasing labor, we have the following definition: *The ratio of the increment in output to a small increment in labor, with capital fixed, is the marginal product of labor.* (If labor were fixed, and capital varied, the analogous ratio would be called the *marginal product of capital.*)

Diminishing Marginal Product. Now let us return to the diagram and consider what increment in labor would be necessary to increase output by an amount ΔQ (the same amount as before) *beyond P.* Again, as a consequence of constant returns to scale, the isoquant (c) corresponding to an output exactly ΔQ greater than at P, will intersect the line OP extended at S, where $PS = PR$ (since PR is proportional to ΔQ).

Draw SN through S parallel to MR. The vertically opposite triangles PRM, PSN have corresponding sides PR, PS equal and so the sides PM, PN are also equal. Thus PN is equal to $(\Delta L)_{12}$.

But the actual increment in labor necessary to attain isoquant (c) from P is given by PT, where isoquant (c) crosses the line along which input changes are taking place. T intersects this line further to the right than the point N, because the part of the isoquant to the right of the line $ORPS$ has a flatter slope than the part of the isoquant to the left of $ORPS$, to which NS is parallel.

Thus PT is greater than MP, and so $(\Delta L)_{23}$ is greater than $(\Delta L)_{12}$. But $(\Delta Q)_{23} = (\Delta Q)_{12}$. So the marginal product of labor is less for the movement 23 than it was for the movement 12.

With a small number of processes, the marginal product of labor changes only at the angles of the isoquants, in between which it is constant. If the number of processes is very large, so that the isoquant curves smoothly, the marginal product changes continuously. Subject to the proviso that the marginal product may change in steps with a small number of processes, rather than continuously, we can state the following result of great importance:

If capital is held fixed, and labor is varied, the marginal product of labor will decline as the quantity of labor is increased, if there are constant returns to scale everywhere.

We do not have to use capital and labor, of course. The equivalent result holds for the marginal product of any variable factor, if there is some fixed factor.

The result has been demonstrated for constant returns to scale. It holds even more so (or *a fortiori* if one prefers the Latin phrase) if there are decreasing returns to scale. This can be seen by referring back to Figure 4.10. If there are decreasing returns to scale, the distance *PS* must be *greater* than the distance *PR* to give the same increment (ΔQ) in output between isoquants (*b*) and (*c*) as between isoquants (*a*) and (*b*). From the geometry of the situation, *PN* will then be *greater* than *MP*, so that *PT* would be greater than *PM* even if the isoquant did not bend at *S*. That is, decreasing returns to scale *reinforces* the effect of declining marginal product.

Increasing returns to scale will, however, work in the opposite direction. *It is possible (we emphasize only the possibility) that the marginal product of labor will increase with increase in the quantity of labor, if there are pronounced increasing returns to scale.*

The result we have been discussing can now be stated in its general form, under the name by which it is best known, *the law of diminishing returns.*

The Law of Diminishing Returns: If only one input is varied, and if there is at least one fixed input, the marginal product of the variable input will decline as the quantity of this input is increased.

The "law" certainly holds for production functions with constant or decreasing returns to scale everywhere. If the number of processes is small, the marginal product will decline in a series of steps, with constant levels in between, rather than continuously.

4.10 Returns to a Variable Input—2

To illustrate the analysis of the preceding section, and as a bridge to the material of the next section, let us consider a specific numerical example.

In Table 4.1 is set out the data for a factory which uses only two inputs, labor and capital, and produces a single output. The technology

TABLE 4.1

Returns to a Variable Factor

Labor L	Process used	Output X	Average product of labor X/L	Increment in labor ΔL	Increment in output ΔX	Marginal product of labor $\Delta X/\Delta L$
10	$10P_1$	100	10			
				20	50	2½
30	$15P_2$	150	5			
				30	50	1⅔
60	$20P_3$	200	3⅓			
				90	100	1⅑
150	$30P_4$	300	2			

Data for Table: Unit levels of all processes produce 10 tons of output and require machine-hours and man-hours, respectively, as follows:
P_1 (6, 1), P_2 (4, 2), P_3 (3, 3), P_4 (2, 5).
Capital is assumed fixed at 60 machine-hours.

· consists of four efficient processes, varying in their capital to labor ratio from 6 machine-hours per man-hour, to ⅖ machine-hour per man-hour, and showing output returns to scale. The factory is assumed to have 60 machine-hours of capital available, and the Table shows the output obtained for various amounts of labor when combined with this amount of capital.

How the outputs are calculated can best be described by referring first to Figure 4.11. This expresses the same data in graphical form. With capital fixed at 60 machine-hours, the combinations of capital and labor available to the factory, as it varies its labor, are represented along the horizontal line *ABCD*. At the point *A*, with 10 man-hours of labor, there is exactly enough of both capital and labor to enable process P_1 to be operated at 10 times its basic level, giving 100 tons.

As labor is increased beyond 10 man-hours, successively higher isoquants are crossed in the diagram. The typical isoquant will be crossed on one of its straight segments where processes are used in combination (like 250-ton isoquants in the diagram), but certain isoquants will be crossed at the kink corresponding to the use of a single process. These will be where the radial lines representing the capital/labor ratios of the individual processes are crossed by the horizontal line at *ABCD* in the figure.

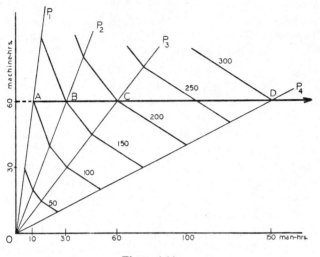

Figure 4.11

To calculate the output and labor corresponding to point *B*, we note that this point represents the use of process P_2 only. Now unit level of P_2 requires four machine-hours and two man-hours and produces ten tons. With 60 machine hours available, this process can be operated at 15 times unit level, producing 150 tons. To operate at this level will require 30 man-hours. Thus the data corresponding to point *B* have been calculated, and data for the other points representing single processes are calculated in the same way.

Calculating output and labor for points in between (where two processes are used in combination) requires solution of simultaneous equations, and we shall not do these calculations here. The figures can more easily be read off the diagram.

Average and Marginal Product. Now turn back to Table 4.1 again. Several figures are given in the table in addition to output and labor at *A, B, C, D*.

One of these is the *average product of labor* for each level of labor used. For a given point, say *B*, this is simply the output represented by that point (150 tons) divided by the labor used (30 man-hours), giving, in this case, 5 tons/man-hour. Note that the average product is in units of "tons per man-hour," not in simple tons like total output.

The other figure given is the increment in output (ΔX) between two points, such as *B* and *C*, divided by the increment in labor (ΔL) between the same two points. This is the *marginal product of labor*. We saw, in the previous section, that the marginal product will change at every kink in the isoquant, so we calculate the marginal product only between these kinks. The marginal product becomes less at each kink when labor is increased, for reasons given previously.

Note that the average product, as well as the marginal product, is also falling as the quantity of labor increases. Note also that the marginal product of labor is *less* than the average product at each point. The two can be compared directly, since both are in units of "tons per man-hour." (We cannot say the marginal product is "less" than total output, since the units are quite different.)

Taking the capital as fixed, we can draw a different set of diagrams, conveying the information in Table 4.1 and Figure 4.11. We can simply graph total product average product and marginal product against labor input, for the given amount of capital.

Product Curves. The result is Figure 4.12. In 4.12(a) is shown the graph of total product against labor. As labor increases from 10 to 150, total

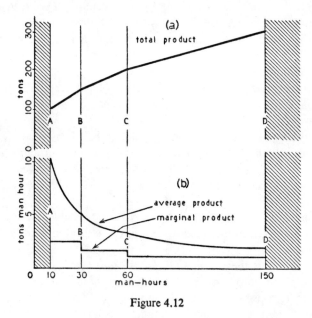

Figure 4.12

product rises from 100 to 300. But it does not do so steadily. Between *A* and *B* (these correspond to *A* and *B* in Figure 4.11 and Table 4.1), the slope of the curve is the increment in output divided by the increment in labor, and is, therefore the marginal product. The marginal product is constant between *A* and *B,* so the slope is constant. Between *B* and *C,* however, the marginal product is less than between *A* and *B* (from Table 4.1), so the graph rises less steeply, and less steeply still from *C* to *D.* Thus the graph for total output rises to the right, but successive segments have flatter slopes. This general shape of the total product curve—rising to the right, but gradually flattening out—is a consequence of two things:

(1) the notion of efficient production, which ensures that output always rises if more of an input is used.

(2) "diminishing returns" (which certainly hold if there are no increasing returns to scale), which gives decreasing marginal product of labor as labor increases.

The same information can be depicted in a different form by graphing average and marginal products (which can be graphed together since the units are the same) against labor input, as in Figure 4.12(b). This shows marginal product decreasing in a stepwise fashion, a consequence of the small number of different processes. Note that average product does *not,* however, fall in a stepwise fashion. It falls continuously, but not in a smooth curve: the graph consists of smooth curved segments meeting at kinks, again a consequence of the small number of processes.

Table 4.2 supplements Table 4.1 by giving a more explicit description of what happens in the intervals *A* to *B, B* to *C, C* to *D.* It should be considered in association with Figure 4.12.

TABLE 4.2

Returns to a Variable Factor

Labor (man-hours)	Process	Output (tons)	Marginal product of labor (tons/ man-hour)	Average product of labor (tons/ man-hour)
Less than 10	If capital is *fixed* at 60 machine hours, a minimum of 10 man-hours is required to operate it.			
From 10 to 30	Combination of P_1, P_2	Rising from 100 to 150	Constant at $2\frac{1}{2}$	Falling from 10 to 5
From 30 to 60	Combination of P_2, P_3	Rising from 150 to 200	Constant at $1\frac{2}{3}$	Falling from 5 to $3\frac{1}{3}$
From 60 to 150	Combination of P_3, P_4	Rising from 200 to 300	Constant at $1\frac{1}{9}$	Falling from $3\frac{1}{3}$ to 2
Over 150	More than 150 man-hours cannot be utilized without increasing capital beyond 60 machine-hours.			

Continuous Curves. If there are a very large number of processes, all the kinks and steps in the curves disappear. The total product curve will flatten smoothly, the marginal product curve will fall smoothly rather than in steps, and the average product will fall smoothly with no kinks.

The Range of Efficient Production. Finally, the reader should note that the graphs *cover only the range of labor inputs for which efficient production with the given capital is possible.*

No producer will choose to employ more labor than the maximum he can actually use as an *input.* He may, however, be deprived of free choice by law or social custom. In some countries it is impossible or difficult to discharge employees who have become surplus to requirements, and in the United States there exist "featherbedding" laws and practices that require the employer to hire men he cannot actually use. Basic production theory is concerned with the relationship between output and *inputs.* Surplus personnel are best considered as special *costs* imposed by law or custom.

It is sometimes contended that surplus personnel will "get in each other's way" and *reduce* output below the maximum. There are many things that can interfere with the efficiency of production, and having too many people around the factory may be one of them. In production theory we concentrate on *efficient* production.

4.11 Indivisibilities

One of the most fundamental characteristics of advanced industrial economics is the existence of "mass production" methods over large sections of manufacturing industry. These are production processes available only when the output is large, that are more efficient than the best available processes for producing small levels of output. It is part of the folk history of the United States that Henry Ford's assembly-line methods of automobile production enabled cars to be sold at a price much lower than would have been the case with small volume production methods.

Economies of Scale. Those factors that enable an industry or firm to produce large outputs at lower average costs than small outputs are loosely referred to as *economies of scale,* and sometimes *decreasing cost.* This term refers primarily to the relationship between average costs and scale of output. We have not yet examined costs, but it is necessary to take note of three different factors that may bring about economies of scale:

(1) A large financial outlay may be required to commence production at all. The larger is output, the less is this outlay per unit of product. This is a *fixed cost* effect, which will be examined in the next chapter.

(2) An individual firm may be able to buy large quantities of an input from another firm or industry at a lower price than small quantities. Presumably the willingness of the supplier to charge less for larger quantities is due to some type of economies of scale in his industry. For the firm buying these inputs, however, any economies of scale accruing to it are derived entirely from the circumstances of the supplying industry, and have nothing to do with the nature of the firm itself. Such economies are *external* to the firm.

(3) The firm may have a technology which is subject to increasing returns to scale in the sense in which we have defined it here. Under these circumstances a firm can double its inputs and *more than double* its output. If the price of its inputs is constant, doubling its outlay on inputs will double the quantity of those inputs, but more than double the output. Thus the average expenditures on inputs per unit of output will be less for larger outputs than for smaller.

Economies of Scale and *Increasing Returns to Scale* are related, but they are not the same thing. Increasing returns to scale are the only *technological* basis for economies of scale, but economies of scale may also be derived from price effects, as in (2), and contractual financial effects, as in (1). On the other hand, increasing returns to scale may fail to lead to economies of scale if the firm or industry must buy its inputs at a price which *increases* with quantity.

How do economies of scale occur? We have already stressed the plausibility of the argument that duplicating a process should lead to doubling both inputs and output, giving constant returns to scale.

But, although we can always *duplicate* a process, we may not be able to *halve* it. Two men with two shovels may dig twice as much as one man with one shovel, but we cannot have half a man with half a shovel. We have an *indivisibility* in the process. Admittedly, we could use one man with one shovel for *half the time,* but we shall assume that other circumstances dictate that all equipment and manpower be used for some unit period.

Indivisibilities become of importance only when there exist processes whose unit level is relatively high, and when *different* processes exist with lower unit levels. The general nature of indivisibilities is best explained by the use of a simple example.

Analysis of Indivisibility. Suppose we have two processes, a small-scale process, *S,* whose unit level requires 1 machine and 1 man, production 1 ton of output, and a large-scale process *L,* whose unit level requires 50 machines and 50 men, but produces 100 tons of output.

We suppose that, although the large-scale process cannot be operated at a level less than the base level, it can be operated at any higher level and shows constant returns to scale. That is, we can use 51 machines and 51 men to produce 102 tons of output, and so on.

Both the small and large processes use capital and labor in the same ratio (one machine to one man), so we can think of our inputs in terms of "doses," each dose consisting of one machine and one man.

For anything less than 50 input doses, the large-scale process cannot be used, so we must use the small-scale process, obtaining one ton of output for each dose. For 50 input doses we can, however, use the large-scale process. Since this gives 100 tons, instead of the 50 tons from operating the small process at level 50, it is clearly efficient to switch to the large-scale process. Output jumps discontinuously from 49 tons with 49 doses to 100 tons with 50 doses.

Obviously, the large-scale process will be used for all outputs above 100 tons.

Now consider some base level of inputs, less than 50 doses—say 20. We can compare multiples of this input with the corresponding output, as in Table 4.3.

TABLE 4.3

Indivisibilities and Returns to Scale

1 *Input* *Doses*	2 *Output*	3 *Inputs as* *Multiple* *of base* *Level*	4 *Output as* *Multiple* *of Base* *Level*	5 *Index of* *Returns to* *Scale* *(4 Divided* *by 3)*
20	20	1.0	1.0	1.0
40	40	2.0	2.0	1.0
50	100	2.5	5.0	2.0
60	120	3.0	6.0	2.0
80	160	4.0	8.0	2.0
100	200	5.0	10.0	2.0
120	240	6.0	12.0	2.0

Column (5) in the table shows the ratio of the output as a multiple of the base level to the input as a multiple of the base level. For constant returns to scale, this ratio would be unity. A ratio higher than unity implies increasing returns to scale, since output increases more than in proportion to the increase in inputs.

As can be seen in the table, the ratio is unity until we read 50 inputs, since we can use only the small-scale process which has constant returns to scale. Once we exceed 50 input doses, the effect of the more productive large scale process becomes apparent, and the ratio rises to 2.

We would obtain an even more pronounced effect if there existed, for example, a "very large-scale" process using 100 inputs but giving 400 tons of output. At 100 inputs, we would not use the large scale process at level 2, but the very large scale process at unit level, and the ratio would rise to 4.0 at this level.

Thus we see that we obtain increasing returns to scale effects if we have indivisible alternative processes with different unit levels, provided the larger scale processes are more productive than the smaller scale processes. (It is easy to see that, if the larger scale processes were *less* productive, they would never be used.) Thus indivisibilities will tend to lead to increasing returns to scale *even though each process, taken by itself, shows constant returns to scale.*

In our example, the switch from the small-scale to the large-scale process gave a discontinuous jump in output from 49 tons at 49 doses to 100 tons at 50 doses. If the producer required only 80 tons (not likely, if he can obtain 100 tons for the same inputs), he would do so by using the large-scale process *inefficiently* (throwing away 20 tons, if necessary). This is one of the rare circumstances in which a process might be used inefficiently by choice, but only because the large-scale process operated inefficiently is still *relatively efficient* compared with the small-scale process.

EXERCISES

(1) The following five processes all produce one ton of the same output when operated at unit level.

Process	Input Capital (machine-hrs.)	Labor (man-hrs.)
P_1	12	1
P_2	10	3
P_3	8	4
P_4	7	6
P_5	6	12

(i) Draw a diagram and plot the points which represent the input combinations for unit level of each of the processes.

(ii) Assuming that the processes can be operated at all levels (including fractions of the unit level), and can be combined without interactions, determine which of these processes is *inefficient.*

(iii) Draw in the unit isoquant for production of the good.

(2) For the production data of (1), determine the rates of substitution of labor for capital when moving from each *efficient* process to the adjacent one.

(3) Determine from the diagram in (1), or otherwise, the increase in output when capital is held constant at 84 machine-hours and labor is increased from 42 man-hours to 72 man-hours. What is the marginal product of labor in this range?

Chapter 5 is concerned with costs in general and costs of production in particular.

CONTENTS

5.1	The Nature of Costs	93
5.2	Production Costs	95
5.3	Isocost Curves	98
5.4	Optimum Input Proportions	101
5.5	"Long-Run" Cost Curves	105
5.6	Costs with a Limited Input	109
5.7	Costs with a Minimum Outlay	114
5.8	Total, Marginal and Average Curves	120
5.9	U-Shaped Cost Curves	125
5.10	Indivisibilities and Economies of Scale	127
5.11	Costs of Fixed Capital	129
	Further Reading and Exercises	133

CHAPTER 5

COSTS

5.1 The Nature of Costs

Economists are interested in costs because of their relevance to decisions and actions. Decision making involves weighing the advantages or *benefits* of a potential action against its disadvantages or *costs*.

Typically, we think of costs as money outlays that must be made. Something in a store costs $10 because an outlay of $10 must be made before the item can be obtained. In straightforward cases, the relationship between costs and outlays accords with this simple view, but we must be prepared to handle cases that are not straightforward. In some cases, a cash outlay may not be a cost, and a cost may not appear as a cash outlay.

To assign an outlay as a cost of a potential action it must be an outlay that can be avoided by not taking the action. If every resident of the United States, whatever his occupation or income, whether he was employed or not, had to pay $100 tax, that tax could not be considered as the cost of any action taken by a resident of the United States. It would be a cost only relative to the action of living in the United States rather than somewhere else.

Although we sometimes use the term *fixed cost,* an outlay that is absolute is not truly a cost—it is better to refer to it as a *charge* or *outlay*. The term is used widely (and rather loosely) in economics, but is most appropriate when there are two layers of decisions—major (such as whether to buy the house or not) and minor (such as day-to-day deci-

sions). Costs which may be varied only by major decision (such as mort-
gage payments) will appear as fixed charges in day-to-day affairs. In the
day-to-day context they are not true costs.

Opportunity Concept. To understand what underlies the concept of cost
we must go deeper than the surface effect which a cash outlay represents.
If one can print one's own money, an outlay of $10 cash represents no
true cost (except a negligible printing cost), because another action requiring $10 outlay can be carried out by printing another $10 bill. It is
precisely because this is not true and an outlay of $10 on one action
eliminates the possibility of carrying out another action for $10 that a cash
outlay represents a cost.

> *The cost of an action is the value of the alternative opportunity given
> up by choosing the action rather than the alternative.*

Making a cash outlay for something precludes spending that amount
on something else. The cash is not the cost, but simply a measure of the
value of other opportunities foregone. It is these lost opportunities that
represent the cost.

To emphasize this aspect of costs, the term *opportunity cost* is often
used. If several opportunities are given up, the relevant cost is the value of
the *best* foregone opportunity.

In any situation in which the assessment of costs for decision making
is called for, the economist will always employ the opportunity cost concept to check whether actual cash outlays properly represent costs.

Consider a small business in which the owner has invested his life
savings of $10,000, and which he operates with his own labor and an
assistant who is paid $4,000 annually. What are his costs? His cash outlays
(assuming no raw materials) may only be $4,000, but we must con-
sider opportunity costs. By using his $10,000 in the business, the owner
has foregone the opportunity to lend this amount at, say, 5 per cent interest. By working in the business, he has foregone the opportunity of man-
aging someone else's for, say $6,000 per year. Thus his costs of operating
the business consist of $500 foregone interest, $6,000 foregone salary,
and $4,000 salary actually paid to his assistant, a total of $10,500, although the actual cash payment is only $4,000.

Opportunity costs of this kind are sometimes known as *implicit
costs* as opposed to cash outlays or *explicit costs*.

External costs. Since we are interested in costs and benefits in relation to
decision making, we need to take note of the fact that all the costs and

benefits of an action do not always accrue to the same person or persons, and may not all accrue to the decision maker himself.

The action of producing certain products may result in air pollution, for example, which is a cost to residents in the neighborhood of a factory but not to the producer himself. Such costs are *external costs,* and the existence of important external costs may make public policy measures desirable, one of which may be to attempt to make the costs fall on the decision maker (by charging him for cleaning and medical bills resulting from his actions, for example). Other actions (building beautiful structures, for example) may give *external benefits* to those who do not pay for costs.

We shall normally consider contexts in which all costs and benefits accrue to the decision maker, that is, in which we have only *private costs* and *private benefits*.

5.2 Production Costs

Let us commence with the simplest situation to analyse, in which we are concerned with production of a single output, which is the only output of all the production processes in the relevant technology.

The only costs associated with using a given production process are presumed to be the payments that must be made to obtain the necessary inputs. We assume for the time being that

(1) all inputs used are purchased in the market, at prices which are independent of the amount of inputs purchased (competitive input markets).

(2) that inputs can be purchased as and when required.

The second assumption may not seem to carry any very strong implications but, in fact, it does. If capital is used in a production process, the relevant input is the *use* of the equipment (machine-hours), not the equipment itself. We are assuming the machine-hours can be purchased directly as and when required. This is not the most typical situation: most production operations are such that, in order to have the machine-hours available when needed, the manufacturer needs to possess the machine itself. The more typical situation will be discussed later, but we shall adhere temporarily to the simplified and atypical situation in which machine-hours, like man-hours, can be purchased as required.

Consider the production of a good for which the available production processes are as in Table 5.1 (these are the same processes as in Table 4.1). The reader can satisfy himself that all processes are technically efficient.

Given the market prices of machine-hours and man-hours, we can

TABLE 5.1

| Process | Inputs at Unit Level | | Output at Unit Level |
	Capital (machine-hours)	Labor (man-hours)	(tons)
P_1	6	1	10
P_2	4	2	10
P_3	3	3	10
P_4	2	5	10

compute the cost of inputs used in each process. At prices of $3 per machine-hour, $2 per man-hour, it is easily seen that the costs of inputs incorporated in the unit levels of the processes are:

$$\begin{array}{ll} P_1 & \$20 \\ P_2 & \$16 \\ P_3 & \$15 \\ P_4 & \$16 \end{array}$$

Least-Cost Presumption. Since each process produces 10 tons, the dollar values shown above represent the costs of producing 10 tons of output by each of the four production processes available. These costs differ, so we make the following behavior presumption of very wide application:

If there are various ways of achieving the same outcome, but with different costs, all decision makers in the economy will always choose the least-cost method from among those known and available to them.

The presumption covers decisions by firms, governments, and consumers alike. It covers monopolies and competitive firms, large corporations and small businesses. We are led directly then to define production costs in a comparable fashion:

The cost of production of a given level of output under given circumstances is always taken to mean the least *cost of producing that output under those circumstances.*

For our example, under the circumstances given (unrestricted opportunity to purchase machine-hours at $3, man-hours at $2, and a technology consisting of processes P_1-P_4), the cost of producing 10 tons of the output in question is $15. This is the least cost possible, and is attained by using process P_3 at unit level.

Input Price Changes. At different input prices, costs would, of course, be different and the relative costs of using the various processes would be expected to change.

In Table 5.2 is set out the costs of operating the processes at unit level (with output 10 tons in each case) for several pairs of input prices. The prices in the first four columns have been deliberately chosen so that the cost of operating process P_3 remains constant at $15.

TABLE 5.2

Production Costs
(For Technology Given in Table 5.1)

		Cost of operating process at unit level (output 10 tons) at various input prices. Machine hire, $ per machine-hour, is represented by r, labor hire, $ per man-hour, is represented by w.				
		(1)	(2)	(3)	(4)	(5)
Process	*r*	3¾	3	2	1	4
	w	1¼	2	3	4	6
	r/w	3	1½	⅔	¼	⅔
P_1		23¾	20	15	10	30
P_2		17½	16	14	12	28
P_3		15	15	15	15	30
P_4		13¾	16	19	22	38

Only at column (2) prices (those used above) is process P_3 the least-cost process. At prices in columns (1), (3), (4), P_3 costs $15, but some other process costs less. Since all processes give output of 10 tons, and since we have defined the cost of production to be the *least* cost of producing 10 tons, the cost of production for 10 tons is $13.75 for column (1) prices, $14 for column (3) prices, and $10 for column (4) prices.

Thus we have the following properties of the situation:

Although at input prices (2), the cost of production is $15 and process P_3 *is used, and although the prices change in such a way that the cost of operating process* P_3 *remains constant, the cost of production changes.*

The cost of production changes in this example as a result of *substitution* between processes when input prices change. The change in prices changes the *relative* costs of the various processes.

Note that it is only the *ratio* of the two prices that is important in determining the *relative* cost status of the various processes. This is illustrated in column (5) of the table, where both input prices are doubled relative to column (3). The price ratio is the same in (3) and (5): the cost of operating any particular process in (5) is double the cost in (3) but the ranking of the processes (from least cost to highest cost) remains unchanged and process P_2 is the least-cost process in both (3) and (5).

Prices and Input Proportions. The relationship between relative input prices, and ratio in which inputs are used in the various processes, and the relative costs of the processes follow a definite pattern which can be illustrated by drawing up the following list:

Input price ratio (r/w)	Least Cost Process	Ratio of machine-hours to man-hours in least-cost process:
3	P_4	⅖
1½	P_3	1
⅔	P_2	2
¼	P_1	6

The *higher* the ratio of machinery hire to wages, the *lower* the ratio of machine-hours to man-hours in the least-cost process. As the input price ratio changes, substitution is always in the direction of replacing the original process by another process which uses relatively less of the input which has risen in price. If there are only a small number of processes, it is obvious that substitution will only occur if a price change is sufficiently large: in Table 5.2 the reader can satisfy himself that P_3 is the least cost process for all price ratios between 1 and 2, switching to P_4 when the ratio rises above 2 and to P_2 when the ratio falls below 1.

This general rule of substitution will later be seen to apply also to choice by the consumer as well as by the producer.

We have investigated how the cost of production changes when the input price ratio changes. In the process we have established the following relationship:

Variation in input prices affects not only the cost of production, it affects the choice of the least cost process and thus of the proportions in which inputs will be used.

We shall concentrate on this aspect of the least-cost choice in Section 5.4 after first introducing some necessary analysis in Section 5.3.

5.3 Isocost Curves

In the example of the previous section, we showed how the choice of process to give minimum cost of production is determined by the input prices. Since there were only a small number of processes, it was simple enough to compute the actual cost of all processes at each set of input prices and then pick out the least-cost combination. Now we wish to give a more general analysis of the choice of input proportions.

First of all, let us introduce a simple analytical device which appears in a variety of forms in basic economic analysis. For two commodities, it is the line which joins the points representing all the combinations of the two commodities which can be purchased for some given dollar outlay. In the context of production and the firm, it is usually called an *isocost* line or curve, sometimes an *iso-outlay* line. In demand theory, the dollar outlay in question is usually the consumer's total budget, and the equivalent line is called a *budget* line.

Consider a simple example with two commodities, machine-hours and man-hours. Suppose machine-hours can be purchased at $2 and man-hours at $3 (the prices being constant to the individual production unit). Given an outlay of $60, what combinations of machine-hours and man-hours can be purchased?

If the whole $60 was spent on machine-hours, 30 could be purchased (K_1 in Figure 5.1). If the whole $60 was spent on man-hours, 20 could

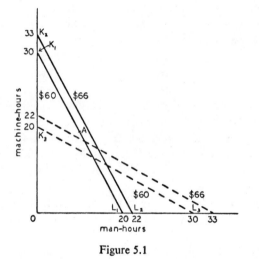

Figure 5.1

be purchased (L_1 in Figure 5.1). If half was spent on machine-hours, half on man-hours, the combination of 15 machine-hours, 10 man-hours could be purchased (A in Figure 5.1). It is easy to see that all the combinations of machine-hours and man-hours that can be purchased lie, like A, on the straight line joining K_1 and L_1. The line K_1L_1 is the *$60 isocost line for prices $2 per machine-hour and $3 per man-hour.*

Change in Outlay. Suppose we considered a 10 per cent increase in outlay, to $66, at the same prices. Obviously the machine-hours that could be purchased by spending the whole amount on these will also rise 10 per cent, to 33 (K_2), while the maximum number of man-hours will rise 10 per cent to 22 (L_2). Thus the $66 isocost line will be K_2L_2, which lies 10 per cent further out along every radial through 0 than does the $60 isocost line, and thus will be parallel to K_1L_1.

For given prices, the isocost lines for different outlays will all be parallel, higher outlays being represented by lines further from the origin.

The isocost lines here are straight lines because of the assumption that the market prices are independent of the quantity purchased by the individual buyer. In those cases, which we shall rarely be concerned with, in which the buyer is, for example, so prominent in the market that his behavior influences market price, the isocost lines will be curves rather than straight lines. We shall always be concerned with the constant price case unless otherwise stated.

Price Changes. Now suppose the prices were different—$3 per machine-hour, $2 per man-hour, for example. Arguing as above, the purchaser could obtain for $60, 20 machine-hours ($K_3$), 30 man-hours ($L_3$) or any combination along the line K_3L_3. At the new prices, we would obtain a new set of isocost curves (the set represented by broken lines in the diagram), all parallel to each other but having a different slope to the first set.

Note that the slope of the isocost curves depends only on *relative* prices. In the last example, if prices rose to $6 and $4 respectively, the $120 isocost curve would be such that 20 machine-hours, 30 man-hours, or linear combinations of these, could be purchased. Thus the $120 isocost line at these prices would be identical with the $60 isocost line at the old prices. Since the prices have changed in the same proportion (doubled), leaving the relative price (1½ machine-hours per man-hour) unchanged, the isocost curves have different $ labels, but the same slope.

Slope and the Price Ratio. Students often have some trouble with the question: In which direction does the slope of the isocost line (or budget line, in demand theory) change when the relative prices change in a certain way? By "slope" we mean the numerical value—algebraically speaking, the slope of a line sloping downward to the right has a negative sign, which we shall ignore.

Any uncertainties about the answer can always be removed by noting that the point where the budget line meets an axis represents the amount of the commodity measured along that axis that could be obtained by devoting the whole outlay to that commodity. Thus the *cheaper* a commodity, other things being equal, the *further* along the axis will be the intersection. Referring back to Figure 5.1 and comparing K_1L_1 with K_3L_3 (ignoring the $ labels), K_1L_1 must represent a *lower* ratio of the price of machine-hours to man-hours than does K_3L_3 because the ratio of OK_1 to OL_1 is *higher* than the ratio of OK_3 to OL_3. To give a simple rule: *the flatter the slope of the isocost curve, the lower the relative price of the commodity measured horizontally.*

We can formalize this relationship. Defining the slope of the isocost line as the ratio of the vertical to the horizontal change between two points on the line, it is equal to the intercept of the vertical axis divided by the intercept of the horizontal axis, since the slope is constant. For the isocost line K_1L_1, then, the slope is OK_1/OL_1. If we denote the price of machine-hours by r, of man-hours by w and the total outlay by m, we have

$$OK_1 = \frac{m}{r}$$

$$OL_1 = \frac{m}{w}$$

$$OK_1/OL_1 = \frac{m}{r} \bigg/ \frac{m}{w} = \frac{w}{r}$$

Thus the slope of the isocost curve is the input price ratio, taken in the proper direction which is the price of the horizontal input over that of the vertical input. The inputs appear reciprocally to the prices, in the sense that the relationship is as follows:

$$\text{Slope of isocost curve} = \frac{\text{vertical intercept}}{\text{horizontal intercept}}$$

$$= \frac{\text{price of horizontal input}}{\text{price of vertical input}} \cdot$$

5.4 *Optimum Input Proportions*[1]

Using isocost lines, we are now in a position to illustrate geometrically the choice of optimum (that is, least-cost) input proportions, given input prices, for the case of a very large number of processes as well as for a small number.

To do this, we combine the isocost lines and the isoquant curves. To concentrate on some particular level of output, we draw the isoquant for that output. Then we draw, on the same diagram, the set of isocost lines for the particular input prices, and observe the relationship between the two.

---

[1] The reader trained in elementary calculus should consult the Mathematical Note on this Section, page 310.

In Figure 5.2, we have drawn the 10-ton isoquant for the industry already examined arithmetically in Table 5.2. Assuming the input prices

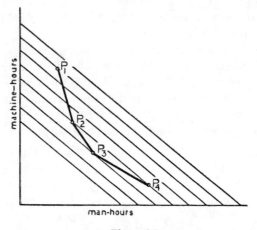

Figure 5.2

to be $3 per machine-hour and $2 per man-hour, we have drawn in the set of isocost lines. Some isocost lines do not intersect the isoquant $P_1P_2P_3P_4$ (at the given prices, it is impossible to produce 10 tons for such a low outlay), but others do. From those isocost lines ($15 and up) which do intersect the isoquant, we choose the least cost (that closest to the origin). This is the $15 isocost, and it intersects the isoquant in only one point, P_3. Thus the least-cost process is P_3, producing 10 tons at a cost of $15: the optimum input proportions are 1 : 1 (the input proportion for P_3). This, of course, is exactly what we found from arithmetic computation.

Smooth Isoquants. We can, however, use the same analysis for the smooth isoquant, representing a large number of processes. This is illustrated in Figure 5.3. With a smoothly curved isoquant, the lowest isocost curve must be that which is *tangent* to the isoquant. The optimum input proportions are given by the ratio of inputs at the point of tangency (T), hence by the slope of OT.

Input Substitution. It is obvious from inspection of the diagram that if the isocost curves had a flatter slope like the broken line, the point of tangency would be at T', to the right of T on the isoquant, and thus the optimum input proportions OT' would give a lower ratio of machine-

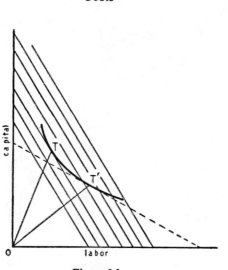

Figure 5.3

hours to man-hours than before. Since a flatter slope to the isocost curve represents (as already pointed out) a lower relative price of the input measured horizontally, man-hours in this case, we have the basic substitution property:

At a lower relative price for labor, the optimum input proportions would represent a higher relative use of labor.

For many purposes, it is convenient to express the relationships that must hold between the isocost line and the isoquant, at the optimum, in a somewhat different form.

Consider Figure 5.4. This represents a magnified view of the parts of an isoquant and isocost line close to P_n, the least-cost process at the given input prices. As in the other diagrams, machine-hours are measured vertically and man-hours horizontally.

P_{n-1}, P_{n+1} are the processes with input proportions closest to P_n. In Chapter 4, we identified the slope of the line $P_{n-1}P_n$ ($\Delta K/\Delta L$) as the rate of substitution of capital for labor in a switch between processes P_n and P_{n-1}, and the slope of P_nP_{n+1} as the equivalent rate of substitution for switching between P_n and P_{n+1}. The slope of the isocost line is, of course, related to the relative prices of the two inputs.

First we note the following:

If P_n is the least-cost process, the isocost line cannot have a slope steeper than P_nP_{n-1} or flatter than P_nP_{n+1}.

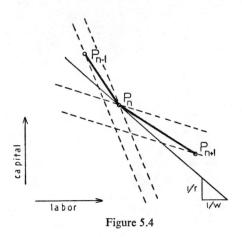

Figure 5.4

The reason for this relationship is clear from considering the set of broken isocost lines which have a slope steeper than P_nP_{n-1}. If this relationship should hold, the isocost line through P_{n-1} is closer to the origin than that through P_n and thus the cost of process P_{n-1} is less than that of P_n. Thus P_n could not be the least-cost process, as asserted. Similarly, for an isocost line flatter than P_nP_{n+1}, P_{n+1} would have lower cost than P_n, contradicting P_n's least-cost property.

We can express this as a relationship between the input price ratio and the marginal rate of substitution, since we showed in the last section that the slope of the isocost curve was w/r, the ratio of the price of labor to the price of capital. We have, formally:

If the efficient processes are numbered so that $\mathbf{P}_{n-1}$, $\mathbf{P}_n$, $\mathbf{P}_{n+1}$ *represent successively lower capital to labor ratios,* $\mathbf{P}_n$ *is the least-cost process at prices* r, w *if and only if*

$$\left(\frac{\Delta K}{\Delta L}\right)_{n,\,n-1} \geqq \frac{w}{r} \geqq \left(\frac{\Delta K}{\Delta L}\right)_{n,\,n+1}.$$

Expressed more verbally, the relationship must be such that the price ratio of *labor to capital* should not be outside the range for the two adjacent rates of substitution of *capital for labor*.

When the number of processes becomes very large, the slopes of P_nP_{n-1} become closer and closer, so that we can take them as equal in the limit and call this slope the marginal rate of substitution of capital for labor at P_n. Thus, for the smoothly curved isoquant we have the more widely used and simple relationship:

For a very large ("infinite") number of processes, giving a smoothly curved isoquant, the point T *on the isoquant represents the least-cost input proportions if and only if the marginal rate of substitution of capital for labor at* T *is equal to the price ratio of labor to capital.*

This is the most standard form in which this condition is used in the literature. It is important for the reader to be completely clear that the three statements

(1) the optimum input ratio is the least-cost ratio,

(2) at the optimum ratio, the isocost line is tangent to the isoquant,

(3) at the optimum ratio, the marginal rate of substitution is equal to the price ratio,

are *absolutely equivalent*. The information content of each statement is precisely the same as that of the others, if the isoquants are smoothly curved and convex to the origin. It is only too easy for the student of economics to be led to believe that he has been given new information, when he has merely been given the same information in a different language.

5.5 "Long-Run" Cost Curves[2]

In the preceding section we showed how, given the technology and assuming all inputs could be freely purchased at fixed prices, the least-cost method of producing any given level of output could be determined. We also pointed out that when we speak of the "cost of production," without qualification, we mean the least cost of producing that level of output.

Given the cost of producing each level of output, we can draw a graph with cost on one axis (traditionally the vertical axis) and output on the other. The graph of cost against output is the *cost curve* of the activity in question.

Since we are assuming that the firm or the factory can purchase inputs as and when required and has no constraints on its use of inputs (such as upper limits on the amounts of some inputs or fixed quantities of an input), the costs, and the associated cost curve, are *unconstrained*. We shall discuss costs of production subject to constraints on inputs at a later stage.

It is traditional to refer to unconstrained costs as *long-run costs*. The name is derived from the general, and valid, notion that the longer the time period over which the firm or factory is allowed to adjust to its circumstances, the more constraints it can dispense with. We shall adhere to the tradition, once the point is quite clear that any idea of time is incidental

---

[2] The reader trained in elementary calculus should consult the Mathematical Note on this Section, page 311.

to the real issue, which is that the firm is able to vary *all* its inputs as it sees fit. For some industries, or in some circumstances, it may be possible to do this even in a short period, in other cases it may take a very long period indeed. For some industries (mining, agriculture) variation of *all* inputs may not be possible at all.

Constant Returns to Scale. We can now establish a fundamental proposition:

> *For a constant returns to scale technology, the unconstrained cost curve with constant input prices is a straight line through the origin.*

If there are constant returns to scale, all processes that produce, say, 10 tons, will produce 20 tons if operated at twice the level. If operated at twice the level, each process will use twice the inputs and, at constant input prices, the cost of inputs will be exactly doubled. Since this is true of all processes, the least-cost process will remain the least-cost process, and the minimum cost of producing double the output will exactly double.

If we consider the technology used earlier in the chapter (Tables 5.1 and 5.2), and suppose input prices are constant at $3 per machine-hour and $2 per man-hour, then producing 20 tons (double the unit level) will cost $40 using $2P_1$, $32 using $2P_2$, $30 using $2P_3$, and $32 using $2P_4$. Process P_3 remains the least-cost process, with the cost doubling from $15 to $30 as output doubles from 10 tons to 20 tons.

The same argument will hold for increasing output in ratios other than 2, so that cost and output will increase in the same proportion. Since there are no constraints on input use, no inputs need be purchased for zero production and the cost of zero production is thus zero. Thus the cost curve must go through the origin and must show costs increasing in the same proportion as output. It is therefore a straight line through the origin, as in Figure 5.5 (a), drawn for the example we have been using.

For many purposes, it is more convenient to consider *average cost* (cost divided by output) rather than simple cost. The graph of average cost against output is the *average cost curve*. For the unconstrained case we refer to the curve as the *long-run average cost curve*, often abbreviated to the initials *LRAC*. Since, if cost is directly proportional to output, average cost is constant ($1.5 per ton in our example), we have the equivalent but more common statement of the preceding proposition:

> *For a constant returns to scale technology, the "long-run" average cost curve, with constant input prices, is a horizontal straight line.*

This is illustrated in Figure 5.5 (b). Note that the average cost curve cannot be drawn on the same axes as the cost curve since the units of meas-

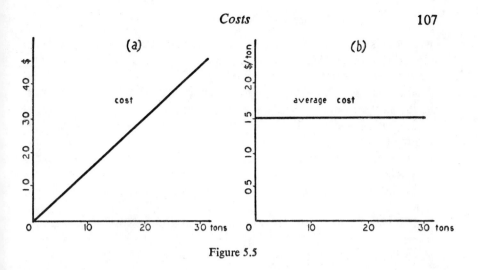

Figure 5.5

urement differ. Costs are measured in *simple $'s*, average costs in *$'s per ton*.

Nonconstant Returns to Scale. Suppose the technology showed decreasing returns to scale everywhere rather than constant returns to scale. If the cost of producing 10 tons was $15 (as before), this would mean that doubling inputs (for a cost of $30) would less than double output to give, say, 15 tons instead of the 20 tons that we would obtain with constant returns to scale. In order to produce double the output with the original proportions, all inputs would have to be more than doubled, so the cost would more than double.

Could we do better, perhaps only doubling our costs, by changing input proportions when we double output? Certainly not if the production function is *homogeneous* (of degree less than one, since we have decreasing returns to scale), since we have already shown (Section 4.8) that the marginal rate of substitution for such a function is constant at given input proportions, whatever the level of output. Since input prices are fixed, the least-cost input proportions will remain those with which we started.

If the function is not homogeneous, the least-cost input combination for producing $2X$ may differ from that for producing X. Suppose that the least-cost method of producing X used amounts K, L of capital and labor, and cost $\$C$, while the least-cost method of producing $2X$ used amounts K', L' and cost $\$2C$. Then by switching input proportions we would double the output at only double the cost. But if this were so, inputs $\frac{1}{2}K', \frac{1}{2}L'$ would cost $\$C$, and they must produce more than X, since otherwise doubling inputs from $\frac{1}{2}K'$, $\frac{1}{2}L'$ to K', L' would be doubling output (or more) in contradiction of the property of decreasing returns to scale everywhere. But this would then imply that, for a cost of $\$C$, inputs K, L produce only X, while $\frac{1}{2}K'$, $\frac{1}{2}L'$ produce more than X, so that K, L cannot be the least-cost method at the low output level.

Thus input substitution cannot be sufficient to make up for decreasing returns to scale everywhere, so that in this case costs increase more than in proportion to output, with the consequence that average costs rise as output increases.

The reverse will be true for increasing returns to scale. Output can be doubled with less than double inputs and less than doubling cost, so costs increase less than in proportion to output and average costs fall as output increases.

We can summarize:

For decreasing returns to scale everywhere, the long-run cost curve is such that costs increase more than in proportion to output, and the average cost curve slopes upward to the right.

For increasing returns to scale everywhere, the long-run cost curve is such that costs increase less than in proportion to output, and the average cost curve slopes downward to the right.

Typical curves are shown in Figure 5.6.

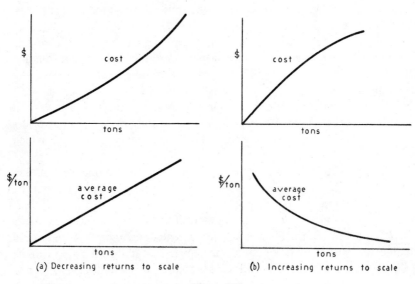

Figure 5.6

5.6 Costs with a Limited Input[3]

In the previous section we assumed that inputs could be purchased as required, in any quantity. We shall turn now to examine a situation which is a common enough one, in which the amount that can be obtained of one or more inputs has an upper limit. If a factory has to adjust output in a matter of a few days (or even a few months), it may well be true that there is simply insufficient time to arrange for, and install, any additional machinery. The result is that the number of available machine-hours has an upper limit, set by the existing installation, for output adjustments over a short period.

Costs associated with adjusting production subject to constraints on inputs are frequently referred to as *short-run costs,* because of the common situation in which the constraints exist primarily because of insufficient time to increase the available quantity of some input. As in the case of long-run costs, however, the important element in the situation is the limit on the input, not the time period itself.

Many input constraints cannot easily be removed, even in the long run. Production on a farm, in which the use of land is an input, tends to be subject to persistent limits on the availability of land. It is difficult for a farmer to expand the quantity of land available to him in anything but a pioneer setting. Even in the long run, it may prove difficult or impossible for institutional reasons to obtain land from adjacent farms, and it is more difficult in the short run. Thus the analysis of this section, although most typically short run, applies also to some types of production (especially farming and extractive industries) *even in the long run.*

We assume, in our analyses, that at least one input is unlimited, and we shall take this to be labor. It is sufficient for obtaining the general picture of the effect of a limited input that we consider a two-input case, with one input limited and the other unlimited. We shall consider the limited input to be machine-hours, while man-hours are unlimited. The prices of both inputs are assumed constant.

Relationship of Short and Long Run. So long as the level of production is such that the optimum (least-cost) combination of inputs requires less machine-hours than the available limit, the analysis is the same as the preceding section, and the cost curves coincide with the long-run cost curves for low output levels. It is only when we reach levels of output at which the optimum input combination would require more than the available number of machine-hours, that the analysis changes.

---

[3] The reader trained in elementary calculus should consult the Mathematical Note on this Section, page 313.

At these levels, since we cannot use inputs in the least-cost combination, we must use them in more costly combinations. Without further information, we then can immediately assert that:

At levels of output for which the input limitation is effective (that is, more of this input would be used but for the constraint), costs will be higher than for the same output without constraints.

That is, beyond a certain level of output, short-run costs of producing a given output will be higher than long-run costs, if the constraint can be relaxed in the long run. This is a particular case of a general proposition, which is intuitively obvious, that a better situation can be achieved without constraints than with them.

Marginal Cost. In the previous chapter, we discussed production with a fixed input. This is clearly appropriate to the present situation. It was shown that, if one input is fixed and the other variable, the marginal product of the variable input declines with output even if there are constant returns to scale.

Since the analysis of production with a fixed input is largely in terms of the *marginal product* of the variable input, it is also convenient in discussing costs under the same circumstances to work with the concept of *marginal cost*. We define this as follows:

The marginal cost at any level of output is the addition to cost that occurs when output is increased by one unit beyond this level. More precisely it is the ratio of the increase in cost to the increase in output for a small increment in output.

If we had a situation in which the cost of producing 100 tons was $200, and the cost of producing 101 tons was $205, then, at output 100 tons, we would have

$$\text{cost (or } total\ cost) : \$200$$

$$\text{average cost} \quad : \$2 \text{ per ton} \left(= \frac{\$200}{100 \text{ tons}} \right)$$

$$\text{marginal cost} \quad : \$5 \text{ per ton} \left(= \frac{\$205\text{-}\$200}{101 \text{ tons-}100 \text{ tons}} \right).$$

The marginal cost, like average cost, is in units of $ per ton, so the two can be directly compared.

Marginal Cost and Marginal Product. Consider the simple case with capital limited and labor variable, price of both inputs being constant. The cost of producing some given level of output is the value of the inputs used, that is, the number of machine-hours times the rent plus the number of man-hours times the wage.

Now suppose we increase output by some small amount beyond the level at which all available capital is in use. What happens to costs? Since capital is limited, the number and value of machine-hours used does not change. The only way in which output can be increased is by using more labor, and so it is only the value of labor used which changes. The cost of labor is the only *variable cost*.

To increase output by an amount ΔX under these conditions, labor must be increased by some amount ΔL. If the wage rate is w, the cost of the additional labor is $w.\Delta L$. This is the only change in cost, since capital is fixed. The change in cost *per unit of output* is

$$\frac{w.\Delta L}{\Delta X} = \frac{w}{\dfrac{\Delta X}{\Delta L}}$$

But $\dfrac{\Delta X}{\Delta L}$ is the marginal product of labor, while the increase in cost per unit of output is the marginal cost. Thus we have

$$\frac{\text{wage}}{\text{marginal product of labor}} = \text{marginal cost} .$$

Using the common abbreviations, *MC* for marginal cost and *MPL* for the marginal product of labor, we have the following result of great importance.

If labor is the only variable input and is available at a constant wage w, *marginal cost is given by the relationship*

$$MC = \frac{w}{MPL} .$$

An equivalent relationship holds for any input which is varied when other inputs are held constant, labor being simply the most usual case.

Variation of All Inputs. The above relationship is one of great importance, and we shall take time off from the main thread of the current argument to show that it holds, for least-cost production, *even if inputs are being varied together.*

Let us suppose there are two inputs, labor (priced at wage w) and capital (at rent r), and that there are no restrictions on the amounts of either. Then we know that the least-cost combination will be such that

$$\frac{w}{r} = \frac{MPL}{MPK}$$

(where *MPK* is the marginal product of capital).

The capital-labor ratio for this least-cost combination will have some particular value. Let us suppose k machine-hours are used per man-hour, where k may be greater or less than one.

For a unit increase in labor (assumed a very small proportion of the total labor in use), output will rise by an amount MPL, and costs will increase by w. The new output level is close to the old, so we can take the marginal products to be unchanged. Now let us increase capital by k machine-hours (k may be a fraction). This will add a further output of $k.MPK$ and a further cost of kr.

By varying labor, then capital, in this way we will achieve the same level of output and of total cost that we would have achieved by varying them together. The addition to output is $MPL + k.MPK$, and the addition to cost is $w + kr$. Thus the *marginal cost* (increase in cost *per unit* increase in output) is given by

$$MC = \frac{w + kr}{MPL + k.MPK} \cdot$$

This can be put in the form

$$MC = \frac{w\left(1 + k\frac{r}{w}\right)}{MPL\left(1 + k\frac{MPK}{MPL}\right)} \cdot$$

But $\dfrac{r}{w} = \dfrac{MPK}{MPL}$, so the two expressions in brackets are equal and can be cancelled, giving

$$MC = \frac{w}{MPL} \cdot$$

We could have manipulated the expression into the equivalent form

$$MC = \frac{r\left(k + \frac{w}{r}\right)}{MPK\left(k + \frac{MPL}{MPK}\right)}$$

giving

$$MC = \frac{r}{MPK} \cdot$$

Thus we can generalize the previous statement:

Even if both capital and labor are variable, but are used in the least-cost combination, the marginal cost is given by both of the relationships

$$MC = \frac{w}{MPL} \quad \text{and} \quad MC = \frac{r}{MPK}$$

where w, r *are the prices of labor, capital.*

Equivalent results hold for any number of inputs.

Rising Marginal Cost. We have already seen, in Chapter 4, that the marginal product of a variable input *declines* (in steps, if there are a small number of processes, steadily, if there are a very large number) when the quantity of the input increases, provided at least one input is fixed. This will be true for both constant and decreasing returns to scale, provided they hold everywhere. With only one variable input (which we take to be labor) output can only be increased if labor is increased, so the marginal product of labor declines as output increases.

If the wage is constant, then, from the relationship $MC = w/MPL$, marginal cost varies inversely with the marginal product of labor. Since the marginal product of labor declines as output increases, marginal cost must rise as output increases. The rise occurs, like the fall in marginal product, in steps if there are few processes and continuously if there are very many processes. Thus we can assert:

If there is a limit on the availability of at least one input, the marginal cost curve must be rising to the right after some level of output.

Figure 5.7 illustrates marginal cost curves for a small and large number of processes. The part of the curve to the left of the vertical line represents outputs for which the input limitation is not effective (that is, the optimum amount of the input is below the limit). The steps in the few process case correspond, of course, to outputs at which one process

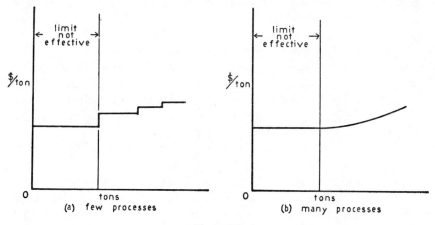

Figure 5.7

is discarded in favor of another. A technology with constant returns to scale everywhere is assumed.

If the limit is not effective, inputs will be combined in the least-cost proportions. Under constant returns to scale, these proportions will be the same for all outputs, and costs will be directly proportional to output. Thus, the ratio of the increment in cost to the increment in output will be constant, so that marginal cost is constant. This is why the left hand portions of the marginal cost curves in Figure 5.7 have been drawn as horizontal straight lines.

All curves have been shown as ending at the right. For a limitation on one input, capital will usually be a level beyond which it is impossible to produce more by using more labor unless some more capital is also available. This occurs when we have reached the process requiring the lowest ratio of capital to labor. However, if there exists a process using labor only, the curve extends indefinitely to the right.

5.7 Costs with a Minimum Outlay

We have investigated the effect on costs of an upper limit to the available amount of some input, so that expansion of output beyond a certain stage depends on expanding the quantity of the variable input only, rather than both (or all) inputs together, and so leads to non-optimal input combinations and to increasing marginal cost.

Here we shall examine an opposite case, also important in practice, in which a certain *minimum* quantity of inputs must be paid for, whether used or not. Such a situation can arise both in the short and long run either because there is a minimum size of one input (typical capital) or because quantities smaller than some minimum cannot be purchased. The latter may occur because delivery may not be worthwhile for small quantities. (Even a worker may not travel to his place of employment unless he is given more than some minimum number of hours of work.)

Suppose that some minimum quantity of machine-hours, say 30, must be paid for, whether this quantity is used or not, and that technical difficulties prevent unused machine-hours being sold. We will assume that the price per machine-hour is $3, so that the minimum payment is $90. Any machine-hours over 30 can be purchased at $3.

Labor is presumed to be obtainable in any quantity at $2 per man-hour.

The cost analysis is straightforward if carried out in the correct way, which is to take the proper view of the cost of machine-hours. Instead of considering the price of machine-hours to be constant at $3, we note that the structure of the situation is as follows:

(1) No outlay is required for zero machine-hours.

(2) To obtain any machine-hours at all, an outlay of $90 (a "fixed cost") must be made.

(3) Once this outlay has been made, no additional outlay is required for any additional machine-hours up to 30. That is, given the initial outlay, *the first 30 machine-hours are free (zero price).*

(4) Any machine-hours beyond 30 have a price of $3.

Thus, in determining the optimum input combination we have two distinct price situations: machine-hours are effectively free (if any at all have been purchased) up to 30, then are $3.

Low Output Levels. For low outputs, with free machine-hours, it is obvious that the least-cost process will be that using the lowest ratio of labor to capital, since labor is the only variable cost. For high outputs, the least-cost process will be determined in the usual way from the relative input prices of $3 per machine-hour and $2 per man-hour.

To make our analysis more concrete, consider the example we have already used several times in this chapter and the last, with four processes having capital to labor ratios ranging from 6 machine-hours per man-hour to ⅔ machine-hour per man-hour.

For low levels of output, the process (P_1) with the lowest labor to capital ratio (1 man-hour and 6 machine-hours for 10 tons output) will be used. This process will be used up to 50 tons output, at which level ($5P_1$) the basic 30 machine-hours will be used up.

Costs for these levels of output will consist of a *fixed cost* of $90 (the cost of using machine-hours at all), and a *variable cost* entirely due to wage payments. The *total cost* is the sum of the two. In this range, the output is increased by operating the same process (P_1) at a higher level. Since this process requires 1 man-hour per 10 tons output, the marginal product of labor is constant at 10 tons per man-hour. Since the price of labor is constant at $2 per man-hour, each 10 tons requires an additional $2 and so the marginal cost is constant at $0.2 per ton. We can easily compute the *average variable cost* and the *average total cost,* to obtain the cost figures in Table 5.3.

Note that average variable cost and marginal cost are constant and equal in this case (not always true), while average total cost falls steadily. The basic relationship between these will be discussed in the next section.

Intermediate Output Levels. Let us now examine the costs for outputs of over 50 tons, for which the 30 free machine-hours included in the initial outlay are no longer sufficient.

TABLE 5.3

Costs with Minimum Outlay
I-Low Output Levels (Process P$_1$ Only)

Output	Variable Cost ($)	Average Variable Cost ($/ton)	Marginal Cost ($/ton)	Fixed Cost ($)	Total Cost ($)	Average Total Cost ($/ton)
10	2	0.2	0.2	90	92	9.2
20	4	0.2	0.2	90	94	4.7
30	6	0.2	0.2	90	96	3.2
40	8	0.2	0.2	90	98	2.45
50	10	0.2	0.2	90	100	2.0

Consider the output of 75 tons. To use process P_1 (at level 7.5) would require 45 machine-hours (15 above the minimum) and 7.5 man-hours, for a total cost of $150. To use process P_3 at level 7.5 would require 22.5 machine-hours (leaving 7.5 paid for, but unused) and 22.5 man-hours, for a total cost of $157.5. We would expect both these to be sub-optimal: P_1 because it is not the optimal process when both inputs must be purchased, P_3 because it fails to use up some free machine-hours which are available.

But if we use the intermediate process, P_2 (also at level 7.5), which uses 4 machine-hours and 2 man-hours at unit level to produce 10 tons, we will require exactly 30 machine-hours and 15 man-hours, for a total cost of $120. Clearly this is better than P_1 or P_3, and can be shown to be optimal.

For outputs between 50 and 75 tons, it will be optimal to use that mixture of P_1 and P_2 that exactly uses 30 machine-hours to produce the given output, and for outputs between 75 and 100 tons, the appropriate mixture of P_2 and P_3.

Thus over the intermediate range, 50 to 100 tons, the analysis is basically that of production with one input (machine-hours) fixed. This was discussed in the previous chapter, the main conclusion being that the marginal product of labor remains constant for mixtures of P_1, P_2, then falls to a lower level for mixtures of P_2, P_3. The point at which process switching occurs is 75 tons: at lower outputs, P_2 is combined with P_1, at higher outputs with P_3. Since the cost of machine-hours is fixed at $90, marginal cost is reciprocally related to the marginal product of labor and will change at 75 tons. We can compute the various costs to obtain Table 5.4.

High Output Levels. Now consider levels of output over 100 tons where machine-hours must be purchased (at $3). From Table 5.2, we saw that the least-cost process for $3 per machine-hour and $2 per man-hour was P_3, having unit level requiring 3 machine-hours and 3 man-hours per 10 tons output. The lowest level at which this process will be used is that level just requiring the basic 30 machine-hours, which is a level of 10, producing 100 tons output. Thirty man-hours of labor will be used, giving a total cost of $150 ($90 plus 30 man-hours at $2 per man-hour). To expand output by 1 ton beyond this minimum level, the process will be operated at level 10.1 (101 tons output). An additional 0.1 level of operation will require an additional 0.3 machine-hours (costing $0.9) and an additional

TABLE 5.4

Costs with a Minimum Outlay
II-Intermediate Output Levels
(Combinations of P_1, P_2, P_3)

Output	Processes Used	Total Cost ($)	Marginal Cost ($/ton)	Average Total Cost ($/ton)
50	$5P_1$	100		2.0
			0.8	
60	$3P_1+3P_2$	108		1.8
			0.8	
75	$7.5P_2$	120		1.6
			1.2	
80	$6P_2+2P_3$	126		1.575
			1.2	
100	$10P_3$	150		1.500

0.3 man-hours (costing $0.6), for an additional cost of $1.5. This is the marginal cost for levels of output beyond 100 tons. Since input prices are constant, the least-cost process remains P_3, and there are constant returns to scale, so marginal cost is constant at $1.5.

For outputs 100 tons and more, the effect of the fixed cost disappears *since the full 30 machine-hours would have been purchased even if there had been no minimum outlay.* The pattern of costs is shown in Table 5.5. At high outputs the cost curve coincides with the corresponding portion of the long-run cost curve.

Synthesis. We can now assemble the three stages together, to show the overall relationship between output and total, marginal, and average cost.

TABLE 5.5

Costs with a Minimum Outlay
III-High Output Levels (Process P$_3$ Only)

Output	Total Cost ($)	Marginal Cost ($/ton)	Average Total Cost ($/ton)
100	150	1.5	1.5
101	151.5	1.5	1.5
110	165	1.5	1.5
200	300	1.5	1.5

The synthesis is given in Table 5.6 and in the curves in Figure 5.8. The curves for the case in which the number of processes is very large (smoothly curved isoquants), but there are still constant returns to scale,

TABLE 5.6

Costs with a Minimum Outlay
IV-Synthesis

Output	Process	Total Cost	Marginal Cost ($ per ton)	Average Total Cost ($ per ton)
0–50	P$_1$	Rises from $90 at 0 to $100 at 50	Constant at 0.2	Falls from over 90 at output 1 to 2.0 at output 50
50–75	Combination of P$_1$, P$_2$	Rises from $100 at 50 to $120 at 75	Constant at 0.8	Falls from 2.0 at 50 to 1.6 at 75
75–100	Combination of P$_2$, P$_3$	Rises from $120 at 75 to $150 at 100	Constant at 1.2	Falls from 1.6 at 75 to 1.5 at 100
100–	P$_3$	Rises from $150 at 100	Constant at 1.5	Constant at 1.5

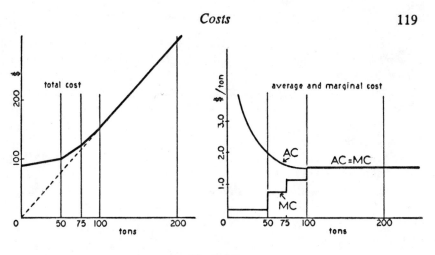

Figure 5.8

are shown in Figure 5.9. For the continuous case, the marginal cost will change smoothly over the intermediate range: it will still be constant (horizontal on the curve) in the low and high output ranges.

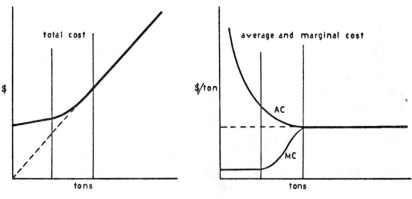

Figure 5.9

If we look more closely at Figure 5.9, the following properties of the curves are apparent:

(i) The total cost curve intersects the vertical axis, since a minimum outlay must be made even to produce the smallest output.

(ii) Over the low-output range, the total cost curve is a straight line of constant slope, the marginal cost curve is flat, and the average total cost curve is falling.

(iii) Over the intermediate range, the total cost curve is bending, the marginal cost curve is rising, and the average total cost curve is falling (although slowly).

(iv) Over the high-output range, the total cost curve is a straight line of constant slope (but steeper than in the low-output range), the marginal cost curve is flat, and the average cost curve is also flat *and coincides with the marginal cost curve.* The high-output part of the total cost curve also has the property that, if extended backward (shown dotted in the diagram), it will pass through the origin.

The relationships between total, marginal, and average cost curves are not accidental, but due to their containing related information, so the curves themselves are necessarily related. The next section is devoted to the analysis of these relationships.

5.8 *Relationship between Total, Marginal and Average Curves*[4]

We shall interrupt our discussion of costs proper at this point to examine the arithmetical and geometrical relationship between total, marginal, and average quantities and their respective curves. Although we shall use as examples total, marginal, and average *costs* (because that is our present context), it is extremely important to realize we are discussing simple arithmetic relationships which apply equally to the relationship between total, marginal, and average *products* of an input, or total, marginal, and average *revenues* (which we shall discuss in the next chapter), or total, marginal, and average *anything.*

Average and marginal must refer to the same total curve. If we are talking of *long-run costs,* we have *long-run* marginal and average costs, if of *short-run costs,* then *short-run* marginal and average costs.

Denote the total cost of producing n units of output by $C(n)$, and the total cost of producing $n + 1$ units by $C(n + 1)$. We shall use the Delta notation, writing ΔC for the difference $C(n + 1)$ less $C(n)$. Since ΔC is the increment in cost incurred by producing an additional unit beyond output n, it is the *marginal cost* at n.

Thus we have our basic relationships:

Total cost at n $= C(n)$.

Marginal cost at n $= \Delta C = C(n + 1) - C(n)$.

Average total cost at n $= \dfrac{C(n)}{n}$.

---

[4] The reader trained in elementary calculus should consult the Mathematical Note on this Section, page 314.

Information Content. Since the marginal and average cost are obtained directly from the total cost, they cannot contain any information not already contained in total cost. Thus we have a simple but important (and sometimes forgotten) fact:

The total cost schedule or curve contains all cost information. Marginal and average costs are used only because they sometimes simplify the analysis, not because they contain additional information.

Average cost contains all the information included in total cost, since we can always reconstruct total cost simply by multiplying average cost by output. Marginal cost, on the other hand, *loses information* contained in total cost. This is because fixed cost does not enter into marginal cost. We can prove this easily by supposing that an additional fixed cost C_0 is added to our original total cost. The total cost of producing n units becomes $C(n) + C_0$ and of $n + 1$, $C(n + 1) + C_0$. The *difference* ΔC is still equal to $C(n + 1) - C(n)$, since the C_0's cancel out, so the new fixed cost affects total cost and average cost, but not marginal cost. Thus we have:

Marginal cost depends only on variable costs, and is independent of any fixed costs.

Marginal and Average. Since marginal and average costs are measured in the same units, and their curves drawn on the same diagram, the relationship between the two is particularly important. A relationship of very great importance can be derived in the following way.

Consider the average cost of $n + 1$ units compared with the average cost of n units. The difference between the two, which we can write as ΔAC, is given by

$$\Delta AC = \frac{C(n + 1)}{n + 1} - \frac{C(n)}{n}.$$

We can multiply top and bottom of the last term by $n + 1$, leaving the value unchanged, to obtain

$$\Delta AC = \frac{C(n + 1)}{n + 1} - \frac{n + 1}{n + 1} \cdot \frac{C(n)}{n}.$$

This can then be rewritten, simply by rearranging, as

$$\Delta AC = \frac{C(n + 1)}{n + 1} - \frac{n + 1}{n} \cdot \frac{C(n)}{n + 1},$$

which then gives

$$\Delta AC = \frac{1}{n + 1}\left(C(n + 1) - \frac{n + 1}{n} C(n)\right).$$

Since $\dfrac{n+1}{n} = 1 + \dfrac{1}{n}$, we then have

$$\Delta AC = \frac{1}{n+1}\left(C(n+1) - C(n) - \frac{1}{n}C(n)\right).$$

But $C(n+1) - C(n) = \Delta C$ (marginal cost), and $\dfrac{1}{n}C(n)$ is the average cost at output n, so we have:

$$\Delta AC = \frac{1}{n+1}\left(\Delta C - \frac{C(n)}{n}\right)$$

or

$$AC(n+1) - AC(n) = \frac{1}{n+1}\left(MC(n) - AC(n)\right).$$

where $AC(n)$, $MC(n)$ mean average and marginal costs at output n.

If we look closely at this final relationship, we see that it implies that the left hand side of the equation is positive or negative according to whether the expression in the brackets is positive or negative. The bracketed expression is positive if the marginal cost at n is greater than the average cost at n, in which case the average cost at $n+1$ is greater than the average cost at n, so that average cost increases with output. If marginal cost is less than average cost, the bracketed expression is negative and average cost falls with output. Should marginal cost be equal to average cost, average cost is unchanged between n and $n+1$, so we have average cost constant at n.

Note that the reverse relationship is also true—if average cost is rising, marginal cost must be greater than average cost, and so on. There is no causal sequence here—marginal and average costs are simultaneously derived from total cost—neither determines the other.

We can summarize these important relationships:

(1) *Average cost rises with output if and only if marginal cost exceeds average cost.*

(2) *Average cost falls with output if and only if average cost exceeds marginal cost.*

(3) *Average cost is steady if and only if marginal and average costs are equal.*

Total and Marginal Curves. Now let us turn to the geometry of the associated curves, commencing with the total cost curve. Figure 5.10 illustrates such a curve (similar to that in Figure 5.9). Take a point on the curve, X, corresponding to output n. $C(n)$ is the vertical height of X above the horizontal axis, while the horizontal distance out to X is simply n. Thus the

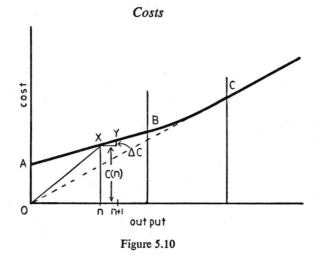

Figure 5.10

average cost $\dfrac{C(n)}{n}$ is the slope of the line OX, from the origin to the point X. The marginal cost, on the other hand, is the vertical rise in the cost curve itself per unit increase in output and is thus the slope of the segment of the curve between the points X, Y.

Using these properties, we can read the total cost curve in Figure 5.10 to obtain the basic cost relationships contained in it:

(1) For the segment AB, the curve has constant slope, so marginal cost is constant. The slope of the curve is less than the slope of any line joining a point on the curve to the origin, so average cost exceeds marginal cost.

(2) For the segment BC, the slope of the curve is increasing, so marginal cost is increasing. Average cost is falling, but still exceeds marginal cost.

(3) For the segment beyond C, the slope of the curve is constant, so marginal cost is constant. Since this segment lies on a line through the origin, the average cost is constant and is equal to the slope of the curve, that is, to marginal cost.

Average and Marginal Curves. Marginal and average cost curves (*not* for the same cost data as the total cost curve in Figure 5.10) are shown in Figure 5.11. To the left of A, the marginal cost is below average cost, so average cost must be falling. To the right of A, marginal cost is above average cost, so average cost must be rising. At A, marginal and average cost are equal, so the average cost curve is neither rising nor falling. Since the average cost curve is falling to the left of A, rising to the right of A, and neither falling nor rising at A, it must have its lowest point at A. This is a simple but important relationship:

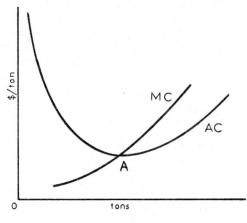

Figure 5.11

If the average cost curve has a lowest point (average cost has a minimum), the marginal cost curve must intersect it at that point.

In an earlier diagram, Figure 5.9, we had a case in which the average cost, having reached its minimum, remains constant. In this case, the marginal cost curve intersects the average cost curve when it first reaches its minimum level, after which the curves coincide. In general, we have:

If the average cost curve is flat (constant average cost) over any range, it coincides with the marginal cost curve over that range.

In the section on long-run cost curves, we did not discuss the associated long-run marginal cost curves. We are now in a position to do this. For constant returns to scale, the average cost curve is flat and the marginal cost curve thus coincides with it. For decreasing returns to scale (Figure 5.6(a)), the total cost curve has a steadily increasing slope, so the marginal cost slopes upward to the right. Since average cost is rising, the marginal cost curve must lie above it. For increasing returns to scale, the slope of the total cost curve is decreasing, so the marginal cost curve must be falling and lie below the average cost curve.

For marginal costs to fall below the horizontal axis (negative marginal cost), total cost would have to be less at higher output than at lower. This would contradict the fundamental presumption of choosing least-cost methods of production, since the producer could obtain the lower output at no more than the *same* cost as the higher by simply throwing away the surplus.

Finally, it should be stressed that whether average cost is rising or falling depends on the relationship between the *level* of marginal cost and that of average cost, *not on the slope of the marginal cost curve*. That is, the marginal cost curve can be rising and the average cost curve falling (as in the left-hand portion of Figure 5.11), or the marginal cost curve falling and the average cost curve rising (not shown on the diagrams), or both curves sloping upward (as in the right-hand portion of Figure 5.11) or downward (not depicted).

5.9 U-Shaped Cost Curves

Earlier in the chapter we discussed costs under two special types of constraint
   (1) with an upper limit to the availability of some input
   (2) with a minimum outlay on some input.

The traditional short-run cost curves for a productive enterprise are obtained by combining these two cases. It is assumed that the enterprise is subject to the double constraint that it must pay for a minimum quantity of some input, and that it cannot obtain any more of that input.

If we draw the average and marginal cost curves under these conditions, the left-hand side of the diagram will be similar to the parts of the diagram covering the low and intermediate ranges in Figure 5.9. Since the upper limit on the input then becomes effective, the right-hand part of the marginal cost curve will be rising, like the right-hand part of the marginal cost curve in Figure 5.7(b). This means that marginal cost is above average cost in the right half of the diagram, so that the average cost curve rises to the right.

The composite effect gives a U-shaped average cost curve similar to that in Figure 5.11.

It is probably more realistic to assume that the minimum input quantity is less than the maximum, so there is a range over which the enterprise can obtain more than the minimum input, up to some upper limit. With constant input prices and constant returns to scale, the average cost curve will now have a flat section in the middle, and the average and marginal cost curves will look like those in Figure 5.12. This flat section will, of course, coincide with the long-run cost curves over this range of output. Empirical evidence seems to support the greater realism of the curve of Figure 5.12 than of the curve of Figure 5.11.

As we shall see in the next chapter, it is the right-hand (upward sloping) portion of the average cost curve that is usually important. In most cases it does not make any difference whether the bottom of the U is flat or not.

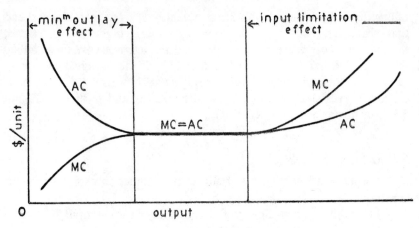

Figure 5.12

In some cases the left-hand (downward sloping) portion may be relevant, but in most it is not. We will find it a convenient simplification later to use a cost curve derived from production with an input limitation but no minimum outlay. With constant returns to scale, this gives average and marginal cost curves like that part of Figure 5.12 to the right of the minimum outlay effect—flat up to the onset of the input limitation effect. The "standard" cost curve of the next chapter is of this kind.

Although we regard the U-shaped curve as primarily short run when there are constant returns to scale, the long-run curve may also have this shape if the constraints (minimum outlay, input limitation) apply also in the long run. Ordinarily, however, we shall assume no constraints in the long run.

Nonconstant Returns to Scale. If there are decreasing returns to scale, even the long-run average cost will be rising (see Section 5.5), with marginal cost necessarily above it. Thus the long-run average and marginal cost curves will be like the right-hand (rising) portion of Figures 5.11 and 5.12. This should be expected, since it was suggested in Section 4.8 that decreasing returns to scale has similarities to, and is probably caused by, a "state of nature" input limitation.

Decreasing returns to scale coupled with a minimum outlay will give a U-shaped cost curve even in the long run (if the minimum outlay effect is long run). In any case we will not obtain a flat bottom to the U with decreasing returns to scale—the curves will either be like Figure 5.11

or will both be rising from the origin—marginal cost above average cost except at the origin.

The analysis of increasing returns to scale is given in the next Section.

5.10 Indivisibilities and Economies of Scale

The "economies of scale" resulting from the effects of indivisibilities can be simply illustrated by considering a technology which consists of two types of process:[5]

(1) "small-scale" or "workshop," capable of producing at low output levels. We shall assume these are subject to constant returns to scale.

(2) "large-scale" or "assembly-line," also assumed to be subject to constant returns to scale. We assume that these processes cannot be operated at *less* than some minimum level, but can be operated at any level above the minimum. In other words, an assembly-line cannot be organised for an efficient output of less than, say, 100 units of output, but assembly lines can be designed to produce 101, 102, 103, . . . units.

For given input prices, and no input limitations, the small-scale process will have a horizontal average cost curve extending from zero output indefinitely, while the large-scale process will give a horizontal average cost curve from 100 units onward. We suppose the average cost of the large-scale process is less than that of the small-scale process, otherwise we should not be interested in the large-scale process at all.

To complete the picture, we must take account of the possibility of operating the large-scale process *inefficiently*. Suppose the minimum size assembly line produces 100 units, but we want only 50 units. We cannot use less inputs than required to produce 100 units, but we can leave every second assembly line position empty and produce 50 units, or, at worst, throw out every second item coming off the line. We can always produce 50 units, one way or another, *but at the same cost as producing 100 units.*

Since the total cost of producing 50 units is the same as that of producing 100 units, the *average cost* of producing 50 units will be double that of 100 units. The average cost of producing any quantity, n, less than 100 units by the large-scale process will be given by $100/n$ times the average cost of 100 units. Thus we can complete the average cost curve for the

---

[5] The model given here, based on stepwise indivisibilities, is believed to provide a more satisfactory picture of observed behavior (especially the observation that small-scale plants do not "creep" steadily towards greater and greater economies of scale) than models assuming steadily decreasing marginal costs.

large scale process: it will be sloping downward from 100 times the minimum average cost at output 1 to the minimum average cost at output 100, after which it will be flat.

We now have two average cost curves, one for the small-scale process, the other for the large-scale process. These are drawn in Figure 5.13, with the downward sloping portion of the large-scale average cost curve intersecting the small-scale average cost curve at A, and joining the horizontal portion of the large-scale average cost curve at B.

Which process will be chosen to produce a given output? Obviously, whichever process gives the least average cost. This is the small-scale process for outputs up to Q_1 (corresponding to A), and the large-scale process for outputs beyond Q_2. For outputs between Q_1 and Q_2, *inefficient use of the large-scale process gives a lower average cost than using the small-scale process.*

Thus the average cost curve is a composite of the two curves, represented by the heavy lines in the figure. It is horizontal at first, followed by an intermediate downward sloping portion (AB), then horizontal again at the lower level.

Production of a commodity under conditions which give rise to such a cost curve is said to show *economies of scale.*

It would be possible to have more than one indivisibility—for example, "small scale," "medium scale," "large scale," giving an average cost curve with several downward steps. The cost curve is sometimes shown as sloping continuously downward, but it seems more consistent with the evidence to consider a stepped curve.

We have drawn the composite average cost curve. The composite marginal cost curve poses some problems. For outputs less than Q_1, marginal cost is equal to average cost for the small-scale process, for outputs greater than Q_2, it is equal to the average cost of the large-scale process. The difficulty is between A and B. Once the large-scale process is in operation (at Q_1), marginal cost is *zero* (since the total cost does not change from Q_1 to Q_2).

It will help here to use an arithmetic example. Suppose the large-scale average cost is $1 per unit for 100 units or more, so the cost of the minimum large-scale process is $100. If the small-scale average cost is $2, Q_1 will be at output 50, since $100/50 \times 1 = 2$ and this is the output at which the average cost of using the large-scale process inefficiently is just equal to the average cost of the small-scale process.

Thus producing 50 units by the small-scale process will cost $50 \times 2 = 100$. If we now shift to the large-scale process to produce 51 units, the total cost is $100, so the marginal cost at 50 units is zero. It continues

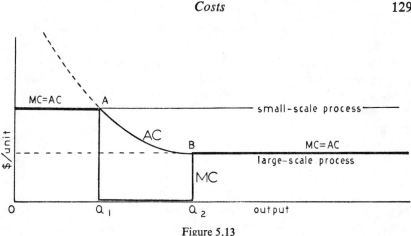

Figure 5.13

at zero until we reach 100 units, when it rises to $1. This marginal cost curve is shown in Figure 5.13.

5.11 Costs of Fixed Capital[6]

In the preceding analysis we have assumed that, although capital services were a necessary input in the production processes, these services ("machine-hours") could be purchased when and however required. But machine-hours are obtained by using machines. In a typical manufacturing concern, the machines themselves are owned by the factory. Even if machine-hours are purchased as required, there must be someone in ultimate charge of the machines who makes such decisions as whether there are enough machines, how much should be charged for their use, and so on.

Machines are one example of an economic category called capital. At the deepest level, the concept of capital is beset with problems, concerning which economists have been disagreeing for decades. For our simpler purposes, we might note the following characteristics typical of a machine which are representative of the properties of *fixed capital in* general:

(1) It must be manufactured or otherwise created all in one piece, before use, although it will be used over some period of time. By contrast,

---

[6] This Section is inserted primarily to illustrate the components of capital costs. Decisions concerning purchase of new capital *(investment decisions)* involve intertemporal considerations and are discussed in Chapter 11, Section 11.3 (page 288).

a *service* or *flow input,* such as labor, comes into existence only as it is actually used.

(2) It is not used up immediately, in a single productive act, but can be used several times or a large number of times. In the older steelmaking processes, steel is first cast into ingots, then the ingots are rolled into finished products. Now the ingots must be made before they can be rolled, but they are not capital equipment because each ingot, once rolled, has ceased to be an ingot. But the rolling mill or the furnace is capital equipment because it is still there (perhaps the worse for wear), after the ingot has been cast and rolled. The ingots are *intermediate goods,* goods produced to be further processed rather than for final use. If the mill likes to keep a large pile of ingots on hand as a buffer against irregularities, this pile is a *stock* or *inventory,* and, as such, is a form of *capital* but not *fixed capital.*

Let us concentrate on a typical piece of fixed capital such as a machine, and analyze the costs associated with using it. First we note that, from the fundamental principles of opportunity cost:

The costs to be assigned to the use of a machine by its owner for his own purposes are the same as the costs to be assigned to it if its services are to be sold on an outside market.

Since we have discussed production theory as though the producer hired machine hours from a contractor, we can separate capital from other costs by now considering the costs associated with capital from the point of view of the contractor. If the producer is also his own machine renting contractor, this makes no difference to the overall cost allocations when correctly made.

Decisions of a Machine Owner. We assume that the contractor already owns the machine, and that its current market price is, say, $10,000. His decision context is whether to rent the machine for some period to be used to give machine-hours in actual use. Assume that the period is a year, and that the machine could continue in use for several years.

What are his alternatives? Apart from renting the machine for the following year, the contractor has the obvious alternatives of (a) selling the machine now, (b) just leaving it idle in the warehouse for the year. Renting the machine and leaving it idle in the warehouse are not, however, complete alternatives, since the machine will still exist at the end of the year. Nor is the alternative of selling the machine now completely specified, since there are various choices to be made concerning the use of the proceeds of sale. To simplify the problem, let us concentrate on three possibilities:

(1) Selling the machine now and lending the money for a year.

(2) Renting it for a year, then selling it.

(3) Leaving it idle for a year, then selling it.

In all three cases, we concentrate on the benefits accrued at the end of the year.

Let us suppose the market rate of interest is 5 per cent. Then the results of (1) are easy to assess: at the end of the year the contractor will have his $10,000 plus $500 interest, total return of $10,500.

Obsolescence. For (3), the return depends on the market price of the machine at the end of the year. If the general price level is steady (which we will assume to be true), the machine may, perhaps, be worth the same at the end of the year as now, in which case the return is $10,000. Clearly, (3) would never be chosen in preference to (1) under these conditions. Actually, it is likely that the machine will be worth less next year than now, not because it is in any worse condition (assuming ideal storage) but because technical progress has made new models of the machine superior and the contractor's machine is an older model. A fall in price simply because the model is old, even though not used, is *obsolescence:* a mint condition 1966 car will be worth less than an equivalent 1968 car simply because the model is outdated. If there is an obsolescence effect, it is even more clear that, in a choice between (1) and (3), (1) will always be chosen.

Thus we can assume that the choice lies between (1) and (2), between selling the machine now and lending the cash value, or renting the machine for a year and then selling.

Maintenance and Depreciation. If the machine is used in production, there will be some costs of keeping the machine in good working order. These are *maintenance costs.* In addition, the fact that the machine is used over the year will result in some wear and tear, even with maintenance, so that the machine is worth less at the end of the year than it would have been if not used at all. The decline in price as a result of use is *depreciation.* It should not be confused with obsolescence: obsolescence occurs whether the machine is used or not, depreciation only if it is used.

Depreciation in the sense we use it here, as an opportunity cost, is not identical with *amortization* or *depreciation allowances,* which are accounting concepts. The latter are cash reserves or bookkeeping entries accumulated in some regular way, designed to be just sufficient to pay for replacement of the machine when it is worn out. Under ideal conditions, depreciation allowances made in a period may be equal to the true value of depreciation. These accounting reserves are, however, severely constrained by institutional factors, such as internal revenue rules on tax deductibility.

An Example. Let us suppose that, for the machine in question, the relevant figures are:

maintenance	$1,000
obsolescence	$1,000
depreciation	$2,000

The price of the machine, after being used over the year, will be $7,000 ($10,000, less $3,000 obsolescence and depreciation—maintenance is not a reduction in price, but payment for man-hours spent during the year by maintenance personnel), so the basic comparison now becomes:

(1) sell the machine now, lend the cash receipts. Return at end of year, $10,500.

(2) Rent the machine for the year, then sell. Return at end of year, rent less $1,000 maintenance, plus $7,000.

The cost of having the machine in use (by the owner or by someone else) thus consists of a cash outlay of $1,000 maintenance, plus the lost opportunity of receiving $10,000 at the end of the year instead of $7,000. The total *opportunity cost* is $3,500, made up of $500 lost interest, $1,000 obsolescence and $2,000 depreciation. We can tabulate the various cost items in the following way

Costs of Using Fixed Capital			
Cash Outlays	maintenance		$1,000
Opportunity Costs			$3,500
	interest	$ 500	
	obsolescence	$1,000	
	depreciation	$2,000	
Total Cost			$4,500

This table sets out the typical items that determine the costs of using fixed capital, assuming that a given number of machine-hours will be used during the year. The cost per machine-hour is obtained by dividing by the number of machine-hours.

The analysis is more complex if the number of machine-hours is variable, and the depreciation depends on the number of hours (as the depreciation on an automobile depends on the mileage run), but the above example is sufficient to give the general pattern.

FURTHER READING

Costs are dealt with, in the traditional manner, in all microeconomics and price theory textbooks. Most devote an undue amount of space to such matters as the "U-ness" of the average cost curve, and the geometric relationship of "short-run" and "long-run" average cost curves. These are of no interest or importance in modern advanced theory and have been omitted here.

For a nontechnical analysis from a different point of view than that given here, see: Stigler, G. J. *The Theory of Price* (3rd ed.), Macmillan, 1966.

EXERCISES

(1) An output is produced by a constant returns to scale technology which consists of 5 processes having the following properties:

Process	Inputs required		Output per period
	capital (machine-hours)	labor (man-hours)	
P_1	7.5	1.0	10 tons
P_2	5.0	2.0	10 tons
P_3	3.75	3.0	10 tons
P_4	2.5	5.0	10 tons
P_5	0.0	12.0	10 tons

(i) Denoting the input prices by r ($ per machine-hour) and w ($ per man-hour), calculate the costs of producing 10 tons by each process for each of the following sets of input prices:

$$\text{(a) } r = 1, w = 2$$
$$\text{(b) } r = 1, w = 1$$
$$\text{(c) } r = 2, w = 1$$
$$\text{(d) } r = 3, w = 1$$

(ii) Which process will be used in each of the cases (a)—(d)?

(iii) What is the average cost of production in each of the cases (a)–(d)?

(2) Assume that input prices are constant at $r = 1$, $w = 1$ with the technology given in Exercise (1) above.

A producer can purchase labor without limit, but can purchase machine-hours only up to a total of 75. Under these conditions:

(i) Give the producer's total and average cost of producing 100, 200, 300, 400 and 500 tons.

(ii) At what output levels will marginal cost change?

(iii) Give the marginal costs and output ranges over which each level of marginal cost is relevant.

(3) Perform the same calculations as in Exercise (2), but for the case in which $r = 1$, $w = 2$. Compare the results with those of Exercise (2).

(4) The following are cost data for some producer:

Output (tons)	Cost ($)
0	0
1	1
2	2
3	3
4	4
5	5
6	6.6
7	9.1
8	12.8
9	18.0
10	25.0

(i) Calculate average and marginal costs, and draw the total, average and marginal cost curves.

(ii) Calculate average and marginal costs, and draw the relevant curves, when the producer must make a *minimum* outlay of $3 which enables him to produce up to 3 tons without any additional purchase of inputs.

(iii) Calculate average and marginal costs, and draw the relevant curves, when the producer must make a *fixed* outlay of $3, in addition to the ordinary costs given in the table, in order to produce any amount at all.

Chapter 6 is concerned with the behavior of producers whose output is determined primarily by profit maximization.

CONTENTS

6.1	The Firm and Its Decisions	137
6.2	Revenue	139
6.3	Cost Curves	145
6.4	The Role of Financing	148
6.5	The Profit Maximizing Output	149
6.6	Perfect Competition	153
6.7	Monopoly	159
6.8	Competition Versus Monopoly	164
6.9	Oligopoly	166
6.10	The Firm's Demand for Inputs	172
6.11	The Giant Corporation	176
	Further Reading and Exercises	178

CHAPTER 6

FIRMS

6.1 The Firm and Its Decisions

The *firm* is the term most widely used in economics to cover all forms of what might be described, in a United States context, as business enterprise. The essential feature of the firm, from the economist's point of view, is that it *controls* some productive activity, taking production in the broad sense in which it was described in Chapter 4. The ultimate decision makers in the economy are often classified in a threefold way, into *consumers* (or households), *firms* (or business enterprises) and *the government* (actually a very large number of Federal, State, and local government authorities). The firm is, in a sense, an *intermediary,* using inputs whose ultimate ownership is in the hands of consumers or government, and producing outputs which are ultimately bought by consumers or government. The firm is considered to have no personality of its own and traditional welfare economics is concerned with discussing benefits and costs to ultimate consumers only. The phrase "good for General Motors" has no meaning in this setting. We may be interested in the welfare of the employees of General Motors, or its stockholders, but not that of General Motors itself.

Thus a firm may be anything from a one-man pretzel stand on a street corner to a giant corporation. We do assume that it makes sense to speak of a decision by the firm, that is, that the firm has some unified decision-making mechanism, however large it may be.[1]

---

[1] But see Section 6.11.

As usual in economic analysis, we commence with simple cases and we shall proceed, until it is stated otherwise, with the analysis of a firm which produces a single product subject to technological constraints of the kind discussed in Chapter 4 and costs of the kind discussed in Chapter 5.

Decisions of the Firm. A simple firm of this kind faces three kinds of decisions, concerning:

(i) *Entry.* Whether to organize itself to produce the particular product under discussion at all.

(ii) *Size.* If inputs cannot be freely purchased as and when required, or if commitments must be made which will limit certain inputs (particularly capital and land), how much of the relatively fixed inputs to acquire or plan for.

(iii) *Output.* What quantity of the product to produce. These three kinds of decisions are not independent of each other.

We assume that the firm, like any other decision maker, considers potential benefits and costs of each possible action as a basis for its choice.

The simple profit maximizing firm is considered to make decisions within the following context:

(1) That the benefits of any action are entirely measured by the revenue obtained by selling the resulting output.

(2) That the costs of any action are entirely measured by the relevant costs of production.

(3) That the decision rule is: take the action that maximizes the *net* benefits, that is the difference between revenue and cost. The term *profit* will be used to refer to the simple excess of revenue over cost.

Motives Other than Profit. Even in an economy such as that of the United States, in which the "profit motive" is supposed to predominate in business behavior, these decision rules represent a simplification. Firms do not always measure benefits by revenue alone, or the net benefits by the excess of revenue over cost. A firm may be motivated by the desire to be large, and may wish to expand output beyond the most profitable level for that reason. It may seek approval for its technical sophistication, or for its social actions, partly at the expense of simple profit. Some authors would even argue that maximization of simple profit is the exception rather than the rule in the contemporary United States, especially among large corporations. Our assumptions that these factors are not taken into account is related to our assumption of the "faceless" firm, already mentioned.

For our basic analysis, we shall adhere to the simple picture of the firm. This is probably a reasonable representation of the small firm. The giant corporation is engaged in so many different activities, in any case, that it cannot be made to fit the simple picture.

6.2 Revenue[2]

A firm's *revenue,* in the simple case, is its receipts from sales of its product (assumed to consist of only one type of good). Just as we used the unqualified term "cost" to mean the *least cost* of producing a given output, so we mean by "revenue" the *maximum revenue* that can be obtained from selling that output, given the market conditions. The revenue clearly depends on the *quantity* of goods sold. In practice, it is not always easy for a firm to predict what revenue will be obtained from selling a given quantity of output, if there is some uncertainty in the situation. This uncertainty may arise for different reasons, and the whole analysis of the firm depends crucially on what kind of uncertainty is involved.

In many cases, the uncertainty is due only to the difficulty of obtaining the appropriate information. *In principle,* with enough market information the revenue could be predicted, at least subject to some random error of a statistical kind.

In other cases, the uncertainty arises from the structure of the situation itself, and cannot be removed by ordinary market information. This is likely to occur when there is a small number of firms whose actions impinge strongly on each other. An action by one firm will affect other firms, and these other firms may react in various ways to the original move. The result (revenue in this case) of the original move will generally depend on the reactions which occur, and these may not be easily predictable. This is the situation in *oligopoly,* which is analogous in some ways to a game in which the results of a move by one player depend on the subsequent moves by other players. Indeed, a branch of mathematics known as the *theory of games* is helpful in analyzing situations of this kind.[3]

The Revenue Function. We shall discuss oligopoly and other complex decision problems of firms at a later stage. Here we shall deal with the simple case, making the assumption that:

---

[2] The calculus-trained reader should consult the Mathematical Note on this Section, page 314.

[3] The classic work is Von Neuman and Morgenstern's *Theory of Games and Economic Behavior.* The theory of games has thrown much light on, but not yet "solved" the theory of oligopoly behavior.

The revenue of the firm is a fully determinate function of the quantity it sells, which can in principle, be predicted. We will assume the relevant information is known to the firm.

Given a known revenue function, we can write the *total revenue* obtained from selling n units of output as $R(n)$. The *average revenue* is then given by $R(n)/n$. We shall be concerned with the case in which the firm sells on an open market to all buyers at the same price. If this is true, the revenue is equal to price multiplied by quantity sold. Thus $pn = R(n)$, so that $R(n)/n = p$ and we have the fundamental relationship:

$$Average\ revenue = price.$$

Since each quantity sold brings in a determinate total revenue, it is associated with a determinate average revenue, hence with a determinate price.

Revenue and Demand. We can draw revenue curves for the firm, just as we can draw cost curves. We draw the *total revenue curve* by plotting total revenue (in dollars measured vertically) against quantity sold. We can also draw the *average revenue curve,* plotting average revenue (dollars per unit) against quantity. (As with cost and other curves, total and average quantities are measured in different units and cannot be plotted together.)

Now every unit sold must be purchased by someone. If we look at the average revenue curve from the point of view of the buyers, we see that it shows how many units of the firm's product will be purchased at each level of average revenue (price), and is thus a demand curve, so that

The average revenue curve of the firm is also the demand curve for the firm's output.

Marginal Revenue. Since we have total and average revenue curves, we will have an associated *marginal revenue curve.* Marginal revenue is defined in a similar way to other marginal concepts, as the *increase in revenue obtained by selling an additional unit.*

It might seem, at first glance, that the increase in revenue obtained by selling an additional unit is simply equal to the price.

This indeed is a possible case. It implies that marginal revenue is equal to the price, and therefore to average revenue. From the general relationship between average and marginal quantities discussed in Chapter 5, equality of marginal revenue and average revenue implies that average revenue is constant. Thus the case in which marginal revenue is equal to price occurs when the average revenue curve (hence the demand curve for the firm's output) is horizontal.

Perfect Competition. A horizontal market demand curve would be an unusual case, but a horizontal demand curve *for the output of a single firm* can be expected to arise when there are a very large number of firms selling the same product. In such a case, buyers will be not willing to pay more for one firm's output than another's, so the market price will be the ruling price for all firms. Since there is a very large number of firms, no single firm's output has a noticeable effect on the market. Thus each firm can expect to sell as much as it wishes at the going price, and the demand for its output is horizontal over the effective range of the firm's output. A firm facing such a market is said to be *competitive,* or in a situation of *pure* or *perfect* competition.[4]

Imperfect Competition. If the demand curve for the output of the firm was downward sloping, rather than horizontal, then average revenue would be falling with output. Again using the relationship between average and marginal quantities from Chapter 5, this would imply that marginal revenue was less than average revenue (or price). We can arrive at the same result by arguing directly that a downward sloping demand curve means that a greater quantity can only be sold at a lower price. Thus selling one more unit implies lowering the price (not only on the marginal unit, but on the whole quantity sold, since the price is the same for everyone) and thus that the addition to revenue from selling one more unit (marginal revenue) is less than the original price (average revenue).

The most obvious case in which a firm faces a downward sloping demand curve is when it is the only firm selling the product (monopoly), so that the demand curve for its output is just the market demand curve for the product. There is a variety of other cases which do not have all the characteristics of the classical picture of monopoly, but in which the individual firm faces a downward sloping demand curve for its product. These cases are collectively known as *imperfect competition.*

Revenue and Elasticity. In discussing elasticity of demand in Chapter 2, we investigated the relationship between elasticity and the way in which expenditure changes with price. Because the demand curve slopes downward a fall in price reduces expenditure insofar as a lower price is paid for every unit purchased, but it increases expenditure insofar as a greater

---

[4] Sometimes a distinction is made between "pure" and "perfect" competition, "pure" being a shade less perfect than "perfect." We shall use the term "perfect," which is a natural partner to *imperfect.*

quantity is purchased. The net effect depends on the price change relative to the quantity change, and thus on the elasticity. It was shown in the earlier analysis that expenditure will rise when price falls if the elasticity of the demand curve is numerically greater than unity (elastic demand), and expenditure will fall when price falls if the elasticity is numerically less than unity (inelastic demand).

Since revenue is simply the seller's view of what the consumer regards as expenditure, we can convert the relationship between price and expenditure into one between quantity sold and revenue.

With a downward sloping demand curve, a greater quantity can only be sold by lowering the price. Thus revenue increases when quantity increases, if expenditure increases when the price falls, that is if demand is relatively elastic. If demand is inelastic, revenue *falls* when the quantity sold is increased by reducing price. Since marginal revenue is the increase in revenue obtained by selling one more unit, marginal revenue is *negative* when demand is inelastic. The relationship between elasticity and marginal revenue can be stated as follows:

Marginal revenue is positive if demand is relatively elastic, negative if it is inelastic, and zero if there is unit elasticity.

Average and Marginal Revenue. We are now in a position to describe average and marginal revenue curves for typical demand situations facing the firm.

If the average revenue curve is horizontal (competitive case), the marginal revenue curve is horizontal and coincides with it. We have a single horizontal line (infinite elasticity of demand for the firm's output) which is both the average and the marginal revenue curve. This is illustrated in Figure 6.1.

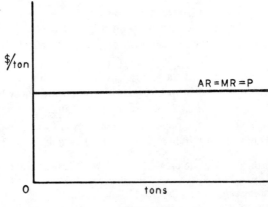

Figure 6.1

If the average revenue curve slopes downward (monopoly case), the marginal revenue curve lies below it everywhere (from ordinary average-marginal relationships). Contrary to what one might be led to believe from standard diagrams, *this does not imply that the marginal revenue curve necessarily slopes downward.*

Straight Line Demand. For a *straight line* average revenue curve, sloping downward and intersecting both axes, the marginal revenue curve can be shown to be downward sloping. In Chapter 2, we showed that a demand curve of this kind passed through all elasticity values. At zero quantity (the intercept with the vertical axis), the elasticity is infinite, implying that marginal and average revenues are equal. Thus the marginal revenue curve starts from the same point as the average revenue curve. At the maximum quantity end of the average revenue is negative. The marginal revenue curve thus slopes downward, crossing the horizontal axis at the quantity for which elasticity is unity. The straight line case is illustrated in Figure 6.2.

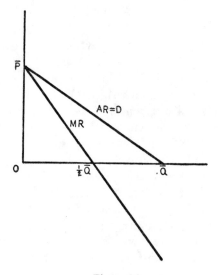

Figure 6.2

There is a special arithmetic relationship for the straight line average curve which is sometimes useful:

For a straight line downward sloping average revenue curve which intersects the horizontal axis at quantity $\overline{Q}$, the corresponding marginal revenue curve commences from the same point on the vertical axis as the average revenue curve and intersects the horizontal axis at quantity $\frac{1}{2}\overline{Q}$.

This relationship is shown in the Figure 6.2. It can be proved geo-metrically by considering Figure 6.3. At the point *B* on the demand curve,

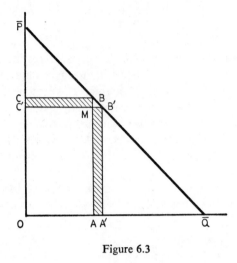

Figure 6.3

price is *AB* and quantity is *OA*, so total revenue is the area of the rectangle *OABC*. At a nearby point, *B'*, the total revenue is *OA'B'C'*. Comparing *OA'B'C'* with *OABC*, we see that we obtain the new rectangle from the old by *subtracting* the horizontal strip *CBMC'* and *adding* the vertical strip *A'AMB'*. The relative thickness of the two strips is *BM/MB'*, the slope of the average revenue curve, which is constant since this is a straight line. Thus the relative areas of the two strips depend on their lengths, *CB* and *A'B'*. If *B* is such that *CB = A'B'*, the areas of the two strips are equal, *OA'B'C'* is equal in area to *OABC*, total revenue does not change, and marginal revenue is zero. If *B*, *B'* are very close together, we will have *B'A'* almost identical with *BA*, and we will have *CB = BA* when *B* is on the mid-point of the average revenue curve. We will then have $OA = \frac{1}{2}\overline{Q}$, proving the relationship. We will also have $OC = \frac{1}{2}\overline{P}$, where $\overline{P}$ is the price at which sales just become zero. Thus:

For the straight line case, the quantity at which marginal revenue is zero corresponds to a price $\frac{1}{2}\overline{P}$, where $\overline{P}$ is the price at which sales just fall to zero.

The General Case. For other cases, the marginal revenue curve can slope up or down, or even slope upward over part of the range and downward over the next. The curves in Figure 6.4 (a), (b), and (c) are all correctly drawn to show some possibilities.

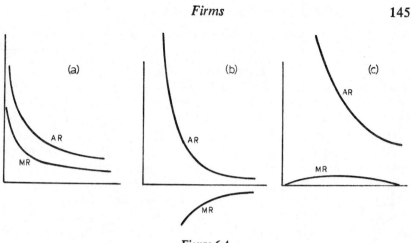

Figure 6.4

If the average revenue curve is downward sloping, we shall usually draw marginal revenue curves sloping downward also, consistent with straight line average revenue curves (Figure 6.2) and with constant elasticity (but greater than one) average revenue curves (Figure 6.4 [a]).

The relationship between average and marginal revenue curves depends on the elasticity of the demand (or average revenue) curve at the output in question. For infinite elasticity (horizontal demand curve), marginal revenue is equal to price so the difference between price and marginal revenue is zero. For unit elasticity, marginal revenue is zero, so that the difference between price and marginal revenue is equal to price. For elasticity less than unity, marginal revenue is negative so that the difference between price and marginal revenue is greater than price. Thus we have the general rule:

The difference between price and marginal revenue is greater for any given quantity, the smaller the elasticity of demand at the point on the demand curve corresponding to that quantity.

6.3 Cost Curves

Cost and cost curves were discussed at length in Chapter 5. The purpose of this section is merely to specify the cost situations with which we shall normally work.

Unless otherwise specified, we shall assume that the firm

(i) has a constant returns to scale technology, with a very large number of processes giving a smooth isoquant,

(ii) faces constant input prices,

(iii) has an upper limit on the availability of one of its inputs, typically to be regarded as "capital" or "land," in the "short run." This upper limit defines the *size* of the firm.[5] (See section 6.4 for the part played by financing in determining this limitation)

The firm's costs depend only on its technology and the conditions under which it can purchase inputs. The assumption that the inputs can be purchased at constant prices is consistent with competitive input markets, and we suppose that these markets are competitive *even for a firm with a monopoly in its output market*. Monopoly in output is perfectly consistent with competition for inputs, since we suppose that the inputs are *unspecialized,* like unskilled labor. At a later stage, we will discuss situations in which input markets are not competitive in the simple sense, but here we shall assume that the cost structures of firms are independent of the market situation for their outputs.

Types of Cost Curve. We shall take as the typical average cost curve the relatively simple kind which is flat up to the point at which the input limitation becomes effective, then rises. This type, shown in Figure 6.5(a) will be referred to as the *standard* cost curve.

Sometimes we will find it relevant to use the U-shaped average cost curve and associated marginal cost curve, either in its traditional form (Figure 6.5[b]) or in the flat-bottomed version of Figure 5.12.

When we discuss *long-run* situations, we shall most typically refer to a situation with no input constraints and with constant returns to scale everywhere, giving the horizontal curve of Figure 6.5(c).

In special cases we may discuss the effect of indivisibilities, using the simple single-step curve discussed in Section 5.10 and shown here in Figure 6.5(d). This curve assumes no input limitation—if there is one at very high output levels, we obtain a hybrid curve by joining Figure 6.5(a) on to the right hand side of 6.5(d). However, if the limitation is effective over the output range in which we are primarily interested, we are probably not then interested in the early part of the curve.

It should be stressed that the relevant cost curve for a given situation is a matter of fact, not assumption. Furthermore, as we shall see, the firm's behavior is determined by the detailed nature of the cost curve over a certain range of output only—outside that range it is sufficient to know, for example, that average cost is nowhere lower than at the lowest point in this range. Thus, if the relevant range was on the upward sloping part

---

[5] We define the *size* of the firm in terms of the *largest* output that can be produced at *minimum average cost.* A firm may also have an absolute upper limit on its possible output, but we do not use this as a "size'" measure.

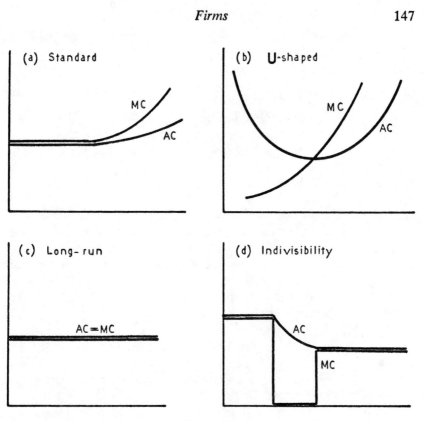

Figure 6.5

of 6.5(a) it would generally matter whether the left-hand part of the curve was like 6.5(a) or 6.5(b). Similarly, if the firm's operations were always in a range of constant costs, it might be irrelevant whether an ultimate input limitation existed or not.

We assume certain cost curves in certain analyses because they are the *simplest* cost curves believed to be "typical" over the relevant range.

In some cases, such as general equilibrium and welfare economics, the economist may be interested in what would happen to the behavior of productive units if they operated at levels well outside their normal range of operation. In such cases, we become interested in the complete cost curves.

In the cost curves for the firm, it is always assumed that proper account is being taken of *opportunity costs*. In particular, whatever the manager or entrepreneur could earn in another firm is a cost to the firm in which his services are being used. Accounting costs, in practice, do not take full notice of opportunity costs and thus do not represent the costs used in economic analysis.

6.4 The Role of Financing

Production processes require time: the inputs are used up in the process before output is produced. If we consider only the central technical aspect of the process, this time may often be short, but if we consider the production process in the full sense, from commencing the collection of inputs to the final dispatch of the output to a customer, it can be quite long.

Thus the costs of production are incurred before the revenues are received. To take a simple example, suppose a firm is producing at a monthly output of 100 tons, with average costs of $10 per ton. We suppose the nature of the production process is such that the inputs are fed in at the beginning of each month, and the output appears at the end of the month. Thus the firm must spend $1,000 on inputs on the first of the month, and only receives revenue on the last day.

Working Capital. Consider the firm's very first production run. It must have $1,000 to pay inputs before production commences, and it will not be able to pay this from revenue which will not appear until the end of the month. This $1,000 is *working capital,* and will typically be borrowed from a bank or other financial institution. At the end of the month, the firm can pay back the loan, but it must then take out another for the next month, and so on. As long as the firm is producing at the rate of 100 tons per month, it requires a permanent working capital of $1,000. This requirement will decline if the firm's output declines and rise if the firm's output rises. It will decline if the *period of production* necessary to maintain the same level of output declines. This can easily be seen by observing that if the period of production falls from one month to half a month, output of 100 tons per month can be met by two successive production runs of 50 tons each, requiring working capital of only $500.

The interest on working capital is one of the firm's costs which was not explicitly mentioned in the previous chapter. Equally important, the ability to finance working capital may be one of the constraints on the operation of the firm.

Ability to *finance* both working capital and fixed capital represents one of the most important factors in determining the size of firms in the economy of the United States. In the industrial sector we can regard the typical input limitation (on capital) as due primarily to financing problems. Fuller discussion requires analysis of investment decisions, given in Section 11.3.

6.5 The Profit Maximizing Output[6]

If the firm faces a clearly determined revenue function in which the revenue depends only on the output sold by the firm and determined cost curves, the relationship between cost and revenue at the most profitable output can be derived easily.

Suppose the firm is producing and selling an output of *n* units. We wish to find out if increasing output by an additional unit will increase profits. The increase in total costs due to producing this extra unit is the marginal cost at output *n*. The increase in total dollar revenue from selling this extra output is marginal revenue at output *n*. We shall suppose initially that total revenue is greater than total cost (profit positive) over the output range under discussion.

If the marginal revenue exceeds the marginal cost, total revenue rises by more than total cost when output increases so surplus profit (revenue less cost) increases. Thus it is profitable to increase output, if it is possible to do so.

If marginal revenue is less than marginal cost, total revenue rises by less than total cost, and profit decreases when output is increased. But in this case, *reducing* output will decrease total cost more than it decreases total revenue, so profit will be increased by reducing output, if this is possible.

From these arguments, we have the basic rules:

If marginal revenue is greater than marginal cost, it will be profitable to expand output, if this is feasible.

If marginal revenue is less than marginal cost, it will be profitable to contract output, if this is feasible.

Thus for any feasible range of output over the whole of which $MR > MC$, the most profitable output in the range will be the *greatest* output. For any range over which $MR < MC$, the most profitable output will be the *least*.

Consider Figure 6.6(a) which shows an unusual (but possible) marginal cost curve intersecting the horizontal marginal revenue curve at two outputs, Q' and Q^*. We can tabulate the relationship between marginal cost and marginal revenue as follows:

---

[6] For the reader trained in calculus, a Mathematical Note on this Section is given on page 316.

Output Range	Relationship of MR, MC	Most profitable output in range
0 to Q'	$MR < MC$ (= at Q')	0 (least)
Q' to $Q*$	$MR > MC$ (= at $Q*$, Q')	$Q*$ (greatest)
$Q*$ and beyond	$MR < MC$ (= at $Q*$)	$Q*$ (least)

The two candidates for "most profitable output" are 0 and $Q*$. Note that, although $MR = MC$ at *two* outputs, only one ($Q*$) is even a candidate for most profitable.

We cannot tell from the marginal curves alone which of 0, $Q*$ is the most profitable output. Let us defer this problem for the moment and assume we know it to be $Q*$.

At $Q*$ we have $MR = MC$, but this relationship also holds at Q'. How do we distinguish between the two cases?

The difference is in the relationship between marginal cost and marginal revenue *near* rather than *at* the two outputs. Near output $Q*$, the MR curve is above MC to the left and below to the right, while the relationships are reversed for Q'. This means it is profitable to move *away* from Q' in either direction, but profitable to move *toward* $Q*$ from either direction, so that Q' cannot be a maximum profit output.

We can check that $Q*$ is indeed the most profitable output, and not 0, only by looking at *average* curves. At $Q*$ we have $AR > AC$ so that positive profit is made. Since profit will be zero at zero output, $Q*$ is more profitable than 0.

On the other hand, in Figure 6.6(b), where the MR (= AR) curve is lower than in 6.6(a), we have $AR < AC$ at output $Q*$, so a loss will be made at that output. In this case zero profit at 0 will be preferable. It should be noted that zero output does not always mean zero profit in the *short run*—there may be costs incurred just to stay in business and it may be more "profitable" to produce something at which the temporary loss is less than for producing nothing.

Note that in the above case we have $MR < MC$ at 0 so that the equality $MR = MC$ is not satisfied as at $Q*$. In this case we have a *corner* or *boundary* solution. (The case in which $MR = MC$ is an *interior* solution.) A boundary solution is also possible at some upper limit to production (if there is one). This is illustrated in Figure 6.6(c). At $\overline{Q}$, $MR > MC$ but it is physically impossible to produce more output given the input limitation, and $\overline{Q}$ is the most profitable output.

We can summarize as follows:

The most profitable output will be
either (1) an output for which MR = MC, *which is also such that the* MR

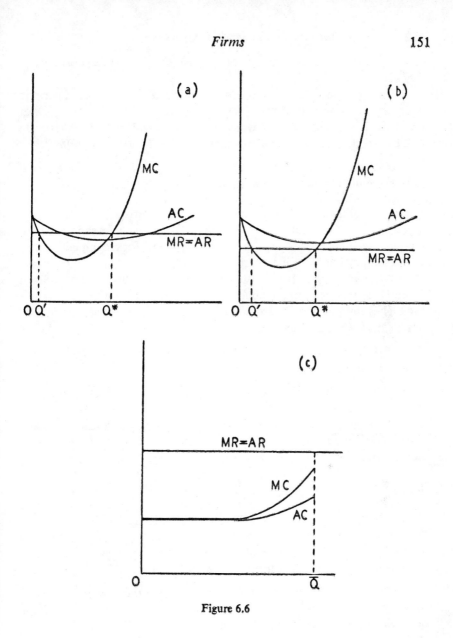

Figure 6.6

curve is above the MC *curve for a slightly lower output and*
below it for a slightly higher output,

or (2) *a boundary solution.*

It will certainly be a boundary solution if $MR \neq MC$ anywhere,
being zero if $MR < MC$ everywhere and at an upper limit if $MR > MC$
everywhere. Even if $MR = MC$ for some output, the solution may still be

on the boundary and examination of the total or average curves is necessary.

Most of the simpler models of the firm are such that either the boundary solution is obvious (*MR < MC* everywhere, for example) or that there is a unique point at which *MR = MC* with the curves crossing in the correct direction for a maximum. Thus we have the *Working Rule:*

Unless otherwise specified, the typical model of the firm is assumed to be such that the most profitable output is that for which MR =MC.

Equally Profitable Outputs. Another problem arises concerning the *uniqueness* of the most profitable output. If marginal cost is equal to marginal revenue over a range of outputs (possible for a competitive firm with a flat portion on its marginal cost curve), *all the outputs in the range are equally profitable.* It is reasonable, in handling this case, to make a special behavior assumption about producers, that they prefer to produce the highest output possible from among those that are equally profitable.

Thus we shall assume:

If there is more than one output giving the same profit, the firm will choose the largest.

This rule also solves a traditional difficulty of perceptive students, who are given numerical examples showing that marginal cost and marginal revenue are equal in going from, say, 100 to 101 tons output, and then puzzle why the firm should choose between 100 and 101 tons as its optimal output.

Information Content. We should note that, if we eliminate the special cases and assume there is a solution of the traditional kind with *MC = MR*, this relationship is *necessarily* true if the firm is operating at its most profitable output. However the firm determines this output, by trial and error or otherwise, and whether the firm has ever heard of marginal cost or marginal revenue, the relationship holds.

The rule MC = MR *has no economic content, it is merely descriptive. To say the firm operates so as to maximize its profit conveys all the information contained in the situation.*

If the aim of the firm is to maximize profits, it will be satisfied with its behavior if, in fact, profits are maximized. Thus the firm has no reason to change its output from the profit maximizing level, unless input prices, demand, or technology change. For this reason, the profit maximizing output is often referred to as the *equilibrium output* of the firm.

It could be argued that "equilibrium" is not a useful term in this context if the firm, in fact, is always at its maximum profit output. The term is only useful if there is some "disequilibrium" with which we can make comparison.

Input Determination. Finally, we can observe that a firm determines its *inputs* when it determines its *output*. For a two-input (capital and labor) firm with an effective limit on capital at its optimum output, marginal cost is entirely due to labor. We showed in Chapter 5 that, in this case

$$MC = \frac{w}{MPL}$$

(MPL = marginal product of labor).

If $MR = MC$, we have a direct relationship linking marginal revenue, the wage and the marginal product of labor:

$$MR = \frac{w}{MPL}, \text{ or } w = MR \times MPL .$$

We shall discuss this in more detail later, but the point should be taken at this stage that *the optimum requirement for inputs is determined simultaneously with the optimum output.*

It should be stressed that the marginal cost/marginal product relationship does not imply that the firm determines the wage w (this is a market price), but that it adjusts output by varying labor until the product $MR \times MPL$ is made equal to the going wage rate w.

6.6 Perfect Competition

Perfect competition is a market structure in which there are a large number of firms producing an identical product, and in which no one firm has more than a negligible share of the total sales. Note that the requirement that no single firm has an important market share requires many firms, but a large number of firms is not sufficient to guarantee a small market share for every firm. It is possible to have sales of, say, 1 million tons of which 900,000 comes from one firm and one ton from each of 100,000 firms. We also assume the existence of *unrestricted entry,* so that new firms can start producing this product if they wish, and *uniform technology,* so that all firms use the same processes under the same conditions.

A perfectly competitive market structure implies that no individual firm can influence the price of the product by its own actions alone. Each firm can sell as much as it is capable of producing, at the going market price. Thus the average revenue of each firm is horizontal and coincides with the marginal revenue curve, and both average and marginal revenue are equal to price.

If an interior profit maximizing solution exists, which will generally be the case, the equality of marginal revenue and marginal cost takes the special form:

At the profit maximizing output under perfect competition, marginal cost will be equal to price (MC = P), *unless there is a corner solution.*

The normal case is drawn in Figure 6.7, with the price ($= MR$) line above the horizontal portion of the standard average cost curve. The

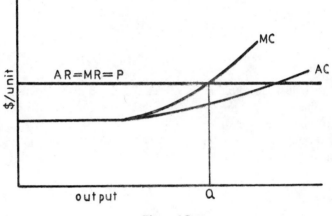

Figure 6.7

profit maximizing output is given by Q, the quantity at which marginal cost is just equal to price.

Consider the effect of a fall in market price (shown in Figure 6.8) from P_1 to P_2. The profit maximizing output will fall from Q_1 to Q_2. A further fall to P_3 (equal to minimum average cost) will cause the quantity to fall to Q_3, on our assumption that the firm produces the maximum output if several outputs give the same profit. If the price should fall to P_4, marginal cost is greater than price everywhere, and the firm will cease production (a corner solution).

At price P_1, the *average cost* is given from the average cost curve at the point X. Each unit sold brings in an average revenue equal to P_1 at an average cost corresponding to X, so the *profit per unit* is equal to the distance AX. The total profit is equal to this multiplied by total output, given by the shaded rectangle in the diagram.

Note that the behavior of the firm at all prices—P_1, P_2, P_3, and P_4 —will be exactly the same as described above if the average cost curve

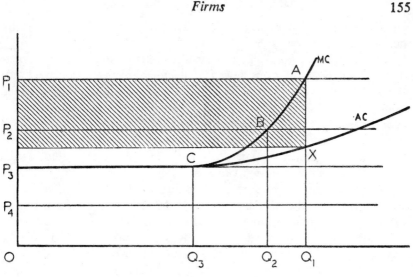

Figure 6.8

has either a traditional or a flat-bottomed U shape, provided Q_3 is produced at minimum average cost equal to P_3 and the right-hand part of the curve is the same as that in the diagram. Thus we do not need to know the shape of the portion of the average cost curve for outputs less than the *largest* output that can be produced at *minimum average cost*.

The Supply Curve. Thus we can read from the firm's marginal cost curve the quantity the firm will supply at any given market price. At price P_1, we read from the point A that the firm will supply quantity Q_1, and so on. But a curve from which we can read the quantity that will be supplied is a supply curve. Thus we can state:

> *The marginal cost curve of a perfectly competitive firm with a standard cost curve is also the firm's supply curve.*

If the average cost curve in Figure 6.8 was U-shaped, rising to the left from C, the supply curve would be that portion of the marginal cost curve to the right of C. Strictly speaking, this supply curve terminates at C, but it is common to draw in a horizontal portion P_3C (thus giving exactly the same supply curve as with a standard cost curve). Considered as part of a *supply curve*, the portion P_3C implies a willingness to supply quantities between 0 and Q_3 at price P_3. This is true for the standard cost case, but with a U-shaped curve the firm is willing to supply 0 or Q_3 at this price, but no quantity in between since average cost will exceed price for such quantities.

The aggregate supply curve for the product is obtained by consolidating the information from the individual supply curves. This is achieved by taking each price (say P_2) and adding together the quantities that each firm will supply at this price, a process often referred to as "adding the individual curves." If all firms have available the same technology and face the same input prices, the flat portion of the curve will correspond to the same price (P_3) for all firms. The output at which the input limitation becomes effective will vary from firm to firm, but not the *price* at which all firms start to move up the sloping portions of the marginal cost curves. Thus the aggregate supply curve will have the same general slope as the marginal cost curve of the individual firm—a flat portion at price P_3, with an upward sloping portion to the right of this. The length of the flat portion will be the sum of the lengths of all the flat points of the individual curves. Since this curve reflects input limitations, it can be regarded as a "short-run" curve. The collection of all perfectly competitive firms producing the same product is usually referred to as an *industry;*[7] so the supply curve we have described is the *short-run industry supply curve.*

The Market. We can now give a market analysis for a perfectly competitive industry, using the short-run industry supply curve in conjunction with the market demand curve. This is given in Figure 6.9.

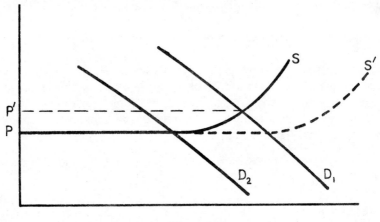

Figure 6.9

The expected events within the industry depend on whether the demand curve intersects the short-run industry supply curve on the rising portion (as D_1 with S) or the horizontal portion (as D_2 with S).

[7] The traditional analysis of the theory of the firm, which commenced with Marshall (*Principles of Economics,* 1890), placed great emphasis on the industry. Modern analysis places much less emphasis here, since general equilibrium analysis (which Marshall did not discuss) does not require such emphasis.

If the intersection occurs on the horizontal portion, the market price *P* will be equal to the minimum average cost for all firms, surplus profits will be zero, and no firms have a particular incentive to expand beyond their present size. At zero surplus profits, firms will have no particular incentive to shut down either, since the value of alternative opportunities for the use of the firm's capital and its organizational and managerial talent has already been included in its costs. Thus there is no incentive for the firms to expand or shut down, or for new firms to enter.[8] Market equilibrium under these conditions will also be a *long-run equilibrium,* a conclusion that could also have been reached by noting that the horizontal portion of the short-run cost curve coincides with the long-run cost curve.

But if the intersection occurs on the rising portion of the short-run supply curve (as the intersection of *S, D_1* in Figure 6.9, giving price *P'*) average cost is less than marginal cost, hence than price, and surplus profit greater than zero will be received. Two types of effect will occur. First, firms already in the industry will attempt to increase their size by obtaining more of their limited input. This will move to the right the point at which the marginal cost curve commences to rise, and so move to the right the point at which the industry supply curve commences to rise. Second, the existence of surplus profits may attract new firms into the industry, again moving the rising part of the industry supply curve rightward.

These tendencies will continue so long as surplus profits exist, which will be as long as the demand curve intersects the rising part of the supply curve. The industry will reach a long-run equilibrium when the rising part of the industry supply curve has moved sufficiently to the right (as the dotted curve *S'* in Figure 6.9) to give an intersection with the demand curve on the horizontal portion of *S'*.

Long-Run Competitive Price. Since the horizontal portion of the industry supply curve is at a level determined by the horizontal portion of the marginal cost curves of the individual curves, this level represents the *minimum average cost,* at which the product can be manufactured, given the technology and the input prices. Thus we have a property of perfectly competitive production in the long run:

---

[8] Under constant returns to scale, the individual firm has no particular economic significance. It makes no difference whether 6 machines and 6 men are legally constituted as one firm, or as six firms each with one man and one machine. Because the size of the firm has no *economic* significance (provided only that there are enough firms to give a perfectly competitive structure) under constant returns to scale, it should not be surprising that *economic* analysis does not determine the sizes of the individual firms. In practice, the size distribution will be determined by large numbers of small influences not taken into account in the broad analysis, from the point of view of which the influences can be considered as random factors.

In the long run (that is, given sufficient time to adjust fully with a constant technology and constant input prices), the price in a perfectly competitive market under constant returns to scale will be equal to the minimum average cost of production.

Modifications. We may well have a situation in which some, but not all, of the conditions of perfect competition are met.

Among the conditions that may not be met is that of a uniform technology. If the technology varies from firm to firm (only some firms being aware of certain efficient processes), the minimum average cost will not be the same for all firms. The short-run industry supply curve may not then contain a long horizontal section, since only firms with the fully efficient technology will produce at the lower price levels. As prices rise, firms with less efficient technologies will commence to produce when their minimum average cost level is reached. The supply curve will slope upward, possibly in a series of steps—each step corresponding to the minimum average cost level of a group of firms at the same technological level.

In the long run, however, we would expect the technology to become uniform at the efficient level. This will occur either by transmission of the technological information from firm to firm or by expansion of the efficient firms and the dropping out of the others. Thus the analysis of the long-run situation is the same as that already given.

If there are decreasing returns to scale (as in some extractive industries and possibly agriculture), rather than the constant returns assumed so far (applicable especially to small-scale manufacturing), average costs rise steadily for individual firms and so for the industry. In this case the industry has no minimum average cost output (except zero), and so:

Under decreasing returns to scale, the long-run supply curve will not be horizontal and no long-run equality of price with minimum average cost will be achieved.

The Industry and General Equilibrium. The concept of the competitive *industry,* larger than the firm, but smaller than the economy, is chiefly useful in deriving the supply curve for a competitive market. The competitive market is itself a partial equilibrium model (as pointed out in Chapter 2) and the industry is a useful model primarily when it is a sufficiently small part of the whole economy for the partial analysis to be appropriate.

For this reason we have concentrated on analysis of the industry under conditions of constant input prices, since this is appropriate for partial analysis. For the watermelon producing industry (appropriate for this analysis) it will be remembered that the farm wage was taken to be independent of the output of watermelons in the analysis of Chapter 2.

If the industry is a sufficiently large part of the economy to affect input prices by the actions of its firms (as would be the case if we took "agriculture" rather than "watermelon production" as our industry) it is more appropriate to move to a general equilibrium setting. An example of industry analysis under these conditions is given in Section 9.6.

6.7 Monopoly

A firm is a monopoly (the Greek roots mean "single seller") in the classical sense if it is the only supplier of a product. The demand curve for the firm's output is thus the market demand curve for the product. Every firm selling a product which is different (in some sense meaningful to the consumer) from that sold by any other firm is a monopolist of a kind.

The simple analysis of monopoly behavior depends, however, on the existence of demand conditions for the product that are stable and (in principle) predictable. This analysis does not hold if, for example, there are strong interconnections between the market for the monopolist's product and the market for the product of another monopolist. A Plymouth is not identical with a Chevrolet, and Chrysler has a monopoly in selling Plymouths. But the demand for Plymouths is very sensitive to the price of Chevrolets, and vice versa, so any market action by Chrysler may lead to reaction by General Motors, and the effect of the action cannot be predicted with certainty without foreknowledge of the reaction by General Motors. Such a market situation is *oligopolistic* and requires special analysis.

On the other hand, if the market for the monopolist's product has strong interconnection with a *perfectly competitive market,* the monopoly analysis holds because no individual firm in the competitive industry has the power to react to the monopolist. A firm selling specially selected wheat under a trademark can be treated as a monopolist, because the market for ordinary wheat is competitive. An oligopoly situation would exist, however, if there were several firms selling selected wheats under different trademarks.

Special treatment used to be given to the analysis of a market situation called *monopolistic competition.*[9] The relevant features of this can

---

[9] The classic work is Chamberlin's *The Theory of Monopolistic Competition* (1933). There is doubt whether the special features of Chamberlin's model which differentiates it from monopoly and oligopoly are relevant. We do not discuss them here.

really be discussed together with monopoly on one hand, and oligopoly on the other.

Thus our analysis of monopoly simply depends on the firm facing a relatively stable and predictable market demand curve,[10] which we take to be downward sloping. The most profitable output will be that for which marginal cost equals marginal revenue.

Monopoly Output. The geometry of monopoly is illustrated in Figure 6.10. Note that the intersection of the marginal revenue and marginal cost curves

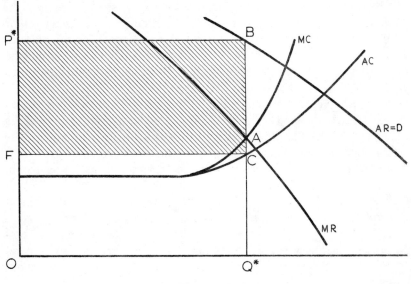

Figure 6.10

(A) merely gives the most profitable output (Q^*). The vertical height of A does not give the price, which must be read from B, the point on the average revenue (demand) curve vertically above A.

The overt action which the monopoly will normally take is to set the *price,* and then offer to sell what the market will take at that price. Thus its sequence of decisions and actions would be:

(1) determine the most profitable output (Q^*)

(2) set the price (P^*) at which the buyers will just buy quantity Q^*, and offer to sell at this price.

---

[10] A monopolist may be able to *shift* the demand curve for his product by advertising and other *selling costs.* Important though such costs are in actual business practice, the general analysis is not greatly changed, and we have chosen to omit them.

If its information on market demand is correct, it will sell exactly Q^* at price P^* and maximize its surplus profit. The average cost of each unit sold is obtained from the point C on the average cost curve, and the average revenue is the price, so that the surplus profit per unit is the vertical distance BC. The total profit is the shaded area in the diagram, equal to profit per unit multiplied by output.

Once the demand and cost conditions are established, the monopolist has a *unique* optimal price[11] and output. It is meaningless to ask what output will the monopolist supply at each of several prices. A monopoly firm determines the price at which it wishes to sell—it is a *price setter,* whereas the perfectly competitive firm accepts the market price as beyond its own control and is a *price taker.*

A market with a monopoly supplier has no supply curve of the ordinary kind.

The monopolist's optimal policy gives rise to *point supply,* given by the point B in Figure 6.10. If its market information has not been exact (almost certain in practice), it must adjust either price or quantity to the demand situation, in the manner discussed in Chapter 2. Monopolists in practice are operating at only an approximation to the profit maximizing output, due to imperfect information about market conditions.

Long-Run Adjustment. A monopolist, like a competitive industry, can make long-run adjustments as well as short-run output decisions. For a monopolist in the short-run situation depicted in Figure 6.10, there will be an incentive to increase size (defined by its input limitation). If the input limitation can be removed, the beginning of the upward slope on the marginal and cost curves can be pushed to the right.

The long-run maximum profit position will be when the marginal revenue curve cuts the marginal cost curve on its horizontal portion, as at A' in Figure 6.11. If demand is unchanged, this increase in size will result in some expansion of output (to Q^{**}) and some reduction in price (to P^{**}), but with profit increasing because of the fall in average costs to their minimum level.

Note that, in the long run, the monopolist will be *producing* at mini-

---

[11] We have assumed throughout that the monopolist faces a single unified market, competitive on the demand side, and such that arbitrage would prevent the use of several prices. Sometimes a monopolist may face *separated* markets in which resale is not possible (one cannot sell one's haircut or medical treatment to another, and tariffs may prevent goods sold abroad being resold at home at an acceptable price). In this case the monopolist can engage in *price discrimination*. It can be shown that it will be profitable to set prices which equate *marginal revenues* in all markets to each other and to the overall marginal cost. Price will thus be higher in the more inelastic market.

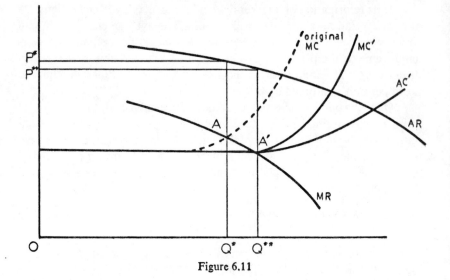

Figure 6.11

mum average cost if there are constant returns to scale but will be *selling* at a higher price.

Preservation of Monopoly. If the monopoly is profitable, other firms will be attracted toward producing the same product. Persistence of a monopoly depends on presenting some barrier to entry by other firms. Among these barriers are:

(1) Legal prohibitions on entry, such as copyrights and franchises (direct prohibition of other firms), patents (which prevent other firms using some essential technique of production), trademarks (which make it difficult for other firms to convince buyers that their product is identical). These are the oldest and most secure foundations for a monopoly. Kings used once to grant the royal franchise over a certain commodity as a reward for services rendered. Nowadays, franchises in the United States are granted mainly for transportation, communications, and public utilities, but copyrights and patents give legal monopolies for a certain number of years.

(2) Economic barriers to entry, derived primarily from the existence of indivisibilities so that a competitor cannot start in a small way and build up, but must operate on a large scale from the beginning. Such barriers are a less secure protection for the monopolist than legal barriers. Their existence usually precludes the industry from ever becoming perfectly competitive, however. Even if other firms enter, they will be few and large, leading to an oligopoly situation.

(3) Informal, and frequently illegal, barriers, such as physical and financial intimidation of potential competitors.

Changes in Demand. In the long run, of course, the demand curves can be expected to shift. Now a shift in demand affects a monopoly in a relatively complex way, since a monopolist's equilibrium position depends on both the "size" of the market and the elasticity of demand. Since we are concerned with long-run changes, we can take the firm's average and marginal cost curves to be horizontal.

Consider Figure 6.12. Initially, demand is given by AR_1 and the cor-

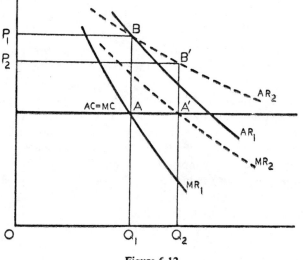

Figure 6.12

responding marginal revenue curve by MR_1. The firm will sell output Q_1 at price P_1. Now suppose demand becomes more elastic, although the new demand curve (AR_2) still passes through the point B corresponding to the original point supply. Since the demand elasticity is higher, the difference between price and marginal revenue is less than it was originally. The new marginal revenue at quantity Q_1 is thus greater than it was originally, so the new marginal revenue curve is like MR_2 and intersects the marginal cost curve at an output Q_2 which is greater than Q_1. The new price P_2 will be lower than the old. Thus, if the demand curve becomes more elastic, but passes through the original point supply, the new equilibrium will be at a higher output and lower price than the old. As a result, price will move closer to average cost as elasticity increases.

It is probable that general economic trends are, and have been for many years, towards increasing the elasticity of demand for products sold under monopoly conditions. Most of the barriers guarding a monopoly can be partially bypassed by technological innovation. The monopolies sustained by railroad franchise in the nineteenth century have been weakened, not by removing the franchise and building competing railroads, but by new technologies which have enabled road, and later air, transport to offer close substitutes for railroad transportation, without coming under the legal definition of railroads. Similarly, many monopolies sustained by patents have been weakened by technologies achieving similar results without using the patented processes.

6.8 Competition Versus Monopoly

In Chapter 10 we shall examine the various market situations in terms of their efficiency in enabling the economy to achieve an optimum level of the general "welfare." The purpose of this section is to examine the effect on output and price in a particular market if the industry was changed from perfectly competitive to monopolistic or vice versa. We shall assume essentially *long-run* equilibrium in both cases.

If there are no indivisibilities, leading to economies of scale, the comparison is direct and simple. The long-run average costs will be the same for the competitive industry and the monopoly, and marginal cost will coincide with average costs. Demand conditions are assumed to be unchanged by the structure of the industry.

The comparison is given in Figure 6.13. For perfect competition, the market equilibrium will be at C, the intersection of the supply and demand curves, giving competitive output Q_c and competitive price P_c.

For monopoly, however, the point supply of the firm will be at the point M, giving monopoly output Q_m and monopoly price P_m. Direct comparison gives the simple rule:

A monopoly will produce a smaller output, and sell at a higher price, than the equivalent competitive industry.

The difference between P_m and P_c can be thought of as the *monopoly markup;* it is the profit maximizing excess over the competitive price which the firm can achieve by virtue of its monopoly position. The shaded area in the figure is the excess profit over and above the profits that could be made by the competitive industry, and is usually referred to as the *monopoly profit.*

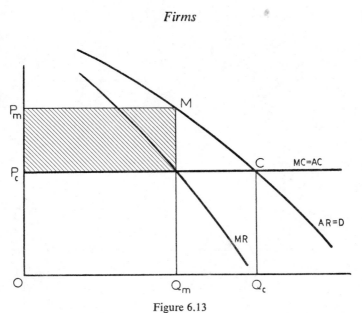

Figure 6.13

Indivisibilities. If there are indivisibilities this simple relationship does not necessarily hold. Consider the case with "small-scale" and "large-scale" processes, leading to a composite average cost curve of the kind discussed in Chapter 5 and depicted in Figure 5.13; and suppose the perfectly competitive industry is made up of firms all producing outputs below the level at which the large-scale process is economical.

The *industry* supply curve will thus be horizontal at the small-scale average cost even though the output of the industry as a whole may be in the range at which large-scale production is economical.

In Figure 6.14, S_c shows the supply curve for the competitive industry, AC_m the average cost curve for the monopoly, which can use the large-scale process. The equilibrium for the competitive industry is at C, giving quantity Q_c and price P_c (= average cost of small-scale process). The equilibrium for the monopoly is at M, giving quantity Q_m and price P_m.

In this case, it is the *monopoly* which produces the greater output and sells at the lower price. This occurs because, although the monopoly sells at a price above average cost, its size of operation enables it to achieve the low average cost of large-scale operation. Even though there is still a monopoly markup, it is less than the cost saving from using the large-scale process.

Economies of scale may lead to an unstable situation in the per-

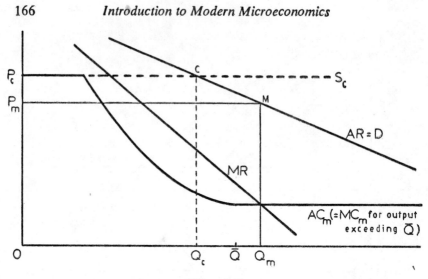

Figure 6.14

fectly competitive case. Any firm that can achieve a size sufficient to use the large-scale process economically can produce at a lower average cost than its competitors. It could afford to sell at a lower price than its competitors and so expand its sales, achieving an even more advantageous situation. Ultimately, the small firms will close down, leaving the large firm with a monopoly. If the demand is sufficiently large compared with the minimum economical level of the large-scale process, it may be possible for several firms to expand to this size, giving an oligopoly rather than a monopoly.

In an extreme case, it may be possible for a very large number of firms to achieve large-scale operation—perhaps 10,000 large firms replacing 1,000,000 small firms—so that the industry is still competitive. Sometimes the existing structure may be *too* stable. It may be so difficult, because of the social, political and legal structure, for small peasant holdings to be consolidated into larger holdings that even economies of scale compatible with competition may not be achieved.

6.9 Oligopoly

The term *oligopoly* means "few sellers," but it is not the actual number of sellers that is important, it is the existence of important interactions between them. Thus we define a market as oligopolistic by its behavioral structure, not by its number of firms.

A market has an oligopolistic structure if action on the part of any one firm may bring on a reaction by other firm or firms having significant effects on the original firm.

Two stores close together, selling similar goods to the same type of customer, will usually have an oligopolistic structure.[12] If one firm cuts its prices, the second firm may well react by also cutting its prices. Obviously the result of price-cutting by the first firm depends on whether the second firm also cuts prices, or leaves prices unchanged. An oligopolist cannot contemplate any action without attempting to guess how his rivals will react, and what the effects of their reaction will be on him.

The most extreme oligopolistic situation will arise when there are only two firms selling exactly the same product. In this case (*duopoly,* if we wish to stress the existence of only two firms), if either firm raises its price above that of its rival it will lose all its sales, while it will gain the rival's customers by lowering its price even by a small amount. The kind of "cutthroat competition" induced by two rival firms with such profound effects on each other conforms to the everyday usage of the term *competition,* but not to the economist's use of the term. The economist's term *perfect competition* refers to a situation in which the individual firms passively adjust their output to market prices over which they have no control and in which the doings of other firms are irrelevant, almost the antithesis of the everyday notion of competitive behavior. From the economist's point of view, the ferocious rivalry of oligopolists is *imperfect competition.*

A large proportion of all markets in the United States are oligopolistic. These vary from the rivalry of a small number of giant corporations each producing a wide variety of products which are closely related —a situation typified by the automobile industry—to the rivalry of gas stations situated on opposite corners of a key intersection. Each oligopolistic market has its own special features, depending on the relationship between the demands for the rival firms, the type of reactions possible, and the tightness of the interconnections between the firms at a variety of levels. It should be made clear that, unlike the cases of perfect competition and monopoly,

There is no general theory of oligopoly, only models of specific oligopolistic situations that provide signposts as to types of possible behavior.

---

[12] Stores were the traditional examples used in the monopolistic competition model. It seems more realistic to assume stores to be part of an *oligopoly* structure, implying that every store has *immediate* rivals who are directly affected by it, rather than to be in *monopolisic competition,* which implies that a store which gains customers does so by taking just a few customers from each of a very large number of other stores.

The Cournot Model. One of these signposts is provided by the analysis of a highly simplified duopoly situation. This analysis was originated by Cournot in 1838 and was the first attempt to discuss the topic. Since it remains one of the analyses that can be carried out without advanced mathematical methods, we shall discuss it here.

We assume that there are two firms selling an identical product. To simplify even further, we assume that the product has zero costs of production—traditionally, we consider the output of a mineral spring with two rival sellers of the spring water, each with his own spring, protected by the local authority from entry by any other sellers. To further simplify, we shall suppose the market demand curve for the spring water to be a straight line and insert some numbers to give the following demand conditions:

Price at which quantity demanded is just zero = $3 per cup.

Quantity demanded at zero price = 300 cups.

Demand equation: $Q = 300 - 100P$.

The behavior of the two sellers, Dupont and Dupres, is presumed to be that:

(1) Each assumes the other will be satisfied if he can continue to sell the *quantity* which he is currently selling, whatever may happen to the price. Therefore each seller will assume he can expect no reaction from the other if he leaves the rival's quantity intact.

(2) Thus Dupont will attempt to set a price which will maximize his profits while leaving Dupres selling his original quantity. Dupres will attempt to set a price which will maximize his profits while leaving Dupont's quantity unchanged.

(3) Since the product is identical, the price charged by *both* sellers must be the same.

The problem is to discover whether there is a *solution* to the market (that is, a price, and quantities sold by both sellers, consistent with market demand) that is *compatible* with the aims of the two rivals.

We approach the problem by supposing that Dupres is selling a quantity q_2, and consider Dupont's most profitable behavior. If Dupres is to continue to sell quantity q_2, the amount Dupont can sell is the total quantity sold less q_2, or $Q - q_2$. Since Dupont's average revenue curve is simply the market demand curve with q_2 subtracted from the market quantity at every price, it will be a straight line parallel to the market demand curve. This is shown in Figure 6.15, where D is the market demand curve and d_1 is Dupont's average revenue curve.

Since Dupont's average revenue curve is a straight line, his marginal revenue curve is also a straight line. We showed earlier in the chapter (Section 6.2) that such a marginal revenue curve would intersect the

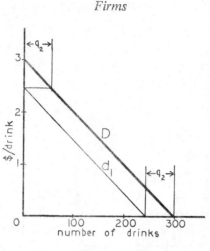

Figure 6.15

horizontal axis at a point halfway out to where the average revenue curve intersects the axis. The market demand intersects the axis at 300, so d_1 intersects the axis at $300 - q_2$, and Dupont's marginal revenue curve intersects the axis at $\frac{1}{2} (300 - q_2)$. Now marginal cost is zero, so the most profitable output will be where marginal revenue is zero, thus at output $\frac{1}{2} (300 - q_2)$.

Denoting Dupont's equilibrium output by q_1, we have:

$$q_1 = \frac{1}{2} (300 - q_2)$$

or,

$$q_1 + \frac{1}{2}q_2 = 150.$$

Thus for each quantity, q_2, which Dupres sells, there will be an optimum quantity, q_1, for Dupont. The relation between q_1 and q_2 is given by the above equation. If $q_2 = 0$, $q_1 = 150$, while if $q_2 = 300$ (the maximum that the market will absorb), $q_1 = 0$.

We can draw a diagram (Figure 6.16), in which q_2 is measured on one axis, q_1 on the other. Plotting the above equation (it is a straight line), we obtain a curve which shows Dupont's optimal position for each possible level of sales by Dupres. Such a curve is Dupont's *reaction curve,* since it shows how Dupont will react to a specific level of sales by Dupres.

A symmetric argument can be given to show how Dupres will react to each level of sales by Dupont. Since the conditions are similar for the two sellers, we will obtain the symmetric equation

$$\frac{1}{2}q_1 + q_2 = 150$$

which can be plotted as Dupres' reaction curve in the diagram.

The behavior of Dupont and Dupres will be compatible only if the *actual* sales by Dupres on which Dupont's optimal behavior is based are

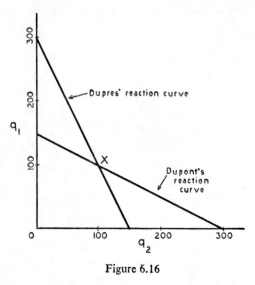

Figure 6.16

also the *optimal* sales by Dupres corresponding to Dupont's actual sales. Compatibility exists only at the intersection of the two reaction curves (X in the diagram). Algebraically, the compatible levels of q_1, q_2 are the solutions of the simultaneous equations of the reaction curves:

$$q_1 + \tfrac{1}{2} q_2 = 150$$
$$\tfrac{1}{2}q_1 + q_2 = 150.$$

The solution is easily found to be $q_1 = q_2 = 100$. Price is found by going to the market demand curve. We have $Q = q_1 + q_2 = 200$, $200 = 300 - 100P$, giving $P = \$1$ per cup.

Since costs are zero, each seller's profit is equal to his revenue which is 100 cups at \$1 per cup $= \$100$. The combined profit of the two sellers is \$200.

Collusion. We might now ask: Is there another market structure which will be more profitable to *both* sellers than the existing duopoly?

This amounts to asking whether *collusion* is profitable, that is, whether it would be advantageous for both sellers to reach some kind of agreement on price and output. The obvious form which collusion would take here would be for the two sellers to act as one, that is to act like a *monopoly,* and agree on division of the profits. A small group of sellers which has agreed on a common price/output policy and on the division of profits is said to form a *cartel,* or a *combine,* if the legal identity of the individual sellers is not preserved.

Consider the effect of Dupont and Dupres jointly acting as a monopoly. The average revenue curve for the monopoly is now the market demand curve for spring water, and the most profitable output is where marginal revenue is equal to marginal cost (zero). Using the property of the straight line demand, this will be at half the quantity which will be bought at zero price. Thus the monopoly equilibrium output will be 150, and the corresponding price satisfies the equation, $150 = 300 - 100P$, giving $1.50.

At price $1.50 and sales of 150, the monopoly will make a profit of $225, *greater than the combined profits of the two sellers under duopoly.* Thus it would be advantageous for both Dupont and Dupres to form a partnership and operate as a monopoly *(combination),* or to agree that each will sell 75 drinks at a price of $1.50 *(cartelization).*

We can compare the market outcome for our example under each of three situations: duopoly, monopoly (already discussed), and perfect competition. In the latter case, since average cost is zero, this will simply amount to allowing free access to the spring for all customers. The comparison is given in Table 6.1.

TABLE 6.1

Market for Spring Water

Market Structure	Equilibrium		Combined Profit of Sellers
	Price	Quantity	
Perfect Competition	0	300	0
Duopoly	1	200	200
Monopoly	1.50	150	225

There is a general presumption that, if there are constant returns to scale, the order of different market structures will be much as in Table 6.1, with perfect competition giving the lowest price, greatest output and least combined profits, monopoly the highest price, least output and greatest profit, and oligopoly in between. This ordering may be upset by a variety of circumstances. Economies of scale might be taken advantage of by the monopolist, but not by individual oligopolistic firms. In this case, the monopoly might give a higher output at a lower price (but with greater profit) than oligopoly.

Alternative Behavior Patterns. One simple analysis of an oligopoly situation has been given. There are other possible analyses, *even for the spring water example,* based on different presumptions concerning the way in which the rivals will react to each other's moves. We could assume, for example, that a rival would remain content if his *share of total sales,* or if his *profits,* remained constant, instead of the *quantity* he sells.[13] In many oligopolistic situations in the United States, *market shares* (proportion of total sales) are very important: firms are considered to behave aggressively if they attempt to increase their share of the market from, say 10 per cent to 15 per cent and strong reactions may occur. If the firm's share continues at 10 per cent, no reaction may take place.

In the absence of good estimates concerning the reactions of other firms, it might be expected that a *status quo* once established, will have a certain inbuilt stability.[14] By each firm continuing to behave as it has in the past, uncertain and possibly disastrous reactions and counter-reactions are avoided.

There will usually be, as demonstrated in our example, gains to be made from collusion. Collusion is illegal in the United States because of antitrust laws. In countries with no such laws, we would expect to find more monopolies and cartels. Broadly speaking, this is the case, but it is also true that the overall market is smaller in these countries.

6.10 The Firm's Demand for Inputs

As pointed out previously, the decision by a firm as to its optimal output is simultaneously and equivalently a decision by the firm as to its optimal input. Given the firm's technology, its input prices, and its output price (perfect competition) or the demand schedule for its product (monopoly), the firm makes a decision as to its optimal behavior which determines how much it will use of every input and how much it will produce. Except in the case of oligopoly (which we shall not discuss here), the information mentioned is sufficient to determine inputs and output.

In analyzing the effects of changes on the behavior of the firm, we have so far assumed costs to remain unchanged while price or demand conditions changed. We shall now turn to discuss, for perfect competition and monopoly, the effect of a change in *input* prices on the firm's output and its use of inputs.

We continue to assume that the firm buys inputs on a competitive market, so that the individual firm does not influence input prices. Consider the effect of a rise in the wage rate, with the other input price (we

---

[13] We obtain a different model of oligopoly in each case, with its own solution. Not all models lead to determinate solutions, especially if the firm is *wrong* in its assessment of the motive of its rival.

[14] A well-known analysis that attempts to establish this stability is that of the "kinked demand curve." Firms may avoid *price* competition for fear of generating strong reactions and concentrate on *nonprice* competition, such as advertising, attractive packaging, and so on.

shall confine ourselves to production with two inputs, capital and labor), and demand conditions for output unchanged.

Suppose, first of all, that the firm in question is perfectly competitive and subject to a limitation on capital such that the firm is operating on the rising part of its average cost curve. If the wage rises, the average cost of producing every output will rise and the cost curve will "shift" upwards: we suppose it does not shift enough to move the equilibrium point off the rising part of the curve.

On this rising part of the curve, we have already seen in Chapter 5 that marginal cost, the wage, and the marginal product of labor are related by

$$MC = \frac{w}{MPL}.$$

Since we have perfect competition, $P = MC$, we can write the relationship as

$$w = P \times MPL$$

(the product $P \times MPL$ is sometimes called the *value of the marginal product of labor:* it is the *marginal revenue product,* a term we shall meet below, for the particular case in which marginal revenue is equal to price).

Since P is constant and w rises, the equation must be balanced by an increase in *MPL*. From productivity theory (Chapter 4), we know that the marginal product of labor usually decreases with more labor (and increases with less). Thus

A rise in the wage rate will cause a decrease in the firm's use of labor.

The decrease in the firm's use of labor, with capital constant at its upper limit, must decrease output. But this is what we expect when the wage rises under these conditions, since the cost curve is higher and the intersection with the price line is further to the left, as shown in Figure 6.17. Output falls from Q to Q'. A fall in the wage rate will, of course, cause a rise in both output and the quantity of labor used.

Demand Curve for an Input. As the wage changes, the relationship $w = P \times MPL$ will be maintained. With P constant, the information for determining the amount of labor used will be contained in the relationship between the quantity of labor and its marginal product.

Now the curve relating the marginal product of labor to the quantity of labor is the *marginal productivity curve* of labor. This is, of course, a curve sloping downward to the right, as in Figure 6.18. The curve relating the value of the marginal product of labor ($P \times MPL$) to output is obtained from this simply by changing the vertical axis to read in appropriate units, depending on the price. This has been done in the figure for two prices.

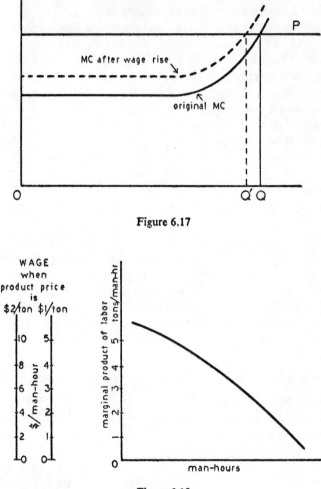

Figure 6.17

Figure 6.18

Once we have the appropriate marginal revenue product curve, we can find out the use of labor by reading from the curve at the point corresponding to the wage (since $w = P \times MPL$). Thus we have established the demand curve for labor:

For a firm with fixed capital and labor as the only variable input, the firm's demand curve for labor is the marginal revenue product curve for labor, which is directly derived from the marginal productivity curve for labor.[15]

----

[15] The demand curve for any other input can be derived in the same way, provided it is the only variable input.

Monopoly. If the firm is a *monopolist* (in the output market), the analysis is changed somewhat. At the equilibrium output, the firm will operate so as to equate marginal cost and marginal revenue. If it is operating on the upward sloping part of the cost curve, the relationship, $MC = w/MPL$ will hold, so that we will have

$$w = MR \times MPL$$

($MR \times MPL$ is the *marginal revenue product* of labor).

It would be simple if we could assume that marginal revenue remained constant, for then the remaining analysis would be identical with that for perfect competition, substituting marginal revenue for price. But this will only be true in the very special case in which the monopolist has a horizontal marginal revenue curve. As pointed out earlier, this is quite possible, but we normally assume a downward-sloping marginal revenue curve.

For the usual case, an increase in the wage will shift the marginal cost curve upward, as in Figure 6.19. The new marginal cost curve will

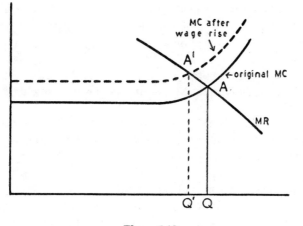

Figure 6.19

intersect the marginal revenue curve (unchanged) at A' instead of A, giving a new equilibrium at a lower output (hence less labor) than the old, and at a higher marginal revenue.

Thus an increase in the wage will result in a decline in the use of labor, just as in the perfect competition case. The demand curve for labor will slope downward, again as in the perfect competition case, but it cannot be derived so simply from the marginal productivity curve for labor since marginal revenue will change as the quantity of labor changes.

Note that, *although a monopoly has no supply curve for output, it has demand curves for inputs.* This is because we assumed it to be competitive in the input markets. The case in which a monopolist is imperfectly competitive in the input market, as well as the output market, is discussed in Section 7.10.

6.11 The Giant Corporation

One of the most spectacular developments over the last half-century in the United States (and to a lesser extent in most Western economies) has been the growth and emergence of the giant multipurpose corporation. Such corporations are not simply direct expansions of simple firms, grown large to take advantage of indivisibilities, but typically produce a very large number of different products and interact with the rest of the economy on many fronts.

Because of their size, the giants are imperfectly competitive in all fields—not only do they sell their products under imperfectly competitive conditions, they buy their primary inputs and intermediate goods, and even raise their finances, under the same conditions. They become institutions in the economy, and their names are household words. No one buys from them, sells to them, or negotiates with them, without being aware of their size and economic power. They are large enough to use direct political pressure to assist in attaining economic goals.[16]

In effect, these corporations are *subeconomies* rather than firms. A corporation such as General Motors is a larger economic unit than some small countries.

As subeconomies, they possess a large and complex internal structure and face many of the same problems as the economy itself—how to allocate resources internally, whether to produce locally or import ("make or buy"), how to send appropriate signals from the central "government" to the individual decision makers in charge of the multitudinous component units. Indeed, modern general equilibrium theory and welfare economics can be applied directly to their analysis, and certain aspects of these (such as decentralized control with shadow prices, discussed in Chapter 9) may come to be used in the internal control of large corporations before they are so used in the economy as a whole.

For our present purposes, we are interested primarily in the extent to which the behavior of such corporations, treated as firms, may differ from what would be predicted from the economist's usual model of the

---

[16] The political power of large corporations has generated much criticism of the industrial structure of the United States in terms of political criteria. This is quite independent of any criticisms of this structure in terms of economic efficiency, as in Chapter 10. See Galbraith, J. K., *The New Industrial State,* Houghton Mifflin, 1968.

firm. However complex the firm, the economist could, in principle, find its profit maximizing set of inputs and outputs. The basic question is, are those the outputs and inputs that the firm would itself choose.

Given complete knowledge and sufficient computer time, the economist's prediction and the corporation's own choice will coincide if the corporation sets out to maximize profits,[17] but will not necessarily do so if the corporation has another aim.

The growth of the modern corporation has been associated with a separation of ownership from control. The "owners" are stockholders who may buy stock with the primary object of resale and may know or care little of what the corporation is really doing, while the managers are professional corporation executives. It has been widely argued in recent years that the managers may have goals other than simply maximizing the profits of the corporation, which they consider "wasted" when paid out to stockholders.

There is no generally accepted idea of what management's other goals may be. For that matter, there is no reason for supposing that goals are necessarily the same from one management group to another. Some executives have technical backgrounds and may be unduly interested in technically advanced products or processes, not necessarily economical,[18] others may be interested in the corporation's "social image" and may use finances for socially desirable but unprofitable purposes.

Most economists who emphasise motives other than profit would agree that there is some level of profit that must be sustained to keep the stockholders "happy" and to ensure that the corporation can always borrow on favorable terms. The corporation is sometimes said to be *satisficing,* that is, ensuring satisfactory but not necessarily maximum profits.

The simplest model of the firm maximizing something other than profit is that of *sales* maximization, subject to some minimum profit level. If the firm is a simple monopoly, it will increase its sales by lowering price and expanding output beyond the profit maximizing point. Each lowering of price will expand sales and lower profit further, the optimum point being where the minimum acceptable profit is being earned. The suggested management motive is that executives' professional prestige is associated with the level of their corporation's sales, rather than the level of its profits. Sales maximization, it will be noted, brings the firm closer to

---

[17] In a less static analysis than we have given here, the definition of profit itself can be a problem. We assume the firm and the economist are maximizing the same profit.
[18] For example, processes may be used which have a higher capital to labor ratio than would give least cost at existing input prices.

the competitive output and price than profit maximization will generally do.[19]

FURTHER READING

The theory of the firm is standard material and available in all microeconomics and price theory texts, not necessarily in the form given here. To continue on from what is given here, the author recommends Cohen, K. J. and Cyert, R. M., *Theory of the Firm,* Prentice-Hall 1965, which covers microeconomic theory generally (including demand theory, general equilibrium and welfare economics) but has special emphasis on the firm. Discussion is given of recent approaches to the behavioral theory of the firm (touched on in Section 6.11 of this book). Calculus is used, but much can be followed without its use. Treatment of costs and production is essentially traditional.

EXERCISES

(1) A competitive industry consists of 1,000 identical firms, each of which has the following marginal costs:

Output (tons)	Marginal cost ($/ton)
to 15	constant at 1.00
16	1.02
17	1.06
18	1.12
19	1.20
20	1.30
21	1.42
22	1.56
23	1.72
24	1.90
25	2.10
26	maximum possible output

Calculate (a) the short-run supply schedule of the industry

(b) the long-run supply schedule for the industry assuming input prices constant at the short-run levels and no limitations for the industry as a whole.

(2) The demand curve for the product of a monopolist is a straight line such that the quantity just falls to zero at a price of $10 per unit and that the maximum quantity (at zero price) is 10,000 units.

The monopolist has no resource limitation and can produce any output at a constant average cost of $2 per unit.

---

[19] If the minimum satisfactory profit is equal to or greater than the maximum profit obtainable, the firm will act as profit maximizer. If its operations become more profitable (lower costs for example), its sales maximization may become apparent.

Find (drawing the graphs is suggested) the profit maximizing output, the price at which it will be sold, and the monopoly profit.

(3) The demand curve facing the monopolist in (2) shifts so that the quantity sold at zero price becomes 12,500 units. The price at which quantity becomes zero, and the cost conditions, remain unchanged.

Find the new output, price and profit. Compare these with the answers in (2).

Is demand more or less elastic at the new equilibrium point than it was at the old equilibrium point?

(4) Assume the demand conditions of (2). Due to indivisibilities, the monopolist can produce at an average cost of $1 per unit, which is constant over the range of his relevant outputs. The average costs of small firms are much higher than this, but constant over their relevant ranges and the same for all.

What is the maximum level of small-firm costs for which the competitive output will be greater than the monopoly output?

(5) A monopolist faces a straight-line demand curve which passes through the point $1/ton on the price-cost axis, and through the point 800 tons on the quantity axis.

The firm has an input limitation which comes into effect at 300 tons, and its marginal costs are as follows:

Constant at 10¢/ton up to and including 300 tons; *increasing by* 0.1¢/ton for each ton beyond 300.

(a) Find the profit maximizing output.

(b) If the firm's input limitation is removed (but input prices are unchanged), to what level of output will it expand?

(6) A perfectly competitive firm has an input limitation on capital that becomes effective at 10 tons output. At this output level, 2 man-hours of labor are used.

Beyond 10 tons, labor is the only variable input. Its marginal product is as follows:

Man-hours	Marginal product of labor (tons/man-hour)
2	4
3	3
4	2
5	1

No more than 6 man-hours can be utilized with the available capital.

(a) Draw up the firm's demand schedule for labor when the produce price is $1/ton.

(b) Draw up the firm's short-run supply curve for its product when the wage is $2/man-hour.

In Chapter 7 we consider human, rather than mechanical, aspects of economic behavior.

CONTENTS

7.1 Who Are the Consumers?   181
7.2 Goods and Consumers   183
7.3 Preference and Choice   185
7.4 Choice with a Budget Constraint   191
7.5 Utility   196
7.6 Income Changes   198
7.7 Substitution   203
7.8 Demand Theory   206
7.9 The Labor-Leisure Choice   210
7.10 Bargaining and Exchange   214
7.11 New and Differentiated Goods   218

CHAPTER 7

CONSUMERS

7.1 Who Are the Consumers?

Fundamentally, consumers are all the individuals of the economy in their role as *human beings*.

Many individuals play several roles. Consider, for example, the manager or entrepreneur responsible for the decisions of a firm. When he is making decisions for the firm, these are not *personal* decisions; in principle, another manager occupying the same position would reach an identical decision. Indeed, for the model of the firm that appears in the economist's simple models of the economy, a computer, fed with information concerning the technology and all relevant price and market data, could easily be programmed to give the profit maximizing output and the amounts of all necessary inputs. In all economic roles except that of being a consumer, decisions are made in accordance with *objective* criteria and could, in principle, be computerized. In practice, people are needed primarily to make judgments, which are decisions based on incomplete information. The incompleteness of information, not the ultimate decision making process, requires people.

Eccentricity and Consistency. As consumers, and therefore as human beings, people are *themselves*. This is the only role in the basic economist's model of society, in which they indulge their personal eccentricities. We assume that the manager of a firm will not insist on producing pink automobiles just because he likes pink, but only if it is profitable to do so.

When he receives his income, as salary or profits, his decisions on what to do with it are in his role as consumer, and he may then choose to live in a pink house and drive a pink car.

We shall see later that, although consumers may be as eccentric as they please, we assume they are eccentric in a *consistent* way. Obviously if consumers behaved capriciously, so that their behavior in one situation was no guide at all to their behavior in another, we would have no structure of consumer behavior with which to work.[1] There is room for caprice, but as random deviation from an underlying pattern.

Supply of Labor. Although the term "consumer" immediately conjures up the vision of a person *buying goods,* it should be made clear from the beginning that a person is equally acting in his consumer role when he is *selling his own services* (primarily labor). The decision, whether to work in some job for 3 hours at $2 per hour is a consumer decision, just as much as the decision whether to buy a pound of coffee at 90¢ per pound. Thus the theory of consumer behavior leads, among other things, to theory of both the *demand for goods* and the *supply of labor.*

Central Role of Consumers. Economists proceed on the fundamental article of faith that the economy is a structure which exists for the benefit of the individuals in it as human beings, and therefore for consumers. Welfare economics, which we shall discuss in a later chapter, is built on the basic assumption that only the views of individuals *as consumers* are to count in attempting to assess how well a given economy is operating. Firms and other decision makers in the economy, as we pointed out in Chapter 6, are treated as faceless and nonhuman. Whether a given firm thrives or goes bankrupt is considered to have no welfare implications, but whether a given individual as a consumer is "better off" or "worse off" is of profound importance.

Consumers are thus central to the economy. They decide how much labor (and, in a "private enterprise" economy such as the United States, how much of other basic inputs) is to be supplied, and how much of all the final outputs of the system they are willing to buy. Their own personal views as to whether they prefer one situation to another are the ultimate assessments from which any attempt to rank one state of the economy as better or worse than another must commence.

Households. We shall consider the consumer to behave as an individual in the analysis which follows. This is somewhat of a simplification, since con-

---

[1]Although we can do many things if *aggregate* consumer behavior can be described in terms of a stable probability distribution.

sumers often act as small groups rather than individuals. Such groups are referred to as *households,* and the most typical is the ordinary family unit. The family must reach joint decisions on many matters, and, while young children's views may not be directly expressed, the household will be taking account of their preferences (or their idea of the children's preferences) in reaching decisions. There are other economic units (churches and clubs, for example) which have some of the characteristics of households. To complicate matters further, a consumer may make some decisions completely as an individual, others as a member of a household. Nevertheless, as we have already done so many times, we mention these complications, then assume them away by supposing the household to behave exactly like an individual.

The individual, even in the context of his own home, is never quite consumer only. He makes some things for himself (if only meals), for which he buys inputs, and thus acts like a firm. He may own a home, again leading to decisions similar to those of the firm. Basically, however, we shall think of him in his prime consumer role, deciding how to sell his personal services and what goods to buy.

7.2 Goods and Consumers

"Commodity" is the economic term frequently used to cover both goods (physical commodities) and services (like medical treatment or transportation). Since it is important only in certain contexts whether we are concerned with a tangible physical good or with a service, we shall use the term "good" in the broad sense, as we have done in previous chapters. It is rather more important in consumer theory to stress the inclusion of services than in the case of the theory of the firm.

Characteristics of Goods. For many years, it has been the tradition in economics to consider the confrontation between a consumer and possible choices among goods as a direct one. Goods are goods, and a consumer exercises his choice among them. But it has become increasingly difficult to describe the consumer choice situation in an advanced consumption economy such as that of the United States without going rather more deeply into what it is about goods that makes the consumer interested in them.

When a consumer is offered a choice between two collections or bundles of goods, his choice is partly determined by his own personality (his preferences) and partly by the properties of the goods themselves. To be more specific, if a consumer can have one of two automobiles, his choice will be determined by (a) the particular properties of the two automobiles in question; (b) his personal view of the desirability to him of the various properties possessed by the automobiles.

Thus a consumer offered a choice between a red Volkswagen and a black Cadillac may choose the Cadillac because it is larger and more powerful, but if offered a choice between a red Volkswagen and a purple Cadillac, he may choose the Volkswagen because he cannot stand the sight of so much purple. (We assume, in this choice, that the consumer cannot sell or repaint the automobile.)

Goods are of interest to the consumer because of the properties or *characteristics* they possess.[2] It is the characteristics, rather than the goods as such, that impinge on the consumer. Thus goods with closely similar characteristics will be related to the consumer in a similar way because they will fulfill similar functions. Given a variety of goods with different characteristics, it may be possible to achieve some particular collection of characteristics in a variety of different ways, so that the consumer may need to choose *efficient* ways of achieving his goals, much as a firm must choose efficient ways of producing.

Identification of a Good. Traditional consumer analysis has always given rise to problems in determining whether two things are to be regarded as the same good or not. To have a consistent theory of consumer behavior, we want to define goods so that the consumer behaves the same with respect to two individual items if they are the same good. We saw, in the example given above, that "automobiles" is too broad a category to be a single good, since a consumer may react quite differently to a Cadillac than to a Volkswagen. But we also saw that even "Cadillac" is too broad a category since a consumer may react differently to a black Cadillac and to a purple Cadillac.

But what happens to the theory of the firm if every color of Cadillac is to be a different good? Are we to consider as a separate firm each segment of Cadillac (itself a division of General Motors) which produces a different colored car?

By noting that certain groups of goods share a great many characteristics, and differ slightly in others, we can treat them together in a rational way that makes for sensible market analysis, while accounting for individual differences in consumer views concerning goods within the group.

Analogy of Consumption and Production. This kind of analysis gives consumption theory many analogies to production theory. Instead of the

---

[2] Further discussion of this idea is given in Section 7.11.

goods being the final object of choice, they are vehicles for obtaining characteristics, and thus are analogous to inputs in a process. The analogy can be extended when we note that, in order to obtain the characteristics, the consumer may have to combine the good with other inputs, perhaps with his own time. A television set may possess some characteristics even when it is not used (at certain stages of social and economic development, its presence in the house may give status), but its primary characteristics require the consumer's time. Thus a very hard-working person may have no interest in a television set simply because he cannot devote time to watching it.

The existence of groups of goods with closely similar characteristics but not identical (often called *differentiated goods*) tends to occur in advanced consumption economics. In simpler societies (including the United States in earlier periods) the variety of goods tends to be smaller, and the goods to be more different in their characteristics. At the extreme, we may have one type of shelter, one type of food, one type of clothing. Whereas there are some characteristics common to pairs of these (shelter and clothing both provide warmth), we can treat them as quite different goods without any problem being posed.

In the simplest analysis of the consumer's behavior, we shall leave the characteristics approach aside and consider the direct relationship of the consumer to goods which each fulfill quite different functions, like food, clothing and shelter. Alternatively, we can consider that, for example, food possesses a characteristic "foodness" which is not possessed, to any degree, by clothing or shelter. The analysis we obtain is then similar to that of the traditional approach.

7.3 *Preference and Choice*

We assume as fundamental that every consumer possesses well defined *preferences* in the sense that, offered a choice between two collections of goods (or characteristics), he either

(1) prefers one collection to the other or

(2) neither prefers the first collection to the second, nor the second to the first.

That is, we rule out the possibility that the consumer has *no* view concerning the two collections. The reader should be careful to distinguish between (2) above, in which the consumer has no preference for one collection over the other (we say he is *indifferent* between them), to a situation in which the consumer *does not know or care* whether he prefers one to the other. In other words, a consumer may be indifferent *between* two collections; he is not indifferent *to* a collection.

We assume, further, that the consumer's preferences are *stable* or *consistent* over some significant time period, so that if he prefers collection A to collection B at one moment, he does not prefer B to A the next. This does not rule out all changes in preferences, only that such changes (usually called a *change in tastes*) should occur only from time to time and, in principle, as a result of a change in some identifiable circumstance of the consumer such as his age or his social context.[3]

To complete the idea of consistent preference, we also suppose that the consumer's preferences are *transitive,* an idea that is very simple and acceptable in spite of the technicality of the name. Preferences are transitive if, among three collections, A, B and C:

Whenever A is preferred to B, which is in turn preferred to C, A is preferred to C.

Put in this straightforward manner, it would seem very unlikely that anyone's preferences should not be transitive. The possibility of intransitive preference is increased, however, if the comparison is more circuitous and particularly if the choices between the different pairs take place in quite different circumstances. From the economist's point of view it is really only important that the consumer have transitive preferences among collections which appear in the same or related contexts.

Revealed Preference. Finally we make the basic presumption without which a consumer's preferences would remain unknown (except, perhaps, to his analyst) and also largely irrelevant:

Action indicates preference. That is, given a choice, a consumer will actually take the collection he prefers.

A consumer's actions are thus considered to reveal his preferences. Analysis based on the use of actions to discover the consumer's preferences is referred to as the method of *revealed preference.*[4]

Preference and Welfare. Later, when we discuss welfare problems, we shall also assume that:

---

[3] It used to be common for economists to take a cowardly shelter behind the phrase "change in tastes" to explain the failure of predictions. Most economists would now consider that, *in principle,* such changes must have some cause which can be identified, not necessarily by economists themselves.

[4] For a direct derivation of the main content of demand theory from revealed preference, see Samuelson, P. A.: "Consumption theorems in terms of 'overcompensation' rather than indifference comparisons," *Economica,* February, 1953.

Preference indicates welfare. That is, if a consumer prefers collection A to collection B, we will presume him to be "better off" (his welfare is increased) if he is given collection A instead of collection B.

This, combined with the assumption that action indicates preference, implies that the choice actually made by a consumer in any given situation gives him the greatest welfare he can attain in the situation.

More Preferred to Less. Let us now turn to consider preferences among collections of goods in a more concrete fashion. We shall, as usual, simplify the problem of two goods, food and clothing. There are no other goods in the system, or, if there are, the quantities of these are fixed. We can draw a diagram in which quantities of food are measured on one axis, quantities of clothing on the other, as in Figure 7.1. Any point on

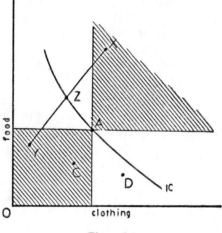

Figure 7.1

the diagram, like the point *A*, represents a specific quantity of food and a specific quantity of clothing. It represents a *collection* or *bundle* of goods.

We now assume:

Goods are things the consumer prefers more of. That is, he always prefers a collection having more of both goods, or more of one good and no less of another.[5]

---

[5] We have implicitly assumed what is technically referred to as *nonsatiation*, that there is no quantity of any good that will lead the consumer to have no interest in an additional amount.

This is an assumption about the class of goods with which we are primarily concerned. There are things, like garbage, that all consumers prefer to have less of,[6] and other things, like foods with unusual tastes or smells, that some consumers prefer more of, others less. We confine ourselves at the moment to cases in which more of the good is preferred.

Consider the collection *A* in Figure 7.1. Vertical and horizontal lines have been drawn through *A*, and the area around *A* is divided into four quadrants, two of which are shaded.

In the northeast quadrant relative to *A*, any point like *X* represents a collection containing more of at least one good and no less of any other than collection *A*. *Thus every collection in the northeast quadrant is preferred to* A.

The southwest quadrant (containing *C*) includes collections all containing less of one good and no more of any other than the collection *A*. *Thus* A *is preferred to every collection in the southwest quadrant.*

What of the collections in the northwest and southeast quadrants (unshaded)? Since the consumer has well defined preferences, he himself knows whether he prefers, say *D* to *A*, or *A* to *D* or is indifferent between them. But we as outsiders cannot reach any simple conclusions about the preference order, as we could for the shaded quadrants.

Indifference Curves. Consider the line *XZY* drawn in the diagram. Clearly *X* is preferred to *A*, and *A* is preferred to *Y*. Let us move down the line from *X* to *Y*, considering the preference relationship between each point on the line and *A*. Somewhere we have two points close together such that one point is preferred to *A*, while *A* is preferred to the other.[7] If we assume some idea of *continuity* of preferences, there will be some point such that the consumer is indifferent between this and *A*. If *Z* is such a point we usually say, rather sloppily, that *Z* and *A* are indifferent, or *Z* is indifferent to *A* (it is the consumer that is indifferent, not the point, and he is really indifferent between the points, not to either of them).

Z can be the only point on *XY* indifferent to *A*. Any point between *Z* and *X* must be preferred to *Z*, and transitivity prevents our having a point which is preferred to *Z* but indifferent to *A*, while *Z* is indifferent to *A*. Similarly *Z* must be preferred to any point between *Z* and *Y*, with the same consequences.

It is clear that, since all points in the northeast quadrant are preferred to *A*, and *A* is preferred to all points in the southwest quadrant, all points between which and *A* the consumer is indifferent must lie in the

---

[6] Sometimes called "bads" instead of "goods."

[7] There are more subtleties involved in the rigorous discussion of this point.

northwest and southeast quadrants. We can join all the points indifferent to A, the resulting curve being known as an *indifference curve*. One property follows immediately from above:

An indifference curve slopes downward to the right.

We can easily deduce the next property. Figure 7.2 shows two hypo-

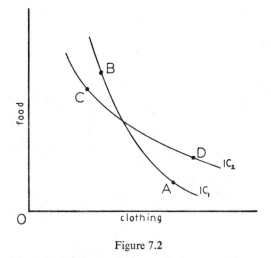

Figure 7.2

thetical indifference curves IC_1, IC_2 which cross each other. Consider the points A, B on IC_1 and C, D on IC_2. Since A, B are on the same indifference curve, and since B is to the northeast of C (on IC_2), A is preferred to C. But C is indifferent to D which is to the northeast of A, and thus C is preferred to A. Thus indifference curves which intersect cannot be associated with consistent preferences, which we have assumed. Thus:

Indifference curves do not cross or intersect each other.

Note that the indifference curves have been drawn convex to the origin, with the same general shape as an isoquant in production theory. The reason for assuming this shape will be brought out in the next section.

Since indifference curves do not cross or intersect each other, we can unambiguously describe one indifference curve as being "further from the origin" or "closer to the origin" than another, in the sense that IC_2 is further from the origin than IC_1 in Figure 7.3.

Comparing IC_1 with IC_2, we see that, for any point like A on IC_1, we can find a point like B on IC_2 such that B represents more of both goods than A and is therefore preferred to A. Since all points on IC_2 are

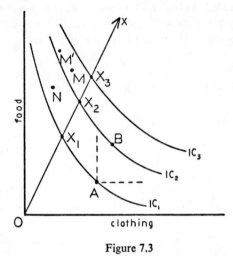

Figure 7.3

indifferent to B, and all points on IC_1 are indifferent to A, it follows that *any point* on IC_2 is preferred to *any point* on IC_1. We say that the further out indifference curve, IC_2, is a *higher indifference curve* than IC_1, meaning that any point on IC_2 is preferred to any point on IC_1.

Indifference Maps. If we take any ray through the origin, like OX in the diagram, any point further out on the ray (like X_2) is preferred to any point closer in (like X_1). Thus the points along OX are in order of increasing preference as we move out. We can draw the indifference curve through every point on OX, obtaining a set of indifference curves called an *indifference map* or a *preference map*: IC_1, IC_2, IC_3 are three of these curves. It follows then that:

> *The consumer's preferences are completely described by his indifference map.*

Once we have the indifference map, we can give the consumer's relative preferences between any two collections by simply noting which lies on the higher indifference curve. A single point can be ranked with respect to all other points from a *single* indifference curve through that point. Suppose B is the point in question. Then M is preferred to B, since it lies further out than any point on the indifference curve through B, and B is preferred to N. But, although we can see that both M and M' are preferred to B, we cannot tell whether M is preferred to M' or not without having the indifference curve through either M or M'.

Indifference maps are simply an analytical device. We do not possess information of this kind about any consumers (and would find it very difficult to draw even our own!). We can, however, deduce something about a person's indifference map from his behavior, and then use this to predict his behavior in a different situation.

7.4 Choice with a Budget Constraint

So far we have discussed the consumer's preferences and choices in a generalized setting. Now we shall turn to discuss choice in the setting in which it is most often exercised, at least as far as economic choice is concerned. This is choice subject to a *budget constraint,* in which the consumer can buy goods at fixed prices subject to his not spending more than some initial money sum (his budget), or not spending more than his receipts from selling some initial holdings of goods.

Let us suppose there are only two goods in the consumer's universe, "food" and "clothing." To give a specific numerical example, we shall suppose that the price of food is $0.50 per pound, the price of clothing $2 per "item," and the consumer's budget is $10.

The Budget Line. The consumer's situation is illustrated in Figure 7.4. Quantities of food are measured on the vertical axis, quantities of cloth-

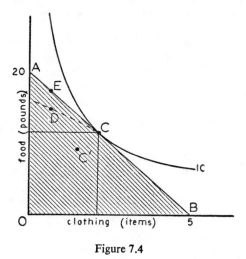

Figure 7.4

ing on the horizontal axis. By spending all his budget on food, the consumer can buy 20 lbs; by spending it all on clothing, he can buy 5 items. These collections are represented by *A, B,* respectively. If the consumer were to buy only two items of clothing, he would have $6 left to spend on food, with which he could buy 12 lbs. Thus he could just buy the collection C (12 lbs food, 2 items clothing) with his budget. It is easy to see that all the collections which the consumer can buy are represented by points on the straight line AB.

This line is the consumer's *budget line* or *budget constraint*. It is analogous to an isocost line, as discussed in Chapter 5, and is, in fact, the *$10 isocost line* for the given prices of food and clothing.

Every point in and on the triangle OAB represents a collection that the consumer is able to buy at the given prices and budget. We can call this shaded area the consumer's *attainable set*: all collections outside it are unattainable. We now have a clear choice situation:

The consumer can choose any collection of goods in the attainable set.

We can immediately rule out many of these collections. For every collection *inside* the area $OAB,$ like C', there is some collection on AB, like C, which has more of at least one good. From the preceding discussion of preferences, we know that the consumer will prefer C to C' and therefore choose C rather than C'. The same arguments can be applied to all collections inside the triangle, so we conclude:

The consumer will choose a collection represented by a point actually on the budget line.

If we take the point C on the budget line every other point on the budget line lies northwest or southeast of it. From the last section, we know we cannot state whether such a point is preferred to C or not, without specific knowledge of the preferences of this particular consumer.

Convexity of Indifference Curves. We already know the consumer's indifference curve through C slopes in a general northwest-southeast direction. Could this indifference curve coincide (by chance) with the budget line AB? If the indifference curve does not coincide with AB, can we tell what relationship will exist between the two curves?

The answer to the first question is that it is *possible,* but if the indifference curve were to coincide with AB, the consumer would be indifferent between any pair of points on the budget line. Since there would be no point on AB which he preferred to all others, he would have no reason for choosing one collection rather than any other. Thus his behavior would be uncertain and possibly random.

Since choice subject to a budget constraint is the normal situation for a consumer, it seems consistent with what we observe to consider that, generally speaking, consumer choices have *in fact* the following properties:

(a) there is one collection that is definitely chosen,

(b) chosen collections typically include some of each good and do not characteristically consist of one of the goods only.[8]

We can deduce the general shape of indifference curves from these two observations. Clear-cut choice implies that there is, *in fact,* one point on the budget line which is preferred to all others. Thus the indifference curve does not coincide with the budget line.

From (b) we can consider the typical collection to consist of a point, like C, with something of both goods (as contrasted with A, B which consist of one good only). Now suppose the indifference curve through C lay inside the attainable set at some stage, like the dotted line CD in Figure 7.4. Then there would be some point on the indifference curve like D such that D is inside the triangle and C, D are indifferent. But there must then be a point E on the budget line which has more of both goods than D, and so is preferred to D. Then we would have E preferred to D and D indifferent to C, so that E must be preferred to C. But C was actually chosen, so that C must be preferred to E, instead of E to C.

Thus we can conclude that, if consumers are observed to consume goods in combination rather than just one good, typical indifference curves through a point on the budget line must be such that all other points on the indifference curve lie to the right of the budget line. If this is to be true for all budget lines, the typical indifference curve (if smoothly curved) must have the shape of IC in the diagram, convex to the origin and touching the budget line at only one point. An indifference curve made up of short straight segments (like the isoquants for a small number of processes that were depicted in Chapter 4) is possible, but we shall assume the traditional smoothly curved kind. In any case:

Indifference curves are convex towards the origin, and every segment slopes downward to the right.

Choice with Budget Constraint. Now that we have given a firm foundation for the previously assumed curvature of indifference curves, we can consider the budget problem in terms of an indifference map. Figure 7.5 shows the budget line drawn over a consumer's indifference map (possible since the axes on both diagrams measure quantities of the two goods). Since the indifference curves are convex to the origin, the budget line

---

[8] The key word here is "typically." Choice of just one of the goods is not ruled out under special circumstances, but there must be some prices at which both goods are consumed.

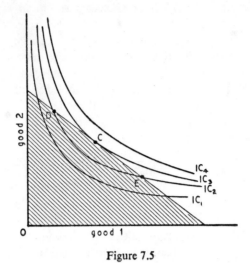

Figure 7.5

will cut or meet various indifference curves (IC_1, IC_2, IC_3 in the diagram), while other indifference curves will lie entirely beyond the budget line.

Now the point most preferred by the consumer, from among those that he can attain with his budget, will be that which is on the highest indifference curve. It is obvious from the diagram that any indifference curve which cuts the budget line and has some portion inside the triangle, cannot be the highest attainable. For IC_2, it is clear that any point on the part DE of the budget line must lie on a higher indifference curve than IC_2.

The highest attainable indifference curve is thus the one that just touches the budget line. In the diagram, it is IC_3, touching the budget line at C.

At C, the slope of the budget line must be equal to the slope of the indifference curve. For other points on the budget line, like D, the slope of the indifference curve is obviously not the same as that of the budget line.

Marginal Rate of Substitution. We met a situation which is *analytically* similar to this in our discussion of cost theory in Chapter 5. There, it was an isocost line for inputs that was tangent to the isoquant at the optimum. Here it is a budget line tangent to an indifference curve. Just as, in production theory, we referred to the ratio between the change in one input and the consequent change in the other just necessary to maintain the same level of output, as the marginal rate of substitution, we make an equivalent definition here:

The marginal rate of substitution at a point is the ratio of the change in the quantity of one good to the consequent change in the other necessary to remain on the same indifference curve. It is the slope of the indifference curve at the point.

In any context in which both indifference curves and isoquants appear together, we distinguish the marginal rates of substitution as the

marginal rate of substitution *in production* (along an isoquant) or

marginal rate of substitution *in consumption* (along an indifference curve).

The condition that the consumer's chosen point will be where the budget line is tangent to an indifference curve can be expressed in terms analogous to those in production theory:

The consumer will choose that point on his budget constraint at which the marginal rate of substitution of food for clothing is equal to the price ratio of clothing to food. At this point the budget line will be tangent to an indifference curve.

This is the way in which the consumer's chosen point is usually described in textbooks. It is often *analytically* convenient to use this formulation, but it adds no *content* to our knowledge of consumer behavior. The following statements are to be regarded as *exactly equivalent* in terms of information about the consumer:

(1) The consumer chooses point C on his budget line.

(2) The consumer prefers point C to all other points on his budget line.

(3) Of all points on the budget line, C lies on the consumer's highest indifference curve.

(4) At point C, one of the consumer's indifference curves is tangent to the budget line.

(5) At point C, the price ratio is equal to the marginal rate of substitution.

(We will add one more alternative in the next section.)

Only if we could probe the consumer's mind could we make any distinctions between these statements.

The collection actually chosen by the consumer is often described as his *equilibrium point*. In spite of its wide use, this is a quite inappropriate term. Equilibrium has no meaning except as compared with *disequilibrium*. But if a consumer always chooses his most preferred point from those available, every action he takes is an equilibrium in this sense. It makes sense to talk of market equilibrium, since we can contemplate disequilibrium situations, but not to talk of the equilibrium of the consumer.

7.5 *Utility*

The analytical similarity between an indifference map for a consumer and an isoquant map for a producer has already been pointed out. Since isoquants represent efficient points, they cannot cross and are convex to the origin. Thus efficient production is analogous to consistent choice.

Suppose we approach the analogy from the other direction. Can we regard goods as inputs into some process analogous to production? This is precisely how the theory of the consumer used to be treated, and it is still useful to look at it this way for some purposes. The "something" that goods produce or give rise to is usually called *utility*. A given collection of goods is associated with a certain level of utility. "Utility" is something such that more of it is always desirable, so a collection with *higher* utility is *preferred,* collections with the same utility are *indifferent*.

Thus indifference curves can be regarded as curves giving the same utility, or *isoutility curves*. Since there is a given utility level associated with each collection of goods, just as there is an output level associated with every collection of inputs, we can speak of a *utility function* in the same way we speak of a production function. The indifference curves are contours of this utility function, just as isoquants are contours of the production function.

There are, however, some fundamental and crucial differences between a production function and a utility function. For a production function we can measure the inputs, then measure the resulting output, and the measurements will be the same whoever carries out the experiment so that a production function is an *objective, fully observable* relationship between inputs and output. For a utility function, we can measure inputs but *we cannot measure output* which is a subjective "something" felt only by the particular consumer. Thus a utility function is not only *subjective* (the relationship will differ from consumer to consumer), but it is not *observable*.

It is impossible for a consumer to communicate how "much" utility he receives from a given goods collection. The things he can communicate are, which of two collections is preferred, or whether he is indifferent between them. There have been ingenious schemes devised which attempt to enable further communication. These include asking a consumer whether he prefers the *difference* between collection *A* and collection

B to the difference between two other collections, and whether he prefers collection *A* with certainty to a gamble that will give him either *B* or *C* with given probabilities.[9] These ingenuities have not received universal acceptance.

If the consumer can communicate only relative preferences, and indifference, then we can tell whether his utility is higher or lower in one situation than another, but not *by how much*. In terms of the indifference map, we know that the higher the indifference curve, the higher the utility, but that is all. Three successive indifference curves might be associated with 1, 1.1, 1.2, utility "units," or with 1, 1.1, 1000, or with 1, 1000, 1001. All would give the same *ordering*.

We usually work with the idea of utility as ordinal. That is, any utility function that gives a higher utility to a preferred collection provides the only information we can obtain. This means that the kind of properties of a production function that depend on measurement of output, such as returns to scale, have no application to utility functions.

If all we know of utility is whether it is higher or lower, then we know which collection a consumer prefers, no more and no less. Thus the idea of a utility function adds no *content* to the theory of consumer behavior, although it may sometimes be a useful analytical tool.

Since "most preferred" and "giving greatest utility" are synonymous, we can make a further addition to the list, given in the last section, of equivalents to the statement that the consumer chooses point *C* on his budget line.

(6) At point *C*, the consumer maximizes his utility for points on the budget line.

The introduction of a utility function does not achieve anything that cannot be achieved by simply discussing preferences, at least in this simple context.[10] On the other hand, ordinal utility does not imply anything about the consumer's behavior not already included in the ordinary preference analysis. Thus it is always acceptable to treat the consumer *as though* he was maximizing a utility function. The decision whether to use utility analysis or direct preference analysis is simply a matter of convenience.

---

[9] A utility function based on the choice between alternatives with stated probabilities is called a *Von Neumann–Morgenstern* utility function, since it was discussed at length in those authors' classic work, *The Theory of Games and Economic Behavior*. Its validity depends very crucially on the consumer having exactly the same viewpoint concerning probabilities as the experimenter.

[10] In the analysis of more complex situations, such as choice among events that are probable but not certain, and between present and future events, the use of a utility function is a great help.

7.6 Income Changes

Consider the consumer with the budget situation used in our earlier example: food at $0.50 per pound, clothing at $2 per item, and a budget of $10. Let the resulting budget line be *AB* in the three diagrams of Figure 7.6, and suppose the consumer chooses point *C*.

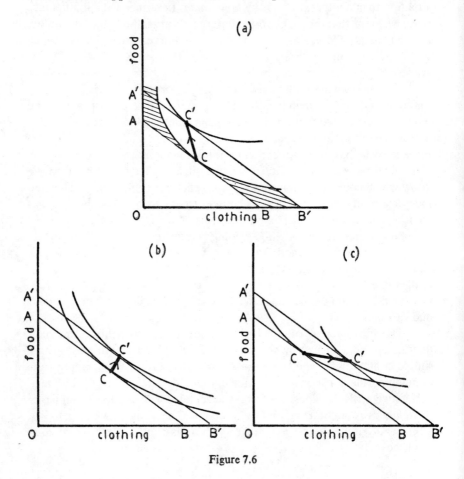

Figure 7.6

Now consider the effect of an increase in the budget from $10 to $12.50, with prices unchanged. This will give a new budget line. Since prices have not changed, the *slope* of the budget line does not change, but since the consumer can obviously buy more of all goods than before, the new budget line is further from the origin than the old. It is depicted as *A'B'* in the diagrams.

In simple models, we consider the consumer's budget to be the same as his money income for the period we are discussing. Consequently we usually refer to a change of the kind we are interested in, where the budget (or money income) changes but prices do not, as a *pure income change*.

Equiproportional Price Changes. The budget line is determined by the price *ratio* for the two goods. Let us suppose we started with the original budget position and, instead of any change in the income, this remained at $10, but *both* prices fell by 20 per cent to $0.40 (food) and $1.60 (clothing). By spending all his income on food, the consumer could buy 25 lbs—exactly what he could buy at income $12.50 and the old prices. Similarly, the clothing he could obtain by spending all his income on clothing would be the same (6¼ items) as at an income of $12.50 and the old prices. The budget line at the reduced prices would thus be $A'B'$, exactly the same as the budget line for the higher income and the old prices.

Thus a fall in all prices *in the same proportion* will have the same effect on the consumer's budget as a rise in money income with prices held constant. We can use the term *rise in real income* to mean that the budget line has moved further from the origin (but without changing slope) either because prices have fallen in the same proportion or because money income has risen, or possibly as a net result of both kinds of change. We shall not stress the term real income here, because it is used in several other different contexts and so has become rather imprecise. But when we speak of a rise in income in this section, we mean any change which shifts the budget line outward without affecting its slope.

Choice and Income. How will the consumer's choice change as a result of the income change? Given his indifference map, we would find the new choice at the point of tangency between the new budget line and an indifference curve. Obviously it will be a *higher* indifference curve. Let us consider the possibilities. There will be some collections on the new budget line which are on a lower indifference curve than the original point C (this area is shaded in the diagrams) and these will obviously not be chosen at the higher income level.

The reader may expect the new point to be like C' in Figure 7.6 (b), where the consumer chooses more of both goods. This is a quite usual case, but it is perfectly possible for the consumer's indifference map to give points like C' in Figures 7.6 (a) and (c) where *less* of one good is chosen, although C' must contain more of at least one good.

Although the consumer is on a higher indifference curve at the higher income, he does not necessarily choose more of both goods. If he chooses more of a particular good when his income rises (like both food and clothing in [b], food in [a], clothing in [c]), we say good is a *normal good* to the consumer. If he chooses less of a particular good when his income rises, like clothing in (a), food in (c), we say that good is an *inferior good* to him.

In spite of the terminology "normal good," "inferior good," the property we are concerned with depends on the consumer's *view* of the good. A good may be normal to one consumer, inferior to another. It is obvious that there must be at least one good which is normal to each consumer.

Inferior Goods. A traditional example of an inferior good is margarine. As income rises, the consumer can afford butter, and uses less margarine. This is the kind of situation which can best be analyzed by considering the consumer's preferences on the *characteristics* of goods rather than on goods. Margarine and butter share one characteristic ("bread lubrication"), but differ in relative amounts of another ("desirable flavor"). The common characteristic is more "essential" so that the low income consumer is chiefly concerned with the cheapest way of lubricating dry bread. At higher incomes, he can afford to pay for the relative "luxury" of butter flavor. Actually, this traditional case has lost a great deal of its force as an example, since technological progress has diminished the flavor difference. Indeed, in recent years a previously ignored characteristic (cholesterol-forming properties) has become important and some consumers, who can afford more meat as their incomes rise, may then switch to margarine to keep down body cholesterol, so that *butter* is inferior.

Other traditional examples of inferior goods are basic filling foods like bread, rice, and pasta. As incomes rise, the consumer no longer needs to concentrate on obtaining the maximum of the most basic characteristic (calories) and can switch to other foods. More modern examples include bus travel (in the United States) and the low quality varieties of all products which come in quality ranges.

Income-Consumption Curves. By increasing income and keeping prices constant we could move the consumer's budget line steadily outwards and note the point he chose at each income level. We could also decrease income below the original level, and trace out points between C and the origin. If we join all the points representing the consumer's choice at each income level, but with prices always constant, the curve we obtain is called the *income-consumption curve*. It joins points on successive indifference curves which have the same slopes, since the slope of the budget line does not change. Figure 7.7(a) illustrates a typical income-consumption curve with both goods normal. Figure 7.7(b) illustrates a case

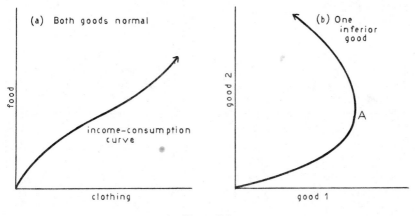

Figure 7.7

in which good *1* becomes an inferior good at the income level corresponding to the point *A*. We expect that goods which are inferior at high income levels will be normal at low income levels, and that no goods will be inferior at sufficiently low incomes.

An income-consumption curve is one variety of *behavior line*. It shows how the behavior of the consumer varies with income.

Engel Curves. The information contained in the income-consumption curve can be treated in another way. Instead of showing how the choice between the two goods varies with income, we can take one of the goods and see how the quantity of this good varies with income. We usually plot the *expenditure* on the good against income. Since prices are constant, expenditure is directly proportional to quantity. Such a curve is called an *Engel curve*.[11]

Examples of Engel curves are given in Figure 7.8(a)-(d). Diagrams (a)-(c) all show expenditure increasing with income, so the good is *normal*. Diagram (d) shows expenditure decreasing with income past income level *Y*, so this good is *inferior* for higher income levels.

Now compare (a), (b), (c). In (a), the Engel curve is a straight line, so the ratio of expenditure on the good to income is constant. In (b), this ratio is falling, while in (c) it is rising.

---

[11] This is not Engels of Marx and Engels but Ernst Engel. He also suggested Engel's Law (see page 203).

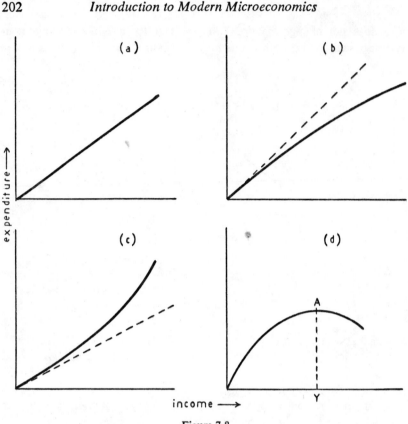

Figure 7.8

Income Elasticity. It is often helpful to make use of a certain elasticity concept as a descriptive term here, just as in the case of demand curves in Chapter 2. We define percentage change in the expenditure on a good for a 1 per cent change in income as the *income elasticity*,[12] price being supposed constant. If the income elasticity is less than unity, expenditure increases by a smaller proportion than income, so that the ratio of expenditure to income falls as income rises, as in (b). If the income elasticity is greater than unity, the ratio of expenditure to income rises, as in (c), while the ratio is constant, as in (a), for unit elasticity.

Goods for which income elasticity is greater than unity are sometimes called *luxury goods,* and goods for which income elasticity is less than unity are called *essential goods.* The terms are not altogether apt.

Thus we have a set of descriptive terms that expresses the relation-

---

[12] For the calculus-trained reader, the Mathematical Note on Section 2.5, page 300, gives a more precise discussion of income elasticity.

ship between income and expenditure on a particular good, with price constant.

If expenditure falls with a rise in income, we have an *inferior* good.

If expenditure rises with income, the good is *normal*. A normal good may be a "luxury" good (income elasticity greater than unity) or an "essential" good (income elasticity less than unity).

These descriptive terms are most often applied to aggregate expenditure relative to aggregate income, but also to family expenditure relative to family income. One of the early empirical observations in this general field was Engel's that income elasticity of food was less than unity—it is often referred to as *Engel's Law*.

Although there are a variety of empirical studies concerning the income-expenditure relationships in the aggregate, it should be emphasized that there is nothing in consumer theory itself to suggest any particular relationship. The various descriptive terms are attached to the goods, but they really refer to patterns of preferences. A particular good may be inferior for one consumer, have a high income elasticity for another, and be normal but with a low income elasticity for yet another.

7.7 Substitution

Given the ratio between the prices of the two goods if we seek to find the smallest income that just enables a consumer to attain a certain indifference curve, say IC_2 in Figure 7.9, we know that this will be the income corresponding to the budget line (ACB in the diagram) which

    (a) has a slope equal to the price ratio,

    (b) is tangent to IC_2 (at C).

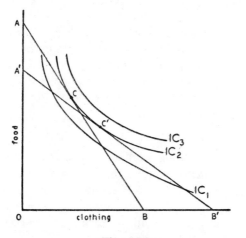

Figure 7.9

If the price ratio now changes, the solution to the new problem will be a new budget line ($A'B'$) with a slope equal to the new price ratio, which is also tangent to IC_2. Assuming the usual case of a smoothly curved indifference curve, the new point of tangency will be C', not identical with C. For the particular type of change shown in the figure, where $A'B'$ is flatter in slope than AB, C' must lie to the southeast of C because the indifference curve is convex to the origin.

The Substitution Effect. Now the change in the slope from budget line AB to budget line $A'B'$ means that the ratio OA'/OB' is less than the ratio OA/OB. If M is the money income corresponding to AB, and P_F, P_C are the dollar prices of food and clothing, OA is the amount of food that can be purchased by spending the whole income on food and so is equal to M/P_F. Similarly OB is equal to M/P_C. Thus we have

$$\frac{OA}{OB} = \frac{M/P_F}{M/P_C} = \frac{P_C}{P_F} .$$

Denoting the prices corresponding to $A'B'$ by P_C', P_F', it follows that

$$\frac{OA'}{OB'} = \frac{P_C'}{P_F'} .$$

The particular change illustrated in the figure, in which $OA'/OB' < OA/OB$, implies $P_C'/P_F' < P_C/P_F$, that is, that the price of clothing falls relative to the price of food in the second situation (and, of course, the price of food rises relative to the price of clothing). The actual change in the consumer's chosen collection from C to C' represents an increase in the quantity of clothing and a decrease in the quantity of food. Thus we have the *pure substitution effect*:

With only two goods, a change in relative prices accompanied, if necessary, by an income change that keeps the consumer on the same indifference curve, will result in the consumer choosing more of the good whose price has fallen relatively, and less of the good whose price has risen relatively. The consumer substitutes some of the relatively cheaper good for the relatively more expensive.

The kind of budget change we are concerned with is often called a *compensated price change*. The qualification, "compensated," refers to the income adjustment which maintains the original indifference level.

The extent of the substitution effect depends on the degree of curvature of the consumer's indifference curve, and thus on his particular preferences. The change in quantities will be greater for a given change in price ratio, the more sharply curved is the indifference curve over the relevant range.

Efficiency Substitution. Substitution effects of a different kind, but giving an effect in the same direction, will occur if we consider cases in which there are different goods with similar characteristics. To take the simplest possible case, suppose there are two characteristics, "nutrition" and "warmth" which are the ultimate objects of the consumer's interest. His indifference map will be similar to that in Figure 7.9, but with "nutrition" on the vertical axis and "warmth" on the horizontal.

If there is only one kind of food (giving "nutrition" but no "warmth") and one kind of clothing (giving "warmth" but no "nutrition"), a change in the relative prices of food and clothing will give results along the same lines as the previous analysis. If the price of food rises relative to the price of clothing, the consumer will substitute some warmth for some nutrition, being a little warmer and a little less well fed but no better and no worse off, taking both nutrition and warmth together.

But suppose there are two kinds of food, both giving the same nutrition per pound. If one is $0.50 per pound and the other is $0.55 per pound, it would be *inefficient* to consume any of the more expensive food. (We are assuming in this simple case that there are no other relevant characteristics, such as taste.) If the price of the second type of food were to fall to $0.45 per pound it would now be inefficient to consume any of the first type of food. Thus a sufficient change in the relative prices of the two foods would cause consumers to *switch* from consuming only the first food to consuming only the second. This substitution effect, which again involves substituting the good whose price has fallen relatively for the good whose price has risen, does not depend on the shape of the consumer's indifference curves, but on simple grounds of making efficient use of the budget to achieve the consumer's object (a certain nutrition level). We call it the *efficiency substitution effect*.

The example given is so simple as to be trivial. The interesting cases arise when we have a variety of goods giving the same characteristics but in different proportions. We shall not analyze these here,[13] but note that they give the same result, existence of an efficiency substitution effect which does not depend on the shape of indifference curves.

Overall Substitution. If we wish to distinguish the substitution effect which arises from the curvature of indifference curves, we shall call it the *private* or *personal* substitution effect, since its extent depends on the preferences

---

[13] For further analysis along these lines, see Section 7.11.

of the individual. The efficiency substitution effect is, however, the same for all consumers.

The overall substitution effect may be made up of a private and an efficiency effect, which reinforce each other. The overall effect will always be in the direction of consuming less of the good whose price has risen relatively, more of the good whose price has fallen.

Whether we are considering the private or efficiency effects, or the overall effect, we are considering changes in prices which are combined with whatever income adjustments are necessary to maintain the consumer at the same indifference level. This is a hypothetical case, since the typical change facing the consumer is one in which price changes are not directly related to income changes.

7.8 Demand Theory

We have now built the component parts from which we can assemble an analysis of the consumer's *demand* for a product. Contrary to what is often expected of demand theory, *we cannot prove, from the theory of consumer behavior, that demand curves slope downward*. We can show that the consumer's demand curve for at least one good must be downward sloping, and we can show that, if a consumer's income-consumption behavior follows a certain path, his demand curves slope downward, but no more.

In previous sections, we discussed the consumer's behavior under a pure income change (with no change in relative prices) and under a price change accompanied by such income change as would maintain the consumer on his original indifference curve. That is, we discussed a *pure income change* and a *compensated price change*.

Here we shall discuss the effect of an *uncompensated price change*, that is, the effect of a change in money prices with money income held constant. We confine the analysis to the case in which the price of *only one good* changes.

In Figure 7.10, AB represents the budget line of the consumer in the original situation, and the consumer chooses point C on IC_1. Suppose the price of clothing falls, but the price of food and money income remains constant. Then, by spending all his income on clothing, the consumer can purchase more (point B') than originally, since the price has fallen. But if he spends all his income on food, he can only purchase the same quantity as before (point A) since neither his money income nor the price of food has changed. Thus the new budget line is AB'. Since AB' is further from

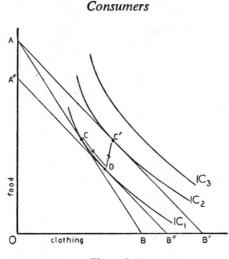

Figure 7.10

the origin than AB (except at A), the consumer can obviously attain a higher indifference curve from budget AB' than from budget AB:

A fall in the price of a good which is actually purchased,[14] *with money income and other prices constant, enables the consumer to attain a higher indifference curve.*

Suppose the point which is chosen on budget line AB' is C', lying on indifference curve IC_2. The effect of the uncompensated price change is a movement from C to C'.

A Hypothetical Experiment. To obtain some idea of how C' might be related to C, we consider a hypothetical experiment in which the consumer is induced to move from C to C' in two steps.

In the first part of the experiment, the price of clothing falls, but the consumer's income is adjusted so that he can just maintain a position on his original indifference curve IC_1. That is, we confront him with a *compensated price change* represented by a budget line parallel to AB', but tangent to IC_1—the line $A''B''$ in the diagram. He will choose point D. The movement from C to D is a *pure substitution effect* and will always result in an increase in purchases of clothing, the good whose relative price has fallen.

In the second part of the experiment, we increase the consumer's

---

[14] Note that if the consumer purchased only food in the initial situation, he may not be able to attain a higher indifference curve as a result of a fall in the price of clothing.

income so that the budget line changes from $A''B''$ to AB'. Since the two budget lines are parallel, this is a *pure income change*. Since the consumer has now reached the budget line AB', his choice will be C', the same point he would have chosen if the budget line had changed directly from AB to AB'. The movement from D to C' is a *pure income effect*. As we saw previously, this effect *could* result in his consuming more clothing at C' than at D (clothing is a normal good) or less (clothing is an inferior good).

Thus, by our hypothetical experiment, we have shown that the effect of the uncompensated price change (movement from C to C') is equivalent to a pure substitution effect (movement from C to D) plus a pure income effect (movement from D to C').

Considering the result of the two effects on the purchase of clothing, we have

(1) the substitution effect (C to D) will increase the purchase of clothing;

(2) the income effect (D to C') will (a) *increase* the consumption of clothing, if clothing is a *normal* good, (b) *decrease* the consumption of clothing, if clothing is an inferior good.

Demand Theory. Since the total effect is the sum of the income and substitution effects, we can make the following statements:

(i) If clothing is a normal good, an uncompensated fall in the price of clothing will certainly result in an increase in purchase of clothing.

(ii) If clothing is an inferior good, an uncompensated fall in the price of clothing will increase the purchase of clothing if the income effect is smaller than the substitution effect. If the income effect is larger than the substitution effect, the purchase of clothing will fall when its price falls.

Thus the consumer's demand for a good will certainly increase when price falls (giving a downward sloping demand curve) if the good is normal, and may still do so if the good is inferior. However, it is possible that the demand for an inferior good may fall when its price falls, giving an upward sloping demand curve.

A good which has an upward sloping demand curve is often called a *Giffen good*.[15] The traditional example of a potential Giffen good is some basic staple food like bread in Europe or rice in Asia. It is then argued that, if a man is consuming both bread and meat and the price of bread rises, he cannot afford to buy the previous quantities of both. Since bread

---

[15] There seems to be some uncertainty as to whether a Mr. Giffen really did note an effect of this kind.

has more calories per unit expenditure the consumer may switch to consuming more bread simply to obtain his basic caloric needs. Note that this is essentially an argument in terms of the characteristics of the goods.

Empirical evidence of the existence of Giffen goods is uncertain, although effects of this same kind are probably important in the supply of personal services, discussed in the next section.

Demand Curves. To predict whether a consumer's demand curve for a particular good will be downward sloping, we need to know whether the good is normal or inferior (to him). That is, we need to know the direction of the income effect. Consumer theory gives no prediction as to this direction, which can only be found by observing the behavior of the consumer under a pure income change. Thus the prediction of the downward slope of a demand curve requires *empirical data,* and cannot be based on theory alone.

We can take it that inferior goods are the minority (hence the term "normal" for goods which are not inferior), and also note that a perverse demand relationship requires an inferior good, the income effect of which outweighs the substitution effect. Our presumption from the beginning that a downward sloping demand curve was the regular case is not upset.

We can also note that at least one good must be normal, since a consumer will not reduce purchases of *all* goods as income rises, so at least one good *must* have a downward sloping demand curve.

At a sufficiently high price, the purchase of any good must start to fall with further price rises simply because the consumer's income is limited.

Consider Figure 7.11. Here we have drawn an original budget line *AB* and a large number of budget lines represent uncompensated changes in the price of clothing. For each budget line there is a particular point chosen by the consumer (the point of tangency to an indifference curve). We can join these points, each of which corresponds to a particular price (of clothing). The resulting curve is called a *price-consumption curve* or *offer curve.* It shows the way in which the goods collection changes as price changes. If we plot, on another diagram, the quantity of clothing chosen at each price we have, of course, an *individual demand curve for clothing, at the given income level.*

Note that we have considered the demand curve to represent the way in which the quantity changes for an *uncompensated* price change. That is, the demand curve shows how quantity of a good varies with changes in its price, other prices and money income being held constant This is the standard definition of the demand curve in modern economic usage.

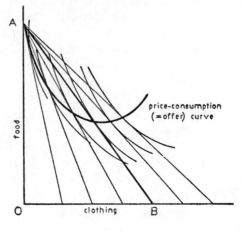

Figure 7.11

7.9 *The Labor-Leisure Choice*

The consumer's decisions concerned with the amount of his own time that he will be willing to sell can be handled by an analysis similar to that of the previous section. In this context we note that the consumer has some fixed endowment of "free" time over and above the time required for such essential purposes as sleep. Let us suppose the available free time is 12 hours. The consumer has a choice between selling any part of this time (as labor) and retaining it for personal relaxation (leisure). We assume that the proceeds of selling labor time are used immediately to buy a generalized good, which we shall call "consumption."[16]

We shall consider the price of consumption to be our basis, so that the wage (price of labor) is expressed in terms of the quantity of consumption that can be purchased with the wage received for one hour's work. The wage, expressed as "consumption goods per hour" rather than "dollars per hour" is called the *real wage,* since it expresses the real consumption possibilities earned for an hour of work. Obviously the real wage can rise either because the *money wage* rises with the price of consumption goods constant, or because the price of consumption goods falls with the money wage constant.

The Budget Line. The consumer's choice situation at a given real wage, *W,* is depicted in Figure 7.12. He can devote all his time (12 hours) to

---

[16] That is, the only reason for working is to obtain income for spending on goods. The analysis requires modification for cases in which labor also possesses desired characteristics—as in the case of the professor who enjoys teaching.

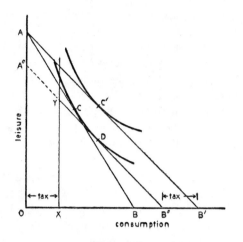

Figure 7.12

leisure, obtaining no earnings and no consumption, a position represented by the point *A*. He can work 12 hours and buy 12*W* units of consumption, represented by the point *B*. Or he can work part of the time and attain points on *AB*, which thus represents his budget line.

Note that the ultimate choice facing the consumer is not really between labor and leisure (for then he would, presumably, always choose maximum leisure), but between *leisure* and *consumption*. His preferences between different collections of these will be expressed by an indifference map of the usual kind, and he will choose the preferred point of *AB*, tangent to an indifference curve. This is the point *C* in the diagram.

Now suppose the wage increases to *W'*. His maximum leisure is still 12 hours (point *A*), but his maximum consumption is now 12*W'*, greater than 12*W*, so the new budget line is *AB'* where *B'* is to the right of *B*. Given his preference map, his new choice can be determined at some point *C'*.

As in analyzing the consumer's demand for goods, however, we are interested in breaking the movement from *C* to *C'* into two parts, corresponding to substitution and income effects.

Comparison with Demand Analysis. Our hypothetical experiment requires rather more ingenuity to devise; however, the endowment of the consumer is his free time, not a money sum, and this cannot be directly manipulated. We could, however, impose a fixed *tax* on the consumer, to be paid in consumption goods. Suppose this tax was an amount of consumption equal to the distance *B''B'* in the diagram. Then the collections attainable by the consumer at wage *W'* would be those on *AB'*, less a quantity $B''B'$ of consumption. These points would lie on $A''B''$, parallel to AB'. Thus a suitable tax can confine the consumer to a budget line lying inside AB'. (Due to the tax, the consumer can no longer choose 12 hours of leisure—he must work at least enough to earn the tax so that he is confined to the section YB'' of the budget line $A''B''$: we assume this section contains his preferred point.)

Thus we can break up the overall effect into a pure substitution effect (the rise in the wage accompanied by a fixed tax keeping him on his original indifference level), and a pure "income" effect (removal of the tax).

There is one more difference from the analysis of the previous section. We are interested in the effect of the wage change on *leisure,* not *consumption.* For a rise in the wage rate the overall effect on leisure will be the combination of the substitution effect (reducing the demand for leisure) and the income effect (which may reduce or increase the demand for leisure).

If leisure is a *normal* good, the effects are in opposite directions, since the income effect will increase the demand for leisure. If leisure is an *inferior* good, effects are in the same direction—the demand for leisure will certainly fall when the wage rises.

Labor Supply Curve. Since the sum of labor supplied and leisure enjoyed is constant (12 hours), the quantity of labor supplied rises when the quantity of leisure demanded falls, and vice versa. When the real wage rises, the supply of labor (by the individual) will rise (giving a regular supply curve) if the quantity of leisure demanded falls. This will certainly occur if leisure is an inferior good, or if it is a normal good but giving an income effect small in relation to the substitution effect. Thus we conclude:

The individual's supply of labor curve will be regular (upward sloping) if leisure is an inferior good, and may be upward sloping even if leisure is a normal good. However, if leisure is a normal good with a high income elasticity, the supply curve may slope downward over part of its length.

There is probably more evidence that leisure is a normal good with high income elasticity and that the supply of labor curve may, therefore, have a "wrong" slope than there is for the existence of Giffen good in demand theory.

The effect of high income elasticity for leisure is usually considered to result in a "backward bending" supply curve for labor. Since some minimum level of consumption is necessary, it is assumed that maximum labor will be supplied at low wages. Above some wage level, however, the consumer will take advantage of being able to sustain a given consumption level with less work, and so will work shorter hours as the wage rises. A curve of this type is illustrated in Figure 7.13.

Effect of Wealth. We can use the general analysis above to investigate the effect of *nonlabor income* (such as interest or dividends from the consumer's *wealth*) on the labor-leisure choice. Consider the situation in Figure 7.14, where the budget line *AB* represents the leisure-consumption

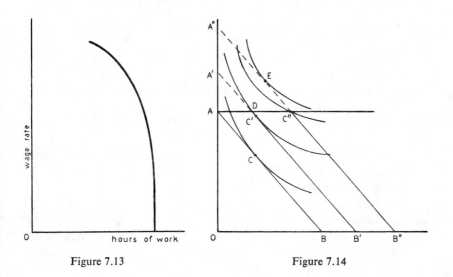

Figure 7.13   Figure 7.14

possibilities at the given wage rate and with no outside income. Now suppose the same consumer receives an outside income equal to the amount of consumption represented by the distance *BB'*. The new budget line will be parallel to the old, but further from the origin by a horizontal distance *BB'* everywhere, and will thus be the line *A'B'*.

But the consumer still cannot obtain more than 12 hours leisure—there is a constraint on the sheer quantity of free time available, similar to a rationing situation. Thus only the solid part *DB'* of the budget line is actually attainable. If leisure has a high income elasticity, the new choice will be a point like *C'*, with more leisure than originally.

If outside income increases sufficiently, to give a budget line like *A"B"*, the consumer will reach a situation in which he chooses to cease work altogether, taking the maximum leisure (12 hours) available at point *C"*. Note that in this case, *the highest indifference curve need no longer be tangent to the budget line*. This is because the point on *A"B"* at which an indifference curve is tangent (E) cannot be reached because of the constraint on leisure.

The same type of analysis, giving a *corner solution,* is relevant whenever there is a constraint on the consumer's choice which is *additional to the budget constraint.*

Note that the analysis here is primarily concerned with hours of work by individuals, and assumes a choice in this respect. For institutional reasons, only self-employed persons (and not always these) are completely free to choose how many hours per day or week they will work.

7.10 Bargaining and Exchange

We have mainly been discussing situations in which the consumer commenced with some budget and was free to purchase any quantities of goods at fixed prices. In this section we shall discuss the exchange and bargaining situation between two individuals who commence with fixed quantities of goods but without any given market prices.

The Edgeworth Box. To carry out the analysis we shall use one of the most ingenious geometric constructions ever devised in economics, the *Edgeworth box diagram.*[17]

Suppose our two individuals have, as initial endowments, quantities a_1, a_2 of good A, and b_1, b_2 of good B. No matter what form of bargaining or exchange takes place, the total quantity of A distributed between the two will always be $a_1 + a_2$, and the total quantity of B distributed between them will always be $b_1 + b_2$.

Consider a rectangle (the "box") with sides $a_1 + a_2$, $b_1 + b_2$. This is the rectangle O_1CO_2D in Figure 7.15. With O_1 as origin and O_1C, O_1D as axes, we measure the quantities of the two goods in the hands of individual *I*. The point X represents quantities a_1, b_1 of the goods for individual *I*.

For individual *II*, we take O_2 as origin and O_2D, O_2C as axes. That is, for individual *II* the normal two axes diagram has been turned around. If the reader takes the page containing Figure 7.15 and turns the book so that the former upper right-hand corner becomes the lower left-hand corner, he will see the normal diagram for individual *II*.

Now the point X represents quantities a_1, b_1 for individual *I*. Thus the vertical distance from O_1D to X is a_1. But the vertical distance between O_1D and O_2C is $a_1 + a_2$, so the vertical distance between O_2C and X is a_2. Similarly, the horizontal distance between O_2D and X is b_2. Thus X

---

[17] Edgeworth's name was also mentioned in connection with the material of Chapter 3. It is also called the *Edgeworth-Bowley* box.

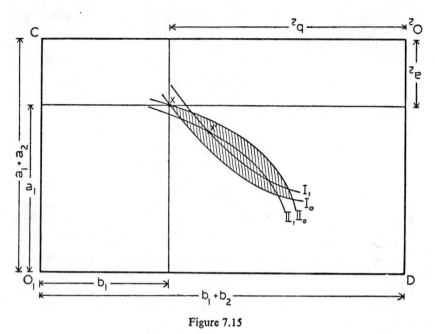

Figure 7.15

represents simultaneously the initial endowments of the two individuals.

If we take *any* point in the box, and measure the quantities of the two goods relative to individual *I*'s axes, then relative to individual *II*'s, we see that the sum of the quantities of Good *A* will always total $a_1 + a_2$, and the sum of the quantities of Good *B* will always total $b_1 + b_2$.

Denoting the totals $a_1 + a_2$, $b_1 + b_2$ by a, b, we see that any point in the box represents an *allocation* of the totals a, b between the two individuals. Change from one point in the box to another represents a *reallocation* such that the increase in quantity of either good by one individual is exactly equal to the decrease in quantity by the other.

Starting from X, every possible result of bargaining and exchange is a reallocation of the fixed totals between the two individuals and is thus represented by some other point in the box.

We now take account of the individuals' preferences, represented by their indifference maps. The map for individual *I* is drawn in the conventional sense, while that for individual *II* is rotated and can be viewed in the conventional sense by turning the page as before. The indifference curves for individual *I* are labelled I_0, I_1 and those for individual *II* are labelled II_0, II_1 and so on.

The initial point X is on some indifference curve for each of the individuals, and these are the curves labelled I_0, II_0.

Bargaining. Each individual would prefer to be on a higher indifference curve than that through *X*, and we shall suppose each tries to improve his position by *bargaining*, that is, by attempting to induce the other to give him some of the goods.

In the absence of physical coercion neither individual will give up goods that put him in a worse position than he was to start with. That is, individual *I* will not be able to induce *II* to accept any reallocation that puts *II* on a *lower indifference curve than* II_0. Similarly, *II* will not be able to induce *I* to accept a reallocation putting *I* on a lower indifference curve than I_0. Thus we can set fundamental limits on the result of any bargaining process:

In the absence of coercion, the result of any bargaining process commencing from X *must be a point lying in the area to the right of* I_0 *and to the left of* II_0. *This is the shaded lens-shaped area in the diagram.*

At any point in the *interior* of this area, *both* individuals are in positions preferred to *X*. Along the boundary, one is in a preferred position, the other is indifferent between this and *X*. Thus it is *mutually advantageous* for the individuals to bargain toward a reallocation from *X* to a point like *X'*.

Any point in the mutually advantageous area is so related to *X* that the reallocation always involves, to either individual, an increase in the amount of one good and a decrease in the amount of the other. Thus the process of moving from *X* to *X'* is a process of exchange: *I* gives up some of his good *A* in exchange for some of *II*'s good *B*.

Let us suppose that the two individuals have, as a result of bargaining, exchanged goods to reach *X'*. At *X'*, both individuals are on higher indifference curves (I_1, II_1) than at *X*. But they are not yet on the highest indifference curves that are attainable, since the lens-shaped area between I_1 and II_1 contains reallocations at which both individuals are on higher indifference levels than I_1, II_1.

So long as the indifference curves of the two individuals, through an allocation point, cross each other, there always remains a mutually advantageous area of further reallocations.

The Contract Curve. Now turn to Figure 7.16, which magnifies the bargaining area of Figure 7.15. If the individuals exchange from *X'* to *X''*, at *which the indifference curves of the two individuals are tangent,* there is no room for further mutually advantageous bargaining. Obviously *I* can now move to a higher indifference curve than I_2 only by a reallocation that puts *II* on to a *lower* indifference curve than II_2.

Thus bargaining will cease once a reallocation has been reached at

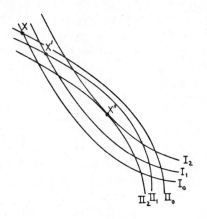

Figure 7.16

which the indifference curves of the two individuals are tangent. A point like *X″* is a *contract point*.

Inside the box there are a continuous series of points at which the indifference curves of the two individuals are tangent. The line joining all these points is the *contract curve* for that particular box. This is illustrated in Figure 7.17.

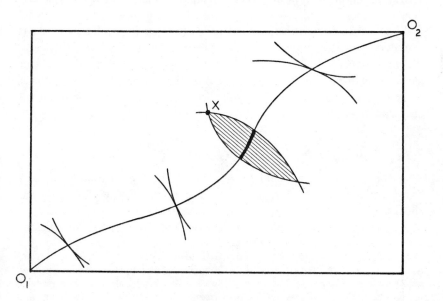

Figure 7.17

Starting from a specific initial allocation, like X, the bargaining process will reach a point at which mutually advantageous exchange is no longer possible only when it reaches a point of the contract curve. From X, the end of the bargaining will not be just anywhere on the contract curve, it must be in the segment (traced heavily in the diagram) which lies between the two original indifference curves. But if we consider all possible initial allocations of the quantities a, b, and thus all possible starting points inside the box, the bargaining process will always end if it reaches some point on the contract curve $O_1 O_2$.

Indeterminateness of Solution. It should be noted that, from a given starting point like X, we know the bargaining can end *somewhere* on the heavy segment, but not *exactly where*. All moves from X into the shaded mutually advantageous area are possible, but it will depend on the detailed bargaining moves, and on the skill and "strength" of the bargains, exactly where each move will lead. Obviously the more successful is I as a bargainer, the further from O_1 along the heavy segment of the contract curve will the final bargain be struck. It is also possible that, from lack of skill or from "cussedness" bargaining will cease *off* the contract curve, even though both could gain from appropriate further moves.

We shall use this Edgeworth box diagram later, for it is a powerful tool. In a single diagram are depicted total quantities of two goods, their allocation among two individuals, and the complete preference maps of those two individuals.

Note that the contract curve depends both on the preferences of the two individuals and on the total quantities of the two goods in the system. If the quantities change even though the individuals are the same, we will have a new box and a new contract curve. But a single box and contract curve will hold for all possible initial allocations of the same totals among the same individuals.

7.11 New and Differentiated Goods[18]

The characteristics analysis of demand theory, mentioned several times earlier in the chapter, can be illustrated very well by discussing the effect of introducing new goods into the system.

Traditional demand theory has never been able to handle satisfac-

---

[18] For development of this idea beyond what is discussed in this book, see Lancaster, K. J., "Change and innovation in the technology of consumption," *American Economic Review/Supplement*, 14–23, May 1966 (nontechnical); and "A new approach to consumer theory," *Journal of Political Economy*, 74, 132–157; 1966 (more advanced).

torily the problem of introducing new goods. The consumer's preference map is given in terms of the original set of goods, and the new good requires that this be thrown away and replaced by a new preference map based on the new set of goods. All the information concerning preferences on the original set of goods is discarded in the process.

For some types of new goods, the same problems might arise even using the characteristics approach. A very large class of new goods, however, are a kind that possesses the *same* characteristics as the old, but *in different proportions.* A new model of automobile is not the same as the old (and thus must be treated as a new good in the traditional approach), but it is not usually different in any fundamental way from existing automobiles. It simply combines the characteristics associated with an automobile in a somewhat different way. A new model would usually be considered a variant or differentiate of an existing product, rather than a new good, but this is a matter of degree, not of kind. Almost all new goods have characteristics or perform functions similar to those of existing goods, but differently combined.

We shall, as usual, take a simple analysis in which we concern ourselves with a class of goods having only two relevant characteristics, which we shall refer to as A and B. We assume that some particular good *G1* possesses these characteristics in fixed proportions, and that the amounts of the characteristics are directly proportional to the quantities of the goods. A simple example would be a food, with calories and protein as the characteristics. A particular kind of food would have so many calories and so much protein per pound, and two pounds would have just twice as many calories and twice as much protein as one pound. We shall also assume that the characteristics from different goods are additive, just as the calorie and protein intake from a meal is the sum of the calories and proteins contained in each of the separate foods.

Suppose initially there are two goods *G1* and *G2*, that 1 pound of *G1* contains 2 units of characteristic A and 1 of characteristic B, and that 1 pound of good *G2* contains 1 unit of A and 2 of B.

Consider a consumer with a budget of $12, and take the prices of both G1 and G2 to be $1 per pound. We are interested in finding the various combinations of *characteristics* rather than just of goods, that the consumer can attain with his budget. In Figure 7.18, the diagram is drawn with characteristics measured on the axes rather than goods. By spending all his budget on *G1*, the consumer can purchase 12 pounds of that good, which will give 24 units of A and 12 units of B. This is the point labelled *G1* on the diagram. By spending all his budget on *G2*, the consumer can purchase 12 pounds of that good, obtaining 12 units of A and 24 units of B—the point *G2* on the diagram. By similar arguments to those used in

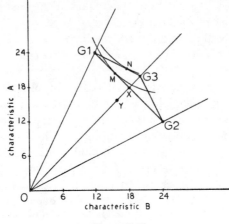

Figure 7.18

discussing the combination of processes in production (Section 4.4), we can see that, by spending part of the $12 on *G1* and the remainder on *G2*, the consumer can attain collections of characteristics represented by the points along the line joining *G1* and *G2*. This line is the attainable characteristics frontier for the given budget and prices. If the budget increased, the frontier would move outward parallel to itself, while it would change its slope if the relative prices of the goods changed.

Since the consumer's preferences are really between collections of characteristics rather than of goods, we can draw the indifference curves between collections of *A* and *B* on the diagram. The preferred collection, as drawn, is *M*, where an indifference curve is tangent to the characteristics frontier. Corner solutions at either *G1* or *G2* might also occur. Since *M* lies between *G1* and *G2*, it will be attained by purchasing a mixture of *G1* and *G2*.

Now suppose a new good (*G3*) is produced, also having characteristics *A* and *B*, but in proportions different from either *A* or *B*. We can suppose a unit of *G3* gives 2 units of *A* and 2 of *B*. *G3* is a more "powerful" good than either *G1* or *G2* since it contains more characteristics per unit than these. This is not relevant to the choice, however, until the price of *G3* is given. The place of *G3* in the system depends on its price. Suppose the price was $1.50. By spending all his budget on *G3*, the consumer could buy 8 units, obtaining 16 units of *A* and 16 of *B*. This is the point *Y* in the diagram. But it would be *inefficient* to consume *G3* at this price, since we can obtain 18 units of *A* and 18 of *B* by spending $6 on *G1* and $6 on *G2*—the point *X*.

Since the relationship between *X* and *Y* would be the same for all consumers on all budgets (but facing the same prices), a firm that introduced *G3* at a price of $1.50 would find no buyers. Suppose the price was now reduced to $1.20. The consumer with $12 could obtain 10 units, giving 20 units of *A* and 20 of *B*. This point (*G3* in the diagram) lies *beyond* the original frontier *G1-G2*, and now it is *X* which is clearly inefficient. The old frontier *G1-G2* is now replaced, since, by spending the budget on combinations of *G1* and *G3*, the consumer can attain characteristics collections along the line *G1-G3*, and also points along *G3-G2* by combining *G2* with *G3*. With the exception of the points *G1* and *G2* themselves, more of both characteristics can be attained by moving from any point on *G1-G2* to some point on either *G1-G3* or *G3-G2*. The frontier is now the bent line *G1-G3-G2*, and we may assume that the consumer of our example will choose some point like *N* on this frontier, attaining a higher indifference level than before.

We can conclude two important things from this simple example. First, that the place of a new good in the system depends on its price —it will sell only at a price sufficiently low to induce consumers to *switch* from combinations of *G1* and *G2* to combinations either of *G1* and *G3* or of *G2* and *G3*. Although the consumer of our example switches from a *G1-G2* combination to a *G1-G3* combination, thus dropping *G2* from his purchases, other consumers may switch from *G1-G2* to *G2-G3*, dropping *G1*. If preferences are dispersed over consumers, we can expect that all three goods will still be consumed. The second point is that, if a new good is introduced and actually sold, at least one consumer must be at a higher indifference level, and none at a lower, so long as all original goods are still sold at the original prices.

As mentioned in discussing oligopoly (Section 6.9), a great deal of competitive behavior among firms in a complex modern economy such as that of the United States consists of devising new products, or product variants. The above analysis gives a framework for examining this behavior from the demand side.

Chapter 8 is concerned with how the distribution of incomes is determined from the distribution of wealth and the prices of factors.

CONTENTS

8.1 Distribution   223
8.2 Wages   226
8.3 Other Factor Payments   230
8.4 Imperfectly Competitive Factor Markets   232

CHAPTER 8

INCOMES

8.1 Distribution

When the economy is in operation, goods are being produced and inputs are being used by the very large number of firms that compose the productive sector of the economy. Some of the goods being produced by one firm are used as inputs by other firms *(intermediate goods),* but other goods are not for such use as inputs (these are *final goods*). All firms use some inputs, such as labor, which are not produced by other firms (*primary inputs* or *factors of production*).

We are interested, in this chapter, in how final goods come to be distributed among consumers, that is, among people. This is the economic study of *distribution.*

Distribution in Economics. It is important to distinguish between what the economist means by distribution, and other uses of the word. In business terminology, "distribution" means how goods are got *to* consumers, the physical process of handling a washing machine, for example, between its leaving the factory and being installed in the home. Although the economist, when handling data, may adhere to the terminology of the statistics which list these processes as "distributive trades," he regards these simply as *production processes* in a theoretical setting. "Distribution" in economics is concerned with *how it is that a certain household can afford to own a washing machine, not with how the washing machine is physically transported to the home.*

A second use of the term that must be distinguished from our use is in a phrase like "income distribution." This often means the *size distribution* of income, such as what proportion of families have incomes between $8,000 and $10,000. Although size distribution interests us, we are chiefly interested in the prior problem of where the incomes are derived from.

Role of the Market. It would be possible to have the total output of final goods in the economy distributed without any use of the market. Everyone, for example, could simply be given a certain number of sacks of flour, a certain number of pounds of meat, and so on, provided the totals added up to the available production of the various goods. Such a distribution system exists in some simple societies and in some special subsocieties, such as the *kibbutzim* in Israel and some monasteries. It does not exist in any complex societies, not even the Soviet Union and other socialist economies.[1]

Most final goods, in all large societies, are distributed *through the market*. That is, consumers have incomes which they use to buy final goods, choosing the collections which they prefer at the market prices.

There may be some final goods in all societies which are not distributed through the market. Government services (such as police, defense, at the minimum) are not sold through the market but are distributed in other ways. Even in the United States there is an important nongovernment service that is not distributed through the market—commercial television and radio. The consumer does not "pay" for these services from his personal income, but from his willingness to watch and listen to advertising. This is one of the more egalitarian forms of distribution in the United States.

When almost all goods are distributed through the market, consumers are free to choose their preferred collections *subject to their budget constraints*. Thus the distribution of goods is ultimately determined by individual preferences and by the distribution of incomes.[2] We have already examined the general properties to be expected of consumer preferences and the general properties of demand that result when incomes are assumed to be given. Here we shall examine the way in which consumer incomes are determined.

Sources of Income. The chief way in which consumers obtain income is by sale of their personal services—labor income in the broadest sense. Almost three quarters of personal income in the United States is obtained by

---

[1] Socialist economies typically allocate *intermediate goods* in this fashion, but not most final goods.

[2] Actually on the distribution of *disposable incomes,* after taxes and quasi-taxes have been paid. See footnote 4.

sale of labor services to employers or by implicit sale of the proprietor's own labor to his profession or business.

Labor is not the only primary resource in the economy. There are others, such as land and capital.[3] The owners of these can obtain income by allowing others (or themselves) to use the resources in productive activity in return for rent and interest payments. Incomes from consumers lending their *wealth* accounts for about one eighth of personal incomes in the United States.

After a firm has paid for all the inputs it uses—intermediate goods, labor, capital, land—it may have a *residual profit,* the excess of total revenue over total cost. This residual may be distributed in a variety of ways, depending on the legal and social institutions. It might, for example, be distributed among the workers in the firm, as in a *cooperative,* or it might be regarded as accruing to the government in some general sense, as in public authority business enterprises. In a *private enterprise* economy, such as the United States, this residual is distributed to persons holding *claims* to a specified share of it. Usually these claims are transferable *stocks,* and the residual is distributed as *dividends* to the stockholders who own the claims. Even in the United States, dividends represent a very small proportion (4 per cent or so) of personal incomes.

Finally, some consumers obtain incomes by *transfer.* Through a variety of social service and similar arrangements, some consumers are simply *given* incomes even though they do not sell their labor and have no wealth from which to derive income. These are transfer incomes in the sense that they are not obtained through a market mechanism but by government giving the incomes to certain consumers and taxing other consumers to an equal amount.[4] Although transfer incomes are almost twice as important as dividend incomes in the United States, we shall not discuss these further since they are directly determined by social policy rather than the working of the economy.

Omitting transfer incomes from further consideration, the major

---

[3] Capital goods are produced by firms and are, in one sense, intermediate goods rather than primary resources. However, if we take the economy at a point in time, the capital goods then existing are not *currently* produced, and are not intermediate goods as far as a time period of a year or two is concerned. Over a period as long as a century, capital goods can be regarded as intermediate goods.

Although a good like electricity, which is produced almost at the instant it is used, is clearly an intermediate good, the definition is not clear for all cases. Distinctions of this kind, between intermediate goods and primary resources, are only made for convenience. In some economic models, labor is treated as a good produced by the use of consumption as an input, and even labor is then treated as an intermediate good!

[4] In the setting of income distribution, personal income taxes are precisely analogous to negative transfer incomes.

source of all incomes is from the sale of services (inputs from the point of firms), either labor services or the services of other productive resources. The income of a consumer from the sale of services depends on two things, the price at which he can sell, and the quantity he has available for sale. The distribution of income between consumers thus depends on the prices of the different types of service the consumer has for sale, and the *initial distribution* of saleable services among consumers.[5]

Distribution of Wealth. The initial endowment of potential raw labor hours (available time) is distributed more or less evenly. But the initial distribution of special abilities and special training, that give different types of labor services, is not uniform. The distribution of wealth (ownership of resources other than labor) depends on the history and the social and economic structure of the country, and may take any form. The economist's contribution to the discussion of income distribution is primarily that of analyzing factor prices rather than the distribution of wealth, and he thus has little to say in the form of predictions concerning the size distribution of income.[6]

8.2 Wages

The potential work force is determined by the population and whatever social and legal institutions determine which members of the population are free to seek work. These institutional constraints vary: in most developed countries, persons below a certain age limit cannot work, while the social permissibility of women working varies from one social group to another, as well as from country to country. At any given time, however, the potential work force is more or less determined.

Within the work force, the labor-leisure choice will determine how much, if at all, any member will wish to work, giving an aggregate *supply curve* for labor, assuming labor to be a single homogeneous input.

Given market prices for goods, the general competitive structure, the technology, and the distribution of capital and other resources (land, for example) among firms, each firm's demand curve for labor is determined

---

[5] If wealth is not privately owned, the return from it and also any residual profit (or surplus) can be distributed however the government chooses. The corresponding income payments then become transfer income.

[6] Economists and statisticians sometimes study empirical generalizations, of which the best known is *Pareto's Law,* about the way that the size distribution of income has been observed to behave in the past. This does not mean there is an economic *theory* of this distribution. In a private ownership economy, the size distribution of income obviously depends on the size distribution of wealth.

as in Chapter 6. From these can be derived an aggregate demand curve for labor, again assuming labor is a homogeneous input.

Thus we can analyze the market for labor, under competitive conditions, in terms of ordinary supply and demand with the wage rate as an equilibrium price.

The purpose of the present section is to examine various aspects of wages which are not covered by the central idea. These include the relationship between markets for different types of labor when it is not homogeneous; constraints on the working of the competitive market; and the observed persistence of disequilibrium in the market, giving unemployment.

If labor is not homogeneous, but takes a variety of forms which are not perfect substitutes in the production process, we can treat each type of labor as a separate input and derive the relevant demand curve. We can derive the supply curve for each type of labor, and then apply supply and demand analysis to each market, rather than to a general homogeneous labor market. However the markets for different types of labor are related in a special way, discussion of which provides a good example of the use of supply and demand analysis in unusual cases.

Skill Differentials. Let us simplify to two types of labor, "skilled" and "unskilled," which are different inputs into production. Like any two inputs, we assume some degree of substitutability due to the existence of alternative production processes employing different ratios of skilled to unskilled labor. Thus the demand curves for the two types of labor can be devised in the ordinary way and have no unusual properties.

On the supply side, however, there is a special asymmetrical link between the two markets. In the simplest case, all skilled workers can also work unskilled, while unskilled workers cannot obtain skilled employment. Let us suppose that the aggregate supply of labor is inelastic (all workers will accept work for whatever wage they can obtain), and that the number of skilled workers in the total is also fixed.

Denote the number of unskilled and skilled workers by U, S, respectively, and the wages and demand curves for unskilled, skilled labor by W_U, W_S and by D_U, D_S.

Because skilled workers can also work as unskilled, they operate (potentially) in both markets. Their opportunity cost in the skilled market is W_U, so the supply curve in the skilled market will be horizontal at wage W_U out to S, then vertical, since S is the number of skilled workers. This is shown in Figure 8.1(a), where the equilibrium is given at W_S with demand curve D_S.

In the unskilled market, the supply curve will be vertical at employ-

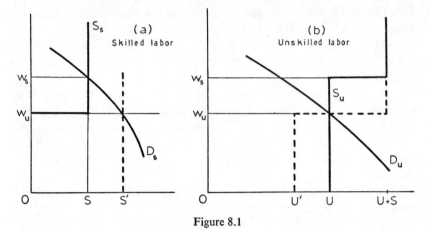

Figure 8.1

ment U up to wage level W_S. At this wage, skilled workers will enter the unskilled market so there will be another horizontal section of employment $U + S$, the total work force, when the supply curve will become vertical. This is shown in Figure 8.1(b), with equilibrium wage W_U under the given demand conditions represented by D_U.

The unskilled wage, in this simple case, puts a *floor* on the skilled wage, since no workers will accept skilled employment at less than the unskilled rate. But the skilled wage does not have the same effect on the unskilled wage, since unskilled workers cannot enter the skilled market. Thus the skilled wage cannot be less than the unskilled wage and the usual case will be that depicted in the figures, where there exists a *skill differential*. But it is possible for this differential to disappear. Suppose demand conditions remained unchanged, but some of the unskilled workers were trained to be skilled, so that the number of skilled workers increased to S', and of unskilled workers decreased to U'. As can be seen from the figure, the skilled wage would come down to equal the unskilled wage.

Insofar as obtaining skills involves some loss of income during a period of training and possibly fees for educational courses, the transfer of persons from unskilled to skilled status could be expected to stop *before* the skilled wage came all the way down to the unskilled. The cost of training represents an *investment* of the worker's money (or time, which could have been used to earn money) in a skill which is then more or less permanent. This has come to be referred to, in recent years, as *investment in human capital*. Unless the worker expects to obtain some return in the form of a wage differential here (but social prestige may be important in a less simplified case), he will not undertake the training.

It is possible to have the skilled wage *lower* than the unskilled wage if the situation is more complex. One reason may be that the "unskilled" labor really requires its own special abilities, such as physical strength, which the skilled worker does not have. Or a particular job may, like a good, possess its own *characteristics* in addition to the wage. A skilled job may be associated with desired characteristics, like pleasant working conditions or social prestige, that partly outweigh a lower wage to some, and so the supply of labor on the skilled market does not necessarily disappear at less than the unskilled wage.

Restrictions on Entry. Another factor that may result in a higher unskilled wage than skilled is *insulation* of the unskilled market from the entry of skilled workers. This involves one of the many forms of interference in the competitive market that exist in labor markets generally. The simplest situation would be monopoly control over the supply of unskilled labor by, say, a trade union. If only union members were allowed to work, either by law or by threat of economic coercion, persons in the skilled market could be prevented from entering the unskilled market if the skilled wage fell below the unskilled. Since the unskilled cannot enter the skilled market, the two markets are then independent, and the relative wages may bear any relation to each other.

Minimum Wages. Attempted restriction of entry is a common form of constraint on the working of competitive labor markets.[7] Another typical constraint is the *minimum wage.* This has the same general effect as any minimum price arrangement. If below the equilibrium price, it has no effect, and if above it results in excess supply (unemployment in this case). Normally it would be expected that the minimum wage would be effective only in the unskilled market (since skilled differentials are the rule), thus causing unemployment among the least skilled, but increasing the wage of those unskilled who are able to find jobs.

Unemployment of this kind can occur if, for example, the supply of unskilled labor in some market increases very greatly—large migration from rural to urban areas, for example. Even without minimum wage laws, the mechanism of the labor market may be such that wages do not fall readily to establish a new equilibrium, as we would expect in the market for a good. Wages are often said to be "sticky."

---

[7] Sometimes the term "skilled" may merely mean that entry into this occupation is restricted, perhaps by some requirement that employers would consider inessential. It is usually easier for skilled occupational groups to obtain official sanction (licenses, state examinations, and so on) for entry restrictions than it is for unskilled. Restrictions on entry into unskilled occupations depend more on sheer organizational strength of the relevant trade union.

Unemployment. It is not, however, appropriate to analyze widespread general unemployment by the simple market model. Since wages represent the greater part of personal incomes, general unemployment will result in a marked change in aggregate incomes and therefore in major shifts in the demand curves for goods and ultimately for labor. Unemployment in this setting requires an analysis taking into account simultaneous changes in all major variables of the economy. It is one of the problems studied in *macroeconomics*.

When unemployment arises in only some labor markets and is due to shifts in demand and supply to which the markets have not adjusted, it is said to be *structural,* and is amenable to partial analysis.

8.3 Other Factor Payments

Economists are less interested than they used to be in elaborate descriptive classifications of the various types of factor payments and in disputes about the "true" nature of profit or rent or interest.

If input markets are competitive, the prices for the inputs, whether intermediate goods or labor or other factors, are determined by supply and demand in the ordinary way. Special features of individual markets are due to particular properties, usually on the supply side.

Land, for example, has the special property that, in its fundamental sense as location and area, its supply to the economy is fixed. The supply curve is inelastic, and all changes in the price of land services *(rents)* are due to demand changes.

Economic Rent. Economists have found it useful to generalize the term *economic rent* to cover factor payments which, like land rent, are not necessary to attract those resources into the economy. Since the stock of buildings and machines in the economy at the beginning of any year is already fixed, and since the stock cannot be rapidly increased or decreased, the returns to the use of fixed capital are often called *quasi-rents* ("almost rents"). Although the population at any time is relatively fixed, people (unlike capital or land) require consumption, hence payments, to keep alive, so wages are not rents or quasi-rents.

A further generalization is to consider the factor payment as sometimes consisting of two parts, an *opportunity cost* and a *rent*. This division is applicable to a right angle supply curve, like the supply curve for skilled labor in Figure 8.1. To obtain any skilled labor at all, a wage equal to the unskilled wage (the *opportunity cost* of attracting workers into the skilled market) must be paid. Since the supply of skilled workers (at wages above the unskilled rate) is fixed, the excess of the skilled wage over the unskilled wage can be regarded as an *economic rent*. If workers are induced to undertake training as a result of the skill differential, the supply curve of skilled labor is no longer vertical and the difference $W_S - W_U$ is no longer a pure rent. It can, however, be regarded as a *quasi-rent* if the process of training is complex or long. Many variations on this particular theme are possible.

It is important to note a certain payment as an economic rent because reduction or removal of the pure rent element will not affect the physical distribution of resources. Reduction of the skill differential in the example above will not change the number of skilled workers, if the skill differential is a pure rent. Attempts to reduce skilled wages by *more* than the skill differential will, on the other hand, reduce the number of skilled workers to zero. Reduction of quasi-rents will have no immediate effect on resources, but may affect the long-run supply. This property of rents has some importance in relation to tax theory, since taxing of pure rents does not affect the supply of the resources to the economy.

Although a pure rent is a payment above the minimum necessary to attract a resource into the economy or a part of it, it is a *necessary* payment to the individual buyer, or for a particular use. The opportunity cost of attracting a resource to an individual buyer, as contrasted with the economy as a whole, is what the resource can obtain from other buyers.

The everyday term "rent" covers a complex of payments for various things, of which only a part is "pure" rent. The rent of an apartment is a payment to the landlord for a product—it is the price of an *output,* not of a factor. The landlord, who is a firm, has costs which include such current costs as heat and janitorial services, capital costs relating to the building, taxes, and also an element which is the rent of the land itself. He may be earning a residual profit over these costs, so the proportion of the total rent which is pure rent for the land may be quite small.

Profits and Return to Capital. In the examples we used in cost theory, the price for the *hire* of capital was symbolized by r, standing for Quasi-Rent or for Return. The net return on capital is sometimes regarded as *interest,* but we prefer to retain this term for its more basic connotation, the return on a loan in the financial sense. The relation between the return on capital and the rate of interest has been touched upon, but will not be seen in its complete form until we have discussed *time* in Chapter 11.

Profits have been treated throughout the book as a *residual,* not as a price. Economists sometimes use the term *normal profit* to mean a kind of price—the price which an entrepreneur (one who runs a firm) can receive for his services. Insofar as an entrepreneur can receive normal profit for operating some *other* firm, it represents his opportunity cost to the firm which he actually operates.

It seems better to treat the opportunity cost of the entrepreneur's executive abilities as a wage, and the opportunity cost of his own capital (if employed in the business) in the ordinary way, treating all the rest as a residual. This is what we have been doing.

8.4 Imperfectly Competitive Factor Markets

We have considered only competitive markets for inputs so far, although we have considered imperfectly competitive output conditions. The restrictions on entry into particular labor markets which were discussed in Section 8.2 did not destroy the essential competitive nature of those markets, they merely changed the supply conditions.

Imperfect competition can arise in the factor market from either the supply side or the demand side, or both. On the supply side, some input (an intermediate good) might be produced by a monopolist, or some primary input might be controlled in a monopoly fashion. This could be because, for example, all land suitable for some special crop was under single ownership, but we shall consider the more typical case in which the supply of some special type of labor is completely controlled by a union.

On the demand side, imperfect competition may arise because of the existence of a single buyer for a specific input *(monopsony)*, or of only a few buyers *(oligopsony)*. Since all firms producing the same product will require the same inputs, we will usually expect to have monopsony only if the firm is also a monopolist in its output market. Perfect competition in output markets with monopsony in input markets is, however, possible —as in the case of a mine or mill which is the only employer in a small, remote town.

Oligopsony can occur with oligopoly, but also with several monopolists who produce different products but use the same input.

Monopoly on the output side need not imply any monopsony or oligopsony on the input side, since a monopolist's inputs may well be the same as those of other firms. We have already been proceeding on the presumption that monopoly on the output side is commonly associated with competition in the input market.

The most extreme case of imperfect competition in a factor market will occur when there is monopoly on the supply side and monopsony or oligopsony on the demand side. This is a common situation in the United States and Europe, where the workers in a monopoly or oligopoly industry are organized into a strong union. Relations between the United Automobile Workers and the automobile manufacturers are of the monopoly-oligopsony kind, while relations between, say, a transit union and a city transit authority will be of a monopoly-monopsony kind.

The outcomes of such situations cannot be classified in any simple way, since they depend on the objects and aims of the union, and the bargaining process itself.

Simple Bargaining Example. To illustrate the above situation, consider the simplest possible example, of a monopolist whose only input is labor, an input controlled by a strong union.

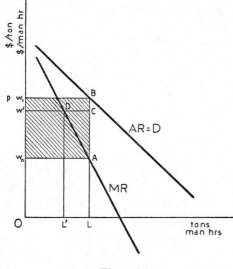

Figure 8.2

We shall simplify further by supposing the monopolist to have a straight line demand curve as in Figure 8.2. Since labor is the only input, we can expect constant average product of labor, equal to the marginal product. Suppose this is 1 ton per man-hour. Then the quantity of labor used is directly proportional to the output, and the horizontal axis in Figure 8.2 has been calibrated in man-hours (labor) as well as in tons (output).

The union is presumed to have a closed membership, which represents L man-hours of labor, and that the aim of the union is to maximize the income of its members, taking the working hours as fixed.

The output corresponding to L man-hours of labor (L tons, in this simple case) will be exactly purchased by consumers at a price equal to $p\$$ per ton. Obviously, the union cannot extract a wage greater than $w_1 = p\$$ per man-hour, since the monopolist would take a loss at any greater wage and go out of business.

On the other hand, the union can obtain a wage w_0 without direct confrontation with the monopolist simply by using its restrictive power. Since A is on the marginal revenue curve, and since the wage is the only marginal cost, an order by the union that its members should not work for a wage other than w_0 would result in the monopolist voluntarily choosing to employ exactly L man-hours. The quantity of labor L is the monopolist's profit maximizing choice if the wage is AL.

But suppose the union wanted to achieve a wage w'. If it simply set this as the going wage, the monopolist would choose to employ only L' man-hours (corresponding to D on its marginal revenue curve), so it can achieve this wage only by *bargaining*.

The typical bargaining procedure would be for the union to demand that the monopolist pay wage w' *and* employ L man-hours of labor, or the union will withdraw all labor. The union, in effect, offers a *point supply*, the point C in the diagram, rather than a perfectly elastic supply curve at wage w'. Such a bargaining move is often called an *all-or-nothing* offer.

Will the monopolist accept the union's demand? If it does so, it will certainly not be in its profit-maximizing position, since it is off its marginal revenue curve. For profit maximizing, the firm would be willing to pay a wage w_0 for employment L, or offer employment L' for a wage w'. But the firm would make *some* profit if it accepted the union demand, since its average profit per unit would be BC. This would be preferable to closing down and making no profit.

The outcome of the bargaining would, however, depend on other factors in addition. The firm might choose to close down temporarily (that is, to initiate a lockout, or to accept a strike) in the belief that cessation of all wage payments will cause the union eventually to reduce its demand.

In a case like this, the union might be able to obtain a wage anywhere between w_0 and w_1, depending on the relative bargaining strength of the firm and the union.

Bargaining and Distribution. This example, the outcome of which can be varied by making different assumptions about union objectives, has been given to establish the basic proposition:

With imperfectly competitive factor markets, the distribution of income between factors no longer depends on factor prices determined by simple supply and demand analysis, but on the outcome of complex bargaining processes.

The analogy of a monopoly-monopsony situation in a factor market to a duopoly situation in an output market should be noted. In both cases, the outcome depends on how the rival is expected to react to a move by one side.

Chapter 9 considers the economy as a whole, rather than the individual parts of the economy that have been studied in the previous chapters.

CONTENTS

9.1 Putting the Pieces Together   237
9.2 General Equilibrium   240
9.3 Information and Decentralization   243
9.4 Stability and Attainment of Competitive Equilibrium   247
9.5 Simplified Models of the Economy   249
9.6 The Two-Good Two-Factor Economy   251

236

CHAPTER 9

THE ECONOMY AS A SYSTEM

9.1 Putting the Pieces Together

Our analysis so far has been devoted to the discussion of the behavior and decision contexts of the individual pieces or components of the economic system. These components are:

(1) *Consumers,* who receive incomes obtained most typically by the sale of their labor services, but also from the sale of other factor services and from shares in residual profits. They allocate the expenditure of these incomes on the purchase of the available goods in accordance with their preferences, but subject to their budget constraints that depend on prices. Furthermore, their labor-leisure choices and thus their incomes are not entirely independent of the prices of final goods. In a *private ownership economy,* all factors are owned and controlled by consumers, and all residual profits distributed among them. In a *mixed economy,* some factors are owned by "government" in the broad sense, some by consumers. In all economies, consumers have ultimate disposition over their labor services at least.

(2) *Producers,* who use inputs obtained either from other producers *(intermediate goods)* or from consumers or governments *(primary factors),* combine these in accordance with a *technology,* and produce outputs. We normally refer to the producers as *firms* in an economy such as that of the United States.

(3) *Markets,* in which producers interact with each other and with consumers. In the economist's basic model of the competitive economy, it

237

is assumed that markets provide the only points of economic interaction between other components of the economy.

(4) *The government,* which is assumed to be the only component of the economy capable of *coercion* and which can therefore do such things as collect taxes and lay down rules by which consumers, producers and markets must operate. In this abstract sense, the government includes not only federal, state and local governments, and all the various public authority agencies, but even private bodies (such as the New York Stock Exchange) which perform regulation with implicit or explicit government blessing.

In this chapter we shall be concerned primarily with fitting together consumers, producers and markets. The government, which can fit itself in as it chooses, is not discussed.

For a centrally planned economy, the basic problems of fitting together are primarily those of *feasibility,* that is, whether the outputs planned to achieve some goal can actually be produced with the given technology and available resources. There are also problems as to which feasible configuration of the economy is "best" in some sense. This is the problem of *optimality.*[1]

If we have a *competitive economy* (by which is usually meant a *perfectly* competitive economy), a different set of problems arise. Here we must be concerned with *compatibility.* Is the behavior assumed of each individual consumer in a competitive economy compatible with the behavior of every other consumer, with that of every producer, and with equilibrium in every market?

To be more specific, we are interested in whether there can *always* be found prices for all goods and all factors such that there is equilibrium in *every* market when:

(a) Each consumer freely chooses his preferred collection subject to his budget constraint, which is in turn determined by his initial endowment of resources (including time), their prices, his share of residual profits, and the prices of goods.

(b) Each producer freely maximizes his profits subject to the technology and any input limitations he faces and to the market conditions for his inputs and outputs.

If such prices can be found, these, together with the quantities produced and consumed of all goods and the quantities of all factors employed for all firms and all individuals, constitute a *general equilibrium* of the economy. The term can also be applied to the state of the economy under these conditions.

---

[1] Problems of optimality are discussed in Chapter 10.

Such an equilibrium need not be *unique*. There may be other prices and quantities which also constitute an equilibrium. In particular, if there are constant returns to scale in production and no input limitations on individual firms, we may well have unique relative prices, a unique list of quantities consumed and services provided by individuals and unique *aggregate* production levels of each good, but an infinite number of ways in which the production is divided among individual firms. This is because the size of an individual firm is indeterminate, even though the "size" of the industry is not. All of the policy implications concerning general equilibrium and welfare are quite independent of how production is divided among the firms in this case, provided the industry is, in fact, competitive.

The Network of Interconnections. Finding out whether the pieces all fit together in this way is not a simple matter, since all are interconnected. Consumer incomes, which determine the demand for goods, are primarily determined by the prices of factors. These factor prices are determined (with perfect competition) by supply and demand in factor markets. But producers' demands for inputs depend on the prices at which they sell their outputs. These, in turn, depend on demand and supply conditions in the goods markets. But demand in the goods markets depends on consumers' incomes, thus on factor prices, and we have come full circle. Furthermore, some part of consumer incomes depends on residual profits, which are determined only after both input and output prices are determined.

The interconnections do not only go from incomes to factor markets to production to goods markets back to incomes, but occur between different goods markets and different factor markets. The demand for labor depends not only on production levels, but also on the quantities of capital and other factors. The demand for one good depends on the prices of other goods, so the goods markets are cross-connected in the same way.

Thus, in general equilibrium, the wage (for example) must:

(i) be exactly the wage at which consumers, exercising their labor leisure choice, choose to supply the number of man-hours actually used,

(ii) generate exactly the amount of labor income which, when combined with income from other sources, gives consumers the incomes at which they will just buy the goods produced at the equilibrium prices,

(iii) be exactly the wage at which producers, given the equilibrium outputs and prices, will choose to employ the number of man-hours consumers chooses to supply,

(iv) be exactly the wage at which, taking account of alternative production processes, the producers will choose to combine the actual quantities of capital (and other inputs) with the equilibrium quantity of labor.

Analogous conditions must be satisfied by the price of every good and every other factor in the economy.

It follows that

All the general equilibrium prices and quantities must be determined together.

We cannot find one price, then another, then another, and so on, since every price must be appropriate in relation to every other. The partial analysis which is so typical a technique of microeconomics is, in principle, unworkable!

Partial Analysis. Our justification for partial analysis, in which we examine one market or the supply or demand conditions of one good, while supposing that incomes, other prices, and production conditions remain unchanged, is based on the *relative* smallness of interconnection effects, for a single market. In discussing the watermelon market (Chapter 2), we really accepted that, in principle, a change in the price of watermelons would change incomes of watermelon producers and thus average incomes. But if the incomes from selling watermelons are a very small part of the total (in the United States, less than one ten thousandth part of total income is derived from watermelons[2]), the effect of the price of watermelons on aggregate consumer incomes can be neglected. Thus we can analyze the watermelon market in terms of demand curves that assume constant average consumer incomes.

Partial analysis becomes less and less appropriate the more the effect of changes in the particular market on the economy as a whole. It is ultimately a matter of *fact,* not of hypothesis, whether partial analysis is appropriate in any given case.

9.2 General Equilibrium

The preceding section introduced the idea of general equilibrium, of a simultaneous equilibrium of all markets in the economy such that all consumers and all producers were acting in accordance with their respective aims, subject to the ordinary constraints. In this section we shall discuss whether such an equilibrium can be expected to exist.

---

[2] In 1965, the value of watermelon production was about $46 million. Only part of this is the income of growers, who must first deduct costs. Total disposable personal income in the United States in 1965 was $465 billion.

The idea of general equilibrium in the full sense was introduced by Walras[3] although, like most ideas, it had antecedents. Walras not only described the general equilibrium, but also enquired as to whether we could be confident of its existence. The answer he gave was a step in the appropriate direction, but not complete. Nevertheless, we shall examine the Walrasian argument.

Only Relative Prices Necessary. Before doing so, we must take note of an important property of the basic model of the competitive economy:

If the competitive economy is in general equilibrium, doubling (or taking any multiple) of all prices (factor and goods prices) will also give an equilibrium, with exactly the same quantities as before.

We have seen (Chapter 7) that doubling all prices facing a consumer, while doubling his money income, will leave his budget constraint, and thus his chosen collection, unchanged. If we double the prices of all inputs used by a firm, and double the price of its output, its marginal cost at every output level will be exactly doubled and, since its price has doubled, its profit maximizing output will be the same as before. Its profit, in money terms, will be exactly doubled. Since factor prices and profits are doubled, consumers' money incomes will also be doubled. This completes the circle, and we have a new equilibrium with exactly the same quantities as before.

It is only *relative* prices that are important in determining equilibrium.

The Walrasian Analysis. Having made this point, we proceed to the Walrasian argument. Suppose there are 1,000 goods and factors, so that there are 1,000 prices to be determined. Supply and demand in each market depend in principle on all 1,000 prices, but there are exactly 1,000 markets for determining these prices. Just as, in elementary algebra, we can usually expect solution of 2 unknowns by 2 equations, so 1,000 prices can presumably be determined from the equilibrium conditions (quantity supplied equals quantity demanded) of 1,000 markets.[4]

This is *too* neat. Since it is only relative prices that are important, we

---

[3] Walras was also mentioned in relation to the material of Chapter 3.

[4] Strictly speaking, equality between the number of equations and the number of unknowns is neither necessary nor sufficient to guarantee a solution, even with the linear equations of elementary algebra. A system of *n linearly independent* linear equations in *n* unknowns always has a solution. The solution may involve negative values, of course, although negative values for prices or quantities have no meaning in most economic models. Modern approaches to general equilibrium analysis (see later in the section) do not count equations. The equation counting approach is discussed here because it is still part of the folklore of economics.

ought to be able to determine only 999 prices independently, since there are 999 relative prices. The good relative to which the other 999 prices are measured is referred to as the *numeraire*.

The difficulty disappears when we take account of the budget constraint that must be satisfied by every consumer. When the consumer has purchased his desired quantities of all goods but one, the expenditure on the last good must be equal to what is left of his income. It follows that when the markets for the 999 goods are all in equilibrium, that for the numeraire must *automatically* be in equilibrium. Thus there are really only 999 *independent* market equilibrium conditions, just matching the 999 independent relative prices.[5]

Modern Analysis. For reasons that are too technical to explain here (one is the possibility of boundary equilibria), the above Walrasian argument, convincing though it may sound, is not complete.

A properly formulated approach to the problem of the existence of a competitive equilibrium has been developed only in recent years.[6] This requires mathematical techniques of an advanced kind, so we shall do no more than note what has been proved by these methods:

An equilibrium exists for a perfectly competitive economy under almost all initial distributions of wealth, provided there are no indivisibilities or increasing returns to scale.

The "almost every" qualification is quite weak, ruling out only initial distributions that leave some consumers with nothing of value (not even labor) to sell and who receive no transfer income.

It is important to note what is *not* covered in the above statement:

(1) Equilibrium cannot be guaranteed if there are major indivisibilities or increasing returns to scale.

(2) Equilibrium cannot be guaranteed for an economy with *imperfect* competition.

(3) The statement gives conditions under which the existence of equilibrium can be *guaranteed*. This does not mean that it is *impossible* to have equilibrium under conditions in (1) and (2).

(4) Economists may, at some later stage, prove that equilibrium exists under conditions (1) and (2). We cannot do so at the moment.

Existence Proofs. Why should we be interested in proving the existence of equilibrium? Some have argued that, since the real economy is observed to

---

[5] But see the comments in Footnote 4.

[6] The modern work on the existence and stability of the competitive equilibrium, in which the central figure has been K. J. Arrow, involves mathematical techniques at an advanced level. The general economist simply needs to know that such proofs exist.

be in equilibrium, that is all we need to know. This is a very naive argument. In the first place, the economy is in operation, but not necessarily in equilibrium. The presence of unemployment (excess supply in the labor market) is a denial of the presumption of an equilibrium condition. In the second place, and much more important:

There is not now, and seems never to have been, any economy that could be considered as perfectly competitive.

If, indeed, the economy of the United States is in equilibrium, it is not the equilibrium of a perfectly competitive economy, but of an imperfectly competitive one. Why interest ourselves at all in the perfectly competitive economy, then? The answer will be clear after the reader has studied Chapter 10. The perfectly competitive economy has certain *ideal* properties in terms of welfare and efficiency. The competitive economy as an ideal would, however, be useless if it could not be guaranteed to work, that is, to have an equilibrium.

It is precisely because the United States is imperfectly competitive that we are interested in the proposition: Would it still work if it was perfectly competitive?

9.3 Information and Decentralization

The economy is a highly complex system composed of a very large number of individual decision making units whose decisions cover a very large number of goods and factors. In the United States, in the mid-sixties, there were approximately:

57,000,000 households,[7]

11,000,000 firms,[8]

3,000 different goods and factors at minimum.[9]

All the decision makers must make compatible decisions with respect to all goods, if the economy is to be at equilibrium. We know that the United States economy works, in some sense, although it is imperfectly competitive and may never be in equilibrium. We also know that a system

---

[7] Census data. The number of consumer decision units is larger than the number of households.

[8] Department of Commerce data. The figure given is the number of legal business entities (sole proprietorships, partnerships, corporations). It is representative of, not necessarily identical with, the number of firms in the economist's sense.

[9] There some 2,200 items in the official wholesale price index, 500 in the retail price index, and the Bureau of Labor Statistics counts about 350 different labor markets. In terms of the most rigorous definition of a single good (viewed as perfectly homogeneous), the number of distinct goods is probably enormous. An estimate of 100,000 would be quite low.

of this kind would possess a *competitive* equilibrium unless the prevalence of indivisibilities was too strong.

Centralized Control.[10] Let us consider an imaginary economy of the same general size as that of the United States, but without the indivisibilities that we know to be characteristic of the American technology. This economy would have a general equilibrium configuration under competitive conditions.

If we supposed the "government" knew all the preference maps of all the consumers, the production technology, and the initial distribution of factors and claims on residuals, then it might compute the prices and quantities corresponding to the equilibrium. The computation would show:

(i) the price of every good and factor,

(ii) the amount produced by every producer of every good, and the inputs of all factors used by all producers,[11]

(iii) the amount consumed of every good, and supplied of every factor, by every consumer.

The computation could also show, on the basis of the equilibrium quantities produced and consumed, the actual deliveries of each good from each producer to each consumer, and of factors from each consumer to each producer.

The *quantities* derived from this computation are precisely those that correspond to equilibrium, so that the government could, without using any market transactions or prices at all, simply order producers to make the deliveries of goods, and consumers those of factors, that were shown by the computation. Thus, *in principle,* a fully centralized system could be organized to achieve exactly the configuration of the economy represented by the competitive equilibrium.

Given the figures for the United States, this would involve issuing up to 210 *billion* orders concerning delivery of a particular good to, or factor by, a particular consumer.

Partial Decentralization. Now consider an alternative approach open to the same centralized authority. It could issue a general instruction to all producers that they were to accept announced prices as given and to pro-

---

[10] This is not meant as a description of any real economy that uses central planning. Neither the information available to, nor the aims of, the governments of such economies are the same as in our example.

[11] But if there are constant returns to scale and no input limitations on individual firms, output in each industry can be divided arbitrarily (equal shares, for example) among the individual firms.

duce whatever output maximized the difference between total revenue and total cost, buying inputs and selling outputs at the announced prices. Consumers are presumed always to act in accordance with their preferences, and thus need no instructions.

Having laid down the general rule of producer behavior, the government would then announce, as the ruling prices, the computed equilibrium prices.

Again, the configuration of the economy would be exactly that of the competitive equilibrium, but achieved this time by the issuance of a general rule (which could be a standing rule), and the announcement of only 3 *thousand* prices. It does not matter whether the producers are government agencies or private firms, provided they obey the rule.

From a comparison of the two schemes described above, we can see that:

Any equilibrium configuration of the economy could be attained under central direction either

(a) by exact scheduling of all quantities of all goods to be transacted between all producers and consumers, or,

(b) by a general rule accompanied by a list of prices.

Prices as Information. In other words, all the *information* necessary to achieve the general equilibrium configuration can be conveyed by *prices alone,* once behavior rules are established.[12] Note that the essence of these rules is that the prices be accepted as inviolable information parameters and no attempt is made to influence them by behavior comparable to that of imperfect competition. As shown by our example, prices are very efficient as information conveyers since there is only one price for each good and this is universal. Individual orders do not have to be issued, as in the direct allocation method, and the price list need only be published in the newspaper.

In effect, the fully centralized decision maker can be replaced by decentralized decision makers, who decide on the detailed production and allocation needs of their own relatively small part of the economy. The decentralized decision makers can be *induced* to act as desired by feeding them appropriate price information, instead of being *ordered* by detailed individual orders. They must, of course, be under general instructions to obey the rules.

Prices which are devised centrally with the object of inducing large numbers of individual decision makers to behave in a certain way are

---

[12] In terms of information theory, the behavior rules are necessary for the price information to be correctly *decoded* into working instructions.

shadow prices.[13] Although prices are not determined centrally in the United States, large corporations which have many divisions using each other's products as intermediate goods are moving towards the use of shadow prices to ensure the proper allocation of these goods. Recent developments in socialist economies have been towards the use of shadow price methods in place of detailed allocation plans.

Role of Markets. Although shadow prices enable a central authority to induce a particular equilibrium configuration, while leaving detailed decisions to be made away from the center, the authority must still *compute* the appropriate prices. This is where the special features of the market economy become apparent. If all works well, the actual *market prices* will be exactly the shadow prices that would be computed. In other words:

The competitive economy computes its own shadow prices.

Thus we can regard markets as not only equating demand and supply for individual goods, but also as generating price information on which individual decision makers can act in a manner compatible with each other.

If firms are *profit maximizing,* they will obey the rule as to choosing the output at which the difference between total revenue and total cost is a maximum, but will accept prices as fixed items of information only if they are also in *perfect competition.* Whereas a centralized economy can order the National Automobile Works to treat the shadow price of automobiles as fixed (and thus act *as if* it were a perfectly competitive firm), a monopolist in a private enterprise economy can be expected to use his monopoly power.

The "competitive equilibrium" can, in principle be achieved by a fully centralized system, or a decentralized system using shadow prices (in both cases centralized computation is required), or by a market economy (computing its own shadow prices). In practice, no existing computer could solve the centralized system, even if the requisite consumer information were available. The market economy has problems of its own, which we shall discuss in the next section.

---

[13] The concept of "shadow prices" has grown out of modern mathematical theory of optimization, especially the particular case known as *linear programming.* The solution of any problem in terms of *quantities* was found always to be associated with an "equivalent" solution (the *dual*) in terms of variables having all the properties of prices. For an exposition of the elements of linear programming, involving only basic algebra, see: Dorfman, Samuelson, and Solow: *Linear Programming and Economic Analysis,* McGraw-Hill,1958, Chapters 1, 2.

9.4 Stability and Attainment of Competitive Equilibrium

As pointed out in the study of the single market (Chapter 3), an equilibrium may *exist* in the sense that an equilibrium configuration is *possible,* but it may not automatically be either *attained or maintained.* The same is true for the general equilibrium of the competitive economy.

We have already noted the conditions under which an economy would possess an equilibrium configuration with perfect competition. If it could be assumed that the known indivisibilities in the technology of the United States economy were not sufficient to rule out a competitive equilibrium, such a configuration would be possible for it. We know that the present state of the United States economy is not that configuration, because of the prevalence of imperfect competition.

If an economy was in a state of competitive equilibrium, we should be interested in whether it would remain in that state when subject to the inevitable random events that occur. That is, we would wish to know whether the competitive economy was a *stable self-regulating system.*

Attainment of Competitive Equilibrium. If a competitive equilibrium is considered desirable, but not actually achieved, we are interested in whether it has any automatic tendency to attain that equilibrium. Commencing from the current configuration of the United States, attainment of a competitive equilibrium would involve:

  (i) attainment of the conditions of perfect competition,
  (ii) attainment of equilibrium under those competitive conditions.

The two phases are separate. The conditions of perfect competition might be achieved (every firm becoming a passive price-taker), with the economy failing to achieve equilibrium (severe unemployment, for example).

Perfection of Competition. With regard to (i), we saw in Chapter 6 that a monopolist tends to generate his own potential competition unless his monopoly position is sustained by legal or other *noneconomic* barriers to entry. To this extent, monopoly could be considered to generate potential self-destruction. The industrial history of the United States suggests, however, that monopolies generate only enough competition to become oligopolies and do not move all the way to anything resembling perfect competition. Even antitrust laws and other government attempts to "improve" competition have created oligopolies rather than competitive industries. Thus, although there is no complete analysis on this topic, most (but not all) economists would doubt the existence of any *automatic* tendency of imperfect competition to become perfect.

Stability. Let us suppose that competitive conditions exist. Will the equilibrium be attained and maintained? Automatic attainment of equilibrium and stability of equilibrium are very close to being the same. If there is an automatic mechanism that moves the economy from *any* disequilibrium position to equilibrium, then the economy will move to equilibrium whether or not it had been there in the first place. The equilibrium is said to be *globally stable* in this case. Sometimes we may have only *local* stability, when equilibrium will be attained automatically only from states of the economy already very close to it.

In Chapter 3, we examined the stability of the single market. It was stated that a continuous adjustment back to equilibrium, with no delay, and at a rate proportional to the deviation from equilibrium, would give stability. The stability of all markets taken together can be shown to be globally stable under analogous adjustment conditions, provided all goods are gross substitutes. On the other hand, lags in adjustment coupled with over-response can create an unstable market system, just as in the "cobweb" model of the single market. Since we have no theoretical backing for supposing adjustment processes to be of any particular kind, and almost no empirical studies, we must consider the stability of the competitive system an open question.

Disequilibrium and Collapse. It is important for the reader to distinguish between instability and collapse. The very simple models used to illustrate stability problems (like the cobweb model) show the unstable market collapsing completely at the slightest provocation. This is due to the sheer simplicity of the model used. There are many reasons for supposing that, if prices move sufficiently far away from equilibrium in real markets, restoring forces which were not apparent for small deviations will then come into operation. The boundedness of incomes is one of these. The "reserve forces" may not move the economy back to equilibrium (because they may disappear again as the deviations become more moderate), but will keep disequilibrium within bounds. Formal analysis on this matter is almost nonexistent, but there seems a strong presumption that any instability in the economy is essentially *bounded*. Perhaps the unemployment levels in the 'thirties represented the boundary of disequilibrium.

Speed of Adjustment. Another aspect of stabilization is the *speed* with which equilibrium is regained. It has often been argued that even long periods of high unemployment do not imply the lack of a stabilizing process, only that the adjustment is slow. The same has been argued concerning the self-destruction of monopolies (or the inevitability of their growth); that it will occur, but slowly. For practical purposes there may be little difference between no adjustment and very slow adjustment. From the policy point of view, an automatic stabilizing mechanism is useful only if it works with sufficient speed. Otherwise, a stabilizing policy must be imposed on the system just as if no automatic tendencies existed, although the degree of regulation may be smaller if the economy is tending in the appropriate direction.

Thus, although the vision of the competitive equilibrium may be very attractive, economists do not yet have a clear answer as to whether the economy will automatically attain, and maintain, this equilibrium. Nor do they have a clear answer as to whether the imperfection of competition has an inbuilt tendency to increase or decrease. In neither case is there any general assessment of the possible speeds of adjustment.

9.5 Simplified Models of the Economy

Because of the fantastic complexity of the complete economic system, and because partial analysis of isolated small portions of the system are inappropriate in many cases, the economist often wishes to give a simplified model that represents some of the character of the economy as a system.

Macroeconomics. One class of such models are *macroeconomic* models. These are studied in macroeconomics texts and in most texts on the principles of economics, so we do not need to discuss them here. In such models, the production sector is highly simplified into an amorphous sector producing a single aggregate good ("output" or "national product") and the analysis is centered on the choice between spending and saving, on money, the rate of interest and investment decisions, and on government policies that affect the aggregate behavior of the economy.

Input-Output. By way of contrast, *input-output* or *Leontief*[14] models concentrate entirely on production, divided into a large number of sectors. A single process is assumed for each industry, with many inputs, almost all of which are intermediate goods. Such models illustrate extremely well the importance of considering interconnections when intermediate goods are involved. For example, suppose that there are only two sectors, "manufacturing" and "mining," and that each requires some of the other's product as one of its own inputs. Consider the problem of producing, say, 100 units of manufactures for consumers (final demand), but no mining

---

[14] For a discussion of these models which uses elementary algebra, see Chapter 9 of Dorfman, Samuelson, and Solow (reference in footnote 13).

output for final demand. To supply manufacturing, we would nevertheless have to operate the mining industry at some level. But, since mining uses manufactured goods, we would have to produce *more than* 100 units of manufactures in order to supply mining and still have 100 units left for final demand. Given actual data (the *input coefficients*) showing how much mining output is required per unit of manufactures and how much manufacturing output is required per unit of mining, we could compute (by solving two simultaneous equations in this case) the actual level at which manufacturing must be operated to leave 100 units to satisfy final demand.

Since an input-output model will prevent a planner falling into the error of supposing he can work out the resource requirements for one sector without solving simultaneously for all sectors, it has been used chiefly for planning purposes. Data can be obtained by direct observations on the economy (assuming that the process actually being used in each industry will remain the only process used), and quantitative planning programs can be computed. Tables of input-output data are published for the United States and the techniques are also used for planning by large firms whose activities can be sectored in an appropriate way.

Input-output models do not, however, take account of possible substitution between processes, of individual resource limitations, or of indivisibilities. They have little theoretical content, apart from the general idea expressed in our simple example, but give quantitative answers to quantitative problems, from quantitative data.

Macro-microeconomics. The type of simplified model most directly related to microeconomics is the class that we may refer to as *macro-microeconomic* models. These models have been in use as long as microeconomic analysis.

In a macro-microeconomic model, we act *as though* the economy has a very much smaller number of goods or factors than is actually the case. A common example, much used in international trade theory, is the *two-good two-factor* model. In this model, we carry out a full general equilibrium analysis exactly as it would be for an economy that really produced only two goods and used only two factors. We know that all economies produce more than two goods, and that there are more than two factors, but we justify the simplification on the ground that we can handle the analysis very much more easily and that the working of the model is, somehow, "representative" of the working of an economy with many goods. A model of this kind is set out in the following section.

In many cases we may have *backup theorems* that assure us that the results for *n* goods are quite analogous to those for 2 goods. This is certainly true of the two-good analysis of consumer behavior, and the two-input analysis of production, the basic components of the two-good, two-factor general equilibrium model.

In other cases, we assume that the "goods" are *aggregates* over some class of goods sharing an important common property, the property depending on the use to which the analysis is put. An important backup theorem assures us that a group of goods (or factors) whose prices all change in the same proportion can be treated, for many purposes, as a single aggregate good. Backup theorems are not always applicable, and macro-microeconomic models must be handled with due caution.

The caution is especially important in using *partial* analysis in a macro-microeconomic model, since effects that are considered negligible for a very small part of the economy may not be so for an aggregate. For example if, instead of the watermelon market in Chapter 2, we had considered the market for an aggregate, "farm products," it would not be possible to carry out the analysis on the assumption that the farm wage rate was independent of the price or quantity of farm products as a whole.

Almost all *empirical* work involving markets, consumer behavior, or production, is carried out on macro-microeconomics models. Most market studies are for an aggregate of similar but not identical goods, or even over much broader aggregates such as "automobiles," or "clothing."

However, in spite of all the problems (many of which have not been fully investigated), almost all applications of microeconomics involve the use of what is, in fact, a macro-microeconomic model of some kind.

9.6 The Two-Good Two-Factor Economy

We can illustrate the use of macro-microeconomic analysis by considering a simple general equilibrium model in which there are two factors and in which two goods are produced. We shall concentrate on the input markets in the model.

The fundamental assumptions are:

(1) The quantity of each resource is fixed to the economy as a whole (no leisure effects, for example), but it can be freely transferred between production of the two goods.

(2) Each good is produced separately (no joint products) in its own industry and requires the use of both resources. There is a uniform technology in each industry and isoquants are of the smoothly curved (many process) kind.

(3) Input markets are competitive and there are no input limitations on individual firms or industries, only on the economy as a whole. The model is, in this sense, "long run."

To simplify the wording of the ensuing discussion we shall call the two factors "labor" and "capital," although the analysis is quite general. The two goods will simply be referred to as *A* and *B*.

Since the quantities of the two factors are fixed to the economy as a whole, we can use a variant of the Edgeworth box diagram which was discussed (for a different purpose) in Section 7.10.

Figure 9.1 is such a box, with labor on the horizontal axes and

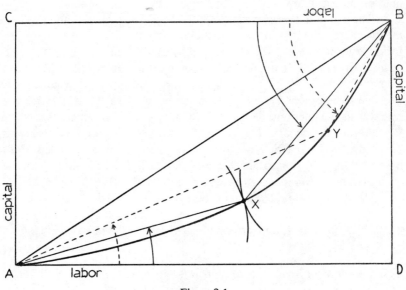

Figure 9.1

capital on the vertical. Any point in the box represents an allocation of the available resources between the two industries. Allocations to industry *A* are measured from *A* as origin, allocations to industry *B* from *B* as origin.

Just as we drew indifference curves for the two consumers in the earlier version of the box, we can draw isoquants for the production of each good in this case, *A*-isoquants relative to *A* as origin, *B*-isoquants relative to *B*. Outputs of the goods for any point in the box are given by the *A*- and *B*-isoquants which pass through that point.

Equilibrium Allocations. Since the economy is competitive, equilibrium allocations and input prices will satisfy the competitive conditions. These are:

(a) Quantity demanded (from both industries together) equals quantity supplied (the fixed totals), for both capital and labor. Thus the total available quantities of both inputs will be exactly used up between the two industries.

(b) Each industry will employ capital and labor in the least cost proportions—that is, in the proportions for which the marginal rate of substitution (ratio of the marginal products) is equal to the input price ratio. Since the input prices (w = wage rate, r = price of capital services) must be the same for both industries because we have competitive input markets, we must have, at equilibrium:

$$MPL_A/MPK_A = MPL_B/MPK_B = w/r.$$

From the ordinary isoquant properties, the ratio MPL/MPK ($=$ MRS) for given inputs is equal to the slope of the tangent to the isoquant at the point in question. Thus any point representing a competitive equilibrium must be such that the A- and B-isoquants through the point have the same slope—that is, it must be a point at which an A-isoquant and a B-isoquant are tangent, if both goods are being produced.

It is possible, of course, that only one of the goods is being produced. Taking this possibility into account, the equilibrium points in the box will be either points A or B (where only one good is produced—B at the point A, and A at the point B), or points like X in Figure 9.1 at which an A-isoquant is tangent to a B-isoquant.

As in the consumer model, there will be a set of points at which there is tangency between an A- and a B-isoquant, and we can join these points by a curve which must pass through A, X, and B in the figure. For convenience, we shall refer to this as the *contract curve* as in the bargaining model, although strictly speaking it should be described as an *input-market equilibrium curve.*

Relative Factor Intensities. Because the properties of production functions under constant returns to scale everywhere are very regular, we have drawn the contract curve as a smooth and regular bowed curve in Figure 9.1, rather than the more irregular curve of the earlier Figure 7.17 (page 217). However the particular shape given is the expression of an important relationship between the technologies in industries A and B, which we now turn to investigate.

Consider the point X and the lines AX, BX. The slope of AX *relative to AD* represents the capital/labor ratio in industry A at the point X, since the height of X above AD represents the amount of capital employed in industry A at the point X and the horizontal distance of X from AC represents the labor employed in A. Similarly the slope of BX *relative to BC* represents the capital/labor ratio in industry B at the equilibrium point X, since capital and labor in B are measured from BD, BC as axes.

It is seen that the capital/labor ratio in industry A is less than the slope of the diagonal (which is the ratio of capital to labor in the economy as a whole), while the capital/labor ratio in B is greater than the ratio for the economy as a whole. Thus the capital/labor ratio is greater in industry B than in industry A at the point X, *although the marginal rate of substitution between the inputs is the same for both industries at* X.

Since, at points corresponding to the *same* marginal rates of substitution, the capital/labor ratio is greater in industry B than in industry A, we say that B is *capital-intensive* relative to A. If we concentrate on the inverse labor/capital ratio, we can see that, by a similar argument, A is more *labor-intensive* than B.

If B remains the capital-intensive good, and A the labor-intensive good, over all marginal rates of substitution, it can be seen that the contract curve will always lie *on the same side of the diagonal as X* (except at A and B), giving the contract curve drawn in the diagram.

We have made an assumption here, that the relative factor intensities of the goods do not reverse (A becoming capital-intensive and B labor-intensive) at marginal rates of substitution ($=$ input price ratios) giving equilibrium points in this economy. This assumption ("no factor reversal") is a *technological* assumption, concerning the relative shapes of the A- and B-isoquants. Whether it is applicable or not is a matter of fact in a model designed to represent some real economy. With factor reversal, some modifications to the analysis need to be made.

Along the Contract Curve. Change from one point on the contract curve, like X, to another which is further from A, like Y, represents a change from one equilibrium point to another such that A uses more of both labor and capital, and B less of both. Thus the output of A is greater and the output of B is less. A movement along the contract curve from A to B represents, in fact, a continuous increase in the output of A and a continuous decrease in the output of B, while maintaining equilibrium in the input markets.

But such a movement changes the capital/labor ratio in both industries, as well as their outputs. Comparison of the slope of AY relative to AX (both measured from AD) shows that of AY to be the larger, while comparison of the slope of BY relative to BX (both measured from BC) shows that of BY to be the larger. That is, an increase in the output of A relative to B (movement from X to Y) has increased the capital/labor ratio in *both* industries.

If this result surprises or puzzles the reader, consider a simple numerical example. Suppose the initial capital/labor ratio in A to be 1/3 and in B (necessarily higher) 1/1, with equilibrium in the input markets. Now let A expand a little at its original capital/labor ratio. It will need, say, 1 machine and 3 men which can only come from contraction of B. But if B contracts at its initial capital/labor ratio just enough to release 3 men, it will also release 3 machines—2 more than A requires. Thus there is an excess of capital in the economy and we do not have equilibrium. We can expect the result to be a downward pressure on the price of capital relative to labor, inducing *both* industries to move to more capital-intensive processes.

Dropping the reference to particular industries A and B, we can express the result in a more general form:

With fixed total quantities of labor and capital, expansion of the labor-intensive industry can only occur if

(i) the capital-intensive industry contracts and (ii) both industries switch to more capital-intensive processes, that is, the capital/labor ratio rises in both industries.

An equivalent result is obtained by interchanging the words "capital" and "labor" everywhere in the above statement.

Input Prices. From the above analysis, it follows directly that *relative input prices* (and thus the relative shares of capital and labor in total income) depend on the *relative outputs* of the two industries.

Since the ratio MPL/MPK is equal to the input price ratio w/r for both industries (competitive equilibrium), and since MPL/MPK increases when K/L increases (from the curvature of the isoquants), an increase in the capital/labor ratio will be associated with an increase in the wage relative to the price of capital services. In other words:

An increase in the output of the labor-intensive industry relative to the capital-intensive industry will raise wages relative to the price of capital services, and result in redistribution of income away from owners of capital towards wage-earners.[15]

General Equilibrium and the Industry. The results we have derived illustrate very well that, if an industry is a major sector of the economy, changes in the industry can be expected to cause changes in

(1) other industries,

---

[15] How, if at all, this affects the distribution of incomes *between persons* will depend on the distribution of wealth. The personal redistribution effect will be greatest if workers own no stocks, and stockholders do not work.

(2) input prices,

(3) the distribution of income.

These changes are sufficient to cause important changes in the demand for the product of the industry, so we cannot use partial supply and demand analysis in such a case.

This is the justification for the assertion made in Chapter 6, that the industry as a partial equilibrium concept is only useful when it is so small a part of the economy (as the watermelon producing industry) that its actions do not influence any important economy-wide variables, including the industry's input prices.

Further discussion of the two-good two-factor model, from a different point of view, is given in the next chapter.

In Chapter 10 we consider the circumstance under which the economist is willing to consider one configuration of the economy as "better" or "worse" than another.

CONTENTS

10.1 Welfare   259
10.2 Efficient Allocation   262
10.3 The Optimal Composition of Output   265
10.4 Efficiency and Competition   270
10.5 Interpretation and Policy Implications   275
     Further Reading   276

CHAPTER 10

WELFARE AND PUBLIC POLICY

10.1 Welfare

We commence with the individual, whose "welfare" is something we investigate to the minimum extent necessary to give some answers to important questions underlying economic policy.

At the outset, we can choose between two different approaches. One is that, whatever individual welfare is, the "government" knows what it is and can assert (without reference to the individual himself) whether the individual is "better off" in one situation than in another. A variation of the same theme is when the "government" can assert that *society* is better off in one configuration than another, without reference to individual welfare at all. Such approaches are referred to as *paternalistic* or *dictatorial* (depending on the emotions of the user of the term), and we shall not pursue them further. This is not because of a moral choice, but simply because the solution of welfare problems under this approach is relatively uncomplicated.

Individual as Judge of Own Welfare. The alternative approach, which raises problems of great magnitude, is to assume that *only* the individual can judge his own welfare. We proceed on the following presumptions, which are very closely related to those used as the foundation for the theory of consumer behavior:

(1) The individual is the sole judge of his own welfare.

259

(2) If the individual prefers A to B, his welfare is "greater" (he is "better off") at A than at B.

(3) The individual acts in accordance with his preferences, so his choice reveals his preferences and thus his welfare.

Thus we take it as fundamental that an individual always attains the highest level of welfare available to him, given the constraints on his choice. In analyzing the position of the individual in two situations, therefore, we need only investigate whether there is a choice available to him in one situation that is preferred to all choices in the other. Furthermore, we can take indifference levels to represent welfare levels, so that the consumer's indifference curves can be regarded as "iso-welfare" curves.

Like all working assumptions in economics, even the idea that the individual is the sole judge of his own welfare is subject to some exception in practice. In the United States, for example, the individual is not free to act upon his preferences if they lead to the use of narcotics.[1]

Interpersonal Comparisons. The most difficult problems in welfare arise when we attempt to establish levels of "social welfare" for groups of individuals. To rank two configurations of the economy, *A* and *B,* when individual *I* is better off in *A* than *B,* while individual *II* is better off in *B* than *A,* involves some judgment of the kind that the improvement in *I*'s welfare between *B* and *A* does or does not outweigh the worsening of *II*'s welfare for the same change. Such a ranking involves *interpersonal welfare judgments.* If we can make such comparisons, by any method, and rank *every* configuration of the economy with respect to every other, where a "configuration" includes distribution of output between persons as well as levels of output, we have a complete *social welfare function.*[2] Such a function is the analog, for society as a whole, of the utility function for the individual.

---

[1] In Section 11.4 we shall see that there can be doubt as to whether the consumer is to be regarded as the best judge of his own welfare over time.

[2] It has been shown (by Arrow) that we cannot, in general, expect a community to produce a consistent welfare function by such methods as simple voting. A well known example of the problems that arise is the "voting paradox." We have three states of the economy, *A, B, C,* and three individuals *I, II, III.* We try to rank the states by majority agreement. Suppose the preferences of the individuals were as follows:

	Individual		
Order of Preference	I	II	III
1	A	B	C
2	B	C	A
3	C	A	B

A majority *(I, III)* prefers *A* to *B,* a majority *(I, II)* prefers *B* to *C,* while a majority *(II, III)* prefers *C* to *A.* Thus the majority rankings are *not transitive* (see

The Pareto[3] Criterion. To avoid making such interpersonal comparisons, economists go as far as they can without them, by dealing only with what can be handled by the following reasonable idea:

Any change which makes at least one individual better off, and none worse off, is an improvement in social welfare. A change which makes none better off, and some worse off, is a worsening of social welfare. We do not attempt any statement concerning a change which makes some better off and others worse off.

Since a very large number of policy changes are of the kind that make some better off and some worse off, this is a very weak criterion. Nevertheless we can draw some very important conclusions from it. It is important to be very clear that the criterion does not imply we are *indifferent* between two situations in which some are better off, some worse off, for the change, only that *we simply do not know what to say.*

Welfare judgments based on the above criterion are said to be *Paretian.* A configuration of the economy such that no one can be made better off without someone else being made worse off (for any feasible change) is said to be *Pareto-optimal.* This does not mean that it is impossible to improve social welfare by a change, on some criterion, only that it is impossible to have an improvement in terms of the Pareto criterion. It would be normal to expect that any complete social welfare function would consider a change to be an improvement if it satisfied the Pareto criterion, so this criterion is not to be regarded as conflicting with other criteria. The Pareto criterion is rather the *common core* of possible social welfare functions—these can be expected to agree in their ranking of configurations which can be ranked by the Pareto criterion, but to disagree on others.

Externalities. The usefulness of the Pareto criterion in simple models depends on the absence of *externalities* in consumption, that is, in the fulfilment of the following condition:

The welfare of each individual depends solely on his own consumption and is not affected in any way by the consumption of others.

Among other things, this implies that no individual feels worse off by observing the consumption of the rich (no envy) or is disturbed by the

---

Section 7.3). Without transitivity, a satisfactory social welfare function cannot be built up.

To obtain a social welfare function, the "government" may *impose* its views, although it need only do so in respect to matters concerning the distribution of income, in which the Pareto criterion is of no help.

[3] Vilfredo Pareto, 1848–1923, was an Italian economist and sociologist.

consumption levels of the very poor (no compassion). Other externalities of a more direct kind (one person being disturbed by the smoke from another's cigarette) must also be ruled out. We can deal with problems involving externalities (which are certainly present, in fact), but at the expense of considerable complication.

Efficiency and Optimality. Sometimes we shall wish to describe a change in which every individual *could* be made better off, without considering whether every individual has been made so in fact. We use the term *efficient* for such a change and for a situation resulting from that change. The clearest example of an efficient change would be one which made more of every good available in the economy. Obviously, the increased output could always be allocated so as to make some better off and none worse off. We reserve the term *optimal* for a situation in which, *in fact,* no one can be made better off without someone else being worse off. The two ideas are related in the following way:

> *An optimal situation is necessarily efficient but an efficient situation is not necessarily optimal.*

Compensation. A related idea is that of *compensation.* If a change makes some individuals better off and some worse off, but the gainers could pay compensation to the losers just sufficient to make the losers no worse off than before, with themselves still remaining better off, then the change should be regarded as

   (i) *efficient,* in any case,
   (ii) *optimal* only if the compensation is *actually* made.[4]

10.2 Efficient Allocation

A configuration of the economy is Pareto-optimal if it is impossible to make someone better off without making someone else worse off. This means that, for optimality, it must be impossible to make someone better off and none worse off by:

(1) Taking the goods actually produced and allocating them differently among consumers.

(2) Taking the existing resources and allocating them differently among producers, so as to produce more of all goods.

(3) Changing the composition of total output, that is, changing the relative amounts of different goods, or of goods and leisure.

---

[4] This is the logical conclusion. Some economists used to argue that we should regard the change as optimal even if the compensation was not made.

It is obvious, of course, that a configuration cannot be optimal unless production is *technically efficient* so that no more can be produced of any single good without more of at least one resource being allocated to it, and that all resources actually supplied and actually productive should be used *(no unemployment of productive resources)*. These conditions are taken to be implicit, and call for no special analysis.

Of the three main conditions, (1), (2), (3), we shall consider the first two in this section. These are efficiency conditions, whose satisfaction is a prerequisite for condition (3). This last condition requires different analysis and is dealt with in the next section.

Efficient Allocation of Goods. Let us consider the efficient allocation of goods among consumers, assuming fixed totals of goods. Two goods, to be allocated among two consumers, is precisely the problem studied in Section 7.10. There we showed that one consumer could always be made better off, without the other being worse off, so long as the allocation was not on the contract curve in the Edgeworth box diagram.

The contract curve is the locus of points at which an indifference curve of one consumer is tangent to an indifference curve of the other. If the indifference curves are tangent, they have the same slope at the point of tangency. The slope of an indifference curve is the *marginal rate of substitution* between the two goods for that consumer. Thus the contract curve is the set of allocations of the two goods such that the marginal rate of substitution is the same for both consumers, so that the equality of this marginal rate is a necessary condition for efficient allocation.

It can be shown that an analogous argument holds for any number of goods and any number of consumers. The condition also holds if one of the goods is leisure, provided that the contract curve represents a feasible allocation of leisure (less than 12 hours for each consumer, on the basis of the assumptions of Section 7.9).

We can now state the first efficiency condition:

I (Efficient allocation of goods among consumers)
The marginal rate of substitution (in consumption) between any two goods, or between any good and leisure, should be the same for all consumers.

Efficient Allocation of Resources. Now let us turn to the problem of efficiently allocating resources among producers. Consider a model with two factors, both used in the production of each of two goods. We shall assume constant returns to scale and smoothly curved isoquants.

The analytical similarity between the isoquant and the indifference curve has already been pointed out. Here we shall draw on this similarity, to use an argument of the same kind as that used above for discussing the allocation of goods among consumers.

Taking fixed totals for the two factors, we can represent these by the sides of an Edgeworth box as in Figure 9.1 (page 252). Allocations of the factors between the production of the two goods are then represented by points within the box. The diagram is shown in Figure 10.1, where *A, B*

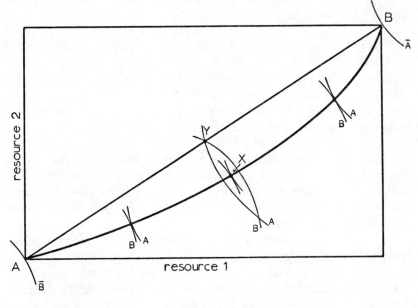

Figure 10.1

represent the origins from which we measure the resources used in the production of the two goods, which we refer to as *A* and *B*.

We can argue, exactly as in the consumer case, that any allocation of resources (like *Y* in the diagram) at which the isoquants of *A* and *B* cross each other is inefficient, since we can find another point (like *X*) at which there is more production (higher level isoquants) for both goods. Thus the only efficient resource allocations will be at points where an *A*-isoquant is tangent to a *B*-isoquant, that is, on the *contract curve,* just as in the consumer case.

As in the consumer case we can generalize to many goods and many factors. Since the slope of the isoquant is the marginal rate of substitution, the second efficiency condition is:

II (Efficient allocation of resources among producers)
   The marginal rate of substitution (in production) between any two re-sources (inputs) should be the same for all producers, whether producing the same or different goods.

10.3 The Optimal Composition of Output

It does not make sense to consider the *composition* of output until we are assured that we cannot have more of all goods (that is, resources are allocated efficiently) and that we cannot make everyone better off by real-locating a given output (that is, allocation of goods is efficient). Once we have efficient allocation of both resources and goods, we are ready to ex-amine whether it is possible to make everyone better off by producing more of some goods, at the expense of less of others.

The Transformation Curve. To investigate this question, we need an ana-lytical device not hitherto used, the *transformation curve* or *production possibility curve* (or surface, if for more than two goods).

Consider an economy with two resources (fixed in total amounts) and producing two goods. The efficient allocations of the resources between the production of the two goods are represented by the points of the contract curve in Figure 10.1. Since we suppose resource allocation to be efficient, we shall consider only points on the contract curve.

The point *A* represents allocation of zero resources to the production of *A* and of the total resources to the production of *B*. The quantity of *B* produced is given by the *B*-isoquant which passes through *A*. It is obvi-ously the *maximum* amount of *B* that the economy can produce with the given resources—we label it $\bar{B}$ (read as "B bar"). As we move along the contract curve from *A* towards *B*, we allocate more of *both* resources to *A*, less to *B*, so the output of *A* is increasing and that of *B* is decreasing. The maximum possible output of *A*, $\bar{A}$, occurs at the point *B*.

Corresponding to any *A*-isoquant, there is a unique *B*-isoquant on the contract curve (that which is tangent to the chosen *A*-isoquant), so that for *efficient production*, there is a unique quantity of *B* corresponding to every choice of *A*.

The relationship between the outputs of *A* and *B* can be illustrated by Figure 10.2, in which the quantities of *A* and *B* are measured along the two axes. The maximum outputs of the two goods, $\bar{A}$ and $\bar{B}$, are shown. All other output combinations must obviously lie along some curve joining $\bar{A}$ and $\bar{B}$.

Let us investigate the possible shape of this curve. By using all the economy's resources in *A*, it can produce $\bar{A}$, and by using all the resources

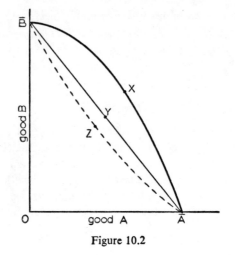

Figure 10.2

in B, it can produce $\bar{B}$. If there are constant returns to scale,[5] by using *half* of *both* resources in A and half in B, and the same production processes as at $\bar{A}, \bar{B}$, (but at half the levels) the economy can produce $\frac{1}{2}\bar{A}$ and $\frac{1}{2}\bar{B}$, the point Y in the diagram. By varying the allocations in this way, but not changing the *proportions* in which factors are used in each of the two industries, combinations of A and B represented by points on the straight line $\overline{AB}$ can *certainly* be attained. Thus a point like Z, lying inside this line, cannot be efficient if there are constant returns to scale.

But the economy may be able to do better than points on $\overline{AB}$ (except, of course, at $\bar{A}$ and $\bar{B}$ themselves). Return to Figure 10.1 (the box diagram). The point Y (half of each resource to each industry) corresponds to Y in Figure 10.2. But Y is off the contract curve, and more of both goods can be produced at a point like X which is on the contract curve. This will give the point X in Figure 10.2, further out than $\overline{AB}$.

The increase in output of both goods between Y and X, for the same total resources, is obtained by using *different* processes (moving around the isoquants) from those used at $\bar{A}$ and $\bar{B}$ and therefore at Y.

We can conclude, therefore, that the curve drawn through all the *efficient* combinations of A and B can never lie *inside* the line $\overline{AB}$ (for constant returns to scale), and typically lies *outside* it (except at $\bar{A}, \bar{B}$),

---

[5] The shape of the transformation curve which is derived here holds also for *decreasing*, as well as constant, returns to scale. The argument is given for constant returns to scale, since it is rather simpler. For *steadily increasing* returns to scale (as contrasted with the stepwise indivisibilities discussed later in the chapter) the transformation curve may not have the shape described.

like the curve on which X lies in Figure 10.2. This gives a curve which is *concave* to the origin, bending the opposite way from an isoquant or indifference curve.

This curve of efficient combinations is called the *transformation curve* or *production possibility curve*. The term "transformation" refers to the idea that we give up some of one product for some of the other as we move around the curve. A is transformed into B, not directly, but by using some resources that could have been used in A to make B instead. We transform the *opportunity* of making A into the actual making of B.

The Marginal Rate of Transformation. Consider Figure 10.3. This shows two adjacent points X, X' on the transformation curve. Moving from X to

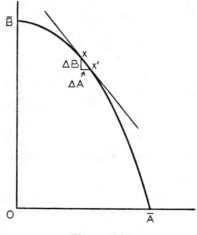

Figure 10.3

X', we give up an amount ΔB of B and obtain an increment ΔA of A. The ratio $\Delta B / \Delta A$ (which is clearly the *slope* of the transformation curve at the relevant point) is referred to as *the marginal rate of transformation between A and* B. Since ΔB, ΔA have opposite signs, the marginal rate of transformation is negative, and is in terms of "units of B per unit of A."

We can relate the marginal rate of transformation to the marginal productivities of resources in the following way:

Consider a small shift in resource allocation from B to A. We shall suppose there are only two factors, labor (l) and capital (k), and that we transfer amounts Δl, Δk from B to A. The change in the output B is given by:

$$\Delta B = -\ (\Delta l.MPL_B + \Delta k.MPK_B)$$

where MPL_B, MPK_B stand for the marginal products of labor and capital in B. The negative sign occurs because we are reducing both labor and capital in B. We can write the above expression in equivalent form:

$$\Delta B = - \Delta l.MPL_B\left[1 + \frac{\Delta k}{\Delta l} \frac{MPK_B}{MPL_B}\right].$$

A similar relationship holds for ΔA:

$$\Delta A = \Delta l.MPL_A\left[1 + \frac{\Delta k}{\Delta l} \frac{MPK_A}{MPL_A}\right].$$

Compare the brackets in the expressions for ΔB, ΔA. Since production is *efficient*, the efficiency condition *II* of the previous section must be satisfied, so that $MPK_B/MPL_B = MPK_A/MPL_A$. Thus the bracketed expressions will be equal and will cancel when we divide ΔB by ΔA, as will the Δl outside the bracket. Thus we obtain:

$$\frac{\Delta B}{\Delta A} = - \frac{MPL_B}{MPL_A}.$$

We could have performed the above analysis a little differently, taking $\Delta k.MPK_B$ and $\Delta k.MPK_A$ outside the brackets, and found that:

$$\frac{\Delta B}{\Delta A} = - \frac{MPK_B}{MPK_A}.$$

Ignoring the negative sign (which we recognize implicitly), we can state the following very important result:

The marginal rate of transformation between two goods is equal to the ratio of the marginal product of any resource in the production of one good, to the marginal product of the same resource in the production of the other.

(This refers, of course, to a resource actually used in the production of both goods).

Goods and Leisure. What of the marginal rate of transformation between goods (consumption) and leisure? Consider a good C and leisure. One hour less labor means one hour more leisure—we can state this as, the marginal product of labor in producing leisure is 1. If we give up an amount ΔL of leisure and use the resulting labor to produce C, the increment in C is given by:

$$\Delta C = \Delta L.MPL_C.$$

Thus the marginal rate of transformation between consumption and leisure $(\Delta C/\Delta L)$ is equal to MPL_C. This is equivalent to the previous analysis if we insert the value 1 for the marginal product of labor in producing leisure.

The Optimal Composition of Output. We are now ready to tackle the main problem, that of the optimal composition of output. Imagine a miniature version of the two-good economy, with a transformation curve of the kind already derived, and a consumer who must choose his preferred output composition.

Since the transformation curve diagram is drawn on axes along which are measured quantities of two goods, we can draw the consumer's indifference curves on the same diagram, as in Figure 10.4. Any point on the

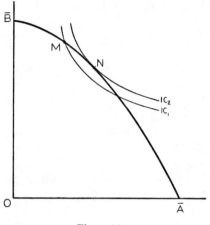

Figure 10.4

transformation curve, like *M*, at which the curve is *cut* by an indifference curve is clearly not optimal, since the consumer can move to a higher indifference curve. The highest attainable indifference curve is obviously attained at the point *N* in the diagram, where the indifference curve is tangent to the transformation curve. At this point the slope of the indifference curve (marginal rate of substitution) is equal to the slope of the transformation curve (marginal rate of transformation).

If allocation is efficient, all consumers will have the same marginal rate of substitution, which we can call *the* rate, and we can generalize the one-consumer case to give our third condition:

III (Optimal composition of output)
If production and allocation are both efficient, the optimal composition of output will be that for which the marginal rate of transformation

between any pair of goods (or between any good and leisure) is equal to the marginal rate of substitution between the same pair in consumption.

Suppose the ratios differed, with the marginal rate of transformation at, say 2 units of *A* for 1 of *B*, with the marginal rate of substitution at 1 for 1. Then the economy could produce 2 units of *A* by giving up 1 of *B*. Since consumers are just as well off if compensated by 1 extra unit of *A* for the loss of 1 of *B*, the change will increase welfare, and the original situation could not have been optimal.

It is important to note that condition *III* is relevant only if conditions *I* and *II* are already satisfied. While *I* or *II* by itself would be an efficiency condition, *III* by itself has no meaning. It is an *optimality* condition, needing efficiency as a prerequisite. If more of *all* goods can be produced by an efficient move, the composition is less important.

10.4 Efficiency and Competition

In the two preceding sections were set out three[6] conditions for Pareto-optimality in the economy. These conditions were given in terms of marginal rates of transformation and substitution. A Pareto-optimal configuration could, in principle, be attained by all-knowing central direction designed to satisfy these conditions. Omniscience would be required because the marginal rates of substitution in consumption can be determined only from knowledge of individual preferences. The purpose here is to relate these conditions to the actual behavior of the ideal perfect economy, or to that of the partly decentralized economy operating with shadow prices.

Efficient Allocation. Condition *I* (efficient allocation of goods) requires that the marginal rates of substitution (in consumption) should be the same for all consumers. From Section 7.4 we know that consumers freely exercising their preferences subject to budget constraints with fixed prices will choose collections for which the marginal rates of substitution are equal to the price ratios. It follows that the marginal rates of substitution will be the same for all consumers if they can freely choose at prices which are uniform for all. Thus:

Allocation among consumers will be efficient if all consumers can exercise free choice (subject to budget constraints) at prices which are uniform for all.

---

[6] By variations in the wording of the conditions, the number can be changed. We can consider *I* and *II* to be essentially the same, and have only two combinations (an amalgam of *I* and *II*, along with *III*), or we can break *III* up in more detail. Some authors make five conditions, but the content is covered by our three.

This will be true if goods are allocated through the market.

Condition *II* (efficient allocation of resources) requires that the marginal rates of substitution between inputs should be the same for all producers. Since the least-cost criterion (Section 5.4) is that the marginal rates of substitution between inputs be equal to their price ratios, and since we presume all producers (whether perfectly competitive or not) will produce at least cost for a given output, the condition requires that all producers buy inputs at the same price.

Allocation of resources among producers will be efficient if all producers are free to buy resources without limit at prices which are uniform for all.

This will be true if all resources are sold on perfect markets and there are no limitations on resources to individual producers.

Barriers to Efficiency. Although there are divergences between prices paid by different consumers due to a variety of influences including lack of information, salesmanship, bargaining and special privilege (the PX, "I can get it for you wholesale"), it is quite clear that the United States economy comes closer to satisfying the condition for efficient allocation of goods than to satisfying either of the other two optimum conditions.

The situation is different when we come to resource markets. Different producers can pay widely different prices for essentially the same type of labor, due to imperfections in the labor market. Capital markets are also highly imperfect—large corporations can obtain capital generally at rates much lower than those paid by small firms. Intermediate goods sold from one firm to another are subject to a variety of special arrangements (antitrust laws notwithstanding) that result in different prices to different producers or classes of producer. Furthermore, the condition that there be no resource limitation is often violated. Farmers with land limitations face different capital limitations (often arbitrarily determined by individual bank executives), so that different farmers may have to operate with different land to capital ratios, thus without equal marginal rates of substitution between land and capital.

Optimal Composition. Condition *III* (optimal composition of output) requires that the marginal rates of transformation be equal to the marginal rates of substitution in production. If there is efficient allocation of goods through the market, the marginal rates of substitution between pairs of goods will be equal to the price ratio. We need to examine the relationship between the marginal rates of transformation and the price ratios.

Denoting the marginal rate of transformation between A and B by MRT_{AB} we have, from the previous section:

$$MRT_{AB} = \frac{MPL_B}{MPL_A} \,.$$

From Section 5.6, we have:

$$MC_A = \frac{w}{MPL_A}$$

giving

$$MPL_A = \frac{w}{MC_A} \,.$$

Similarly,

$$MPL_B = \frac{w}{MC_B} \,.$$

(Where MC stands for marginal cost, and where we assume the satisfaction of Condition *II*, so that the same wage is paid for equivalent labor in both industries.)

Together, these relationships give:

$$MRT_{AB} = \frac{MC_A}{MC_B} \,.$$

If *both* firms operate so that they produce the output at which marginal cost is equal to price, we have:

$$MRT_{AB} = \frac{p_A}{p_B} \,.$$

Thus perfectly competitive firms (or production units operating in response to fixed shadow prices) will operate in such a way as to make the marginal rate of transformation equal to the price ratio. Since the price ratio is equal to the marginal rate of substitution, we have:

The composition of output will be optimal if all production units choose outputs that equate marginal cost to price, provided allocation of goods and resources is efficient.

This will be true if all firms operate under conditions of perfect competition.

The composition of output between goods and leisure will also be optimal under the same conditions, since the marginal rate of transformation between good C and leisure is given by

$$MRT_{CL} = MPL_C = w/MC_C = w/p_C \,.$$

The last expression is the "real wage," to which the marginal rate of substitution between good C and leisure was shown to be equal in Section 7.9.

The Perfectly Competitive Economy. Taking all three conditions together, we are in a position to make the following statement:

> *In the absence of indivisibilities and increasing returns to scale, of resource limitations to individual producers, and of corner solutions, the equilibrium of the perfectly competitive economy is also a Pareto-optimal configuration of the economy. A partly decentralized economy guided by appropriate shadow prices will also be Pareto-optimal.*

This is the reason, mentioned but not demonstrated in Chapter 9, that the perfectly competitive economy is, in certain senses, an "ideal" configuration.

The qualifications in the statement should be noted. The effect of resource limitations to individual producers has already been discussed. We rule out corner solutions because these may prevent some of the marginal equalities from holding. Corner solutions do not necessarily prevent the attainment of a Pareto-optimal configuration, but the conditions must be stated somewhat differently.

The major qualification is, however, that concerning indivisibilities. As is apparent from the analysis of Section 6.8, indivisibilities may result in perfectly competitive firms operating at too small a size to take advantage of large-scale processes. We could obtain more of the good, *with the same resources,* by operating with large-scale methods. Thus the economy will have two "transformation curves," one false, but possibly observed, for production by small-scale methods, the other representing truly the *production possibilities* for production by large-scale methods, with the former lying inside the latter and representing points which are inefficient relative to it. Under perfect competition, the marginal rate of substitution will equal the marginal rate of transformation, *but on the wrong curve.*

Distortions. We can think of behavior or policies which result in inequality between the marginal rates of transformation and substitution as introducing *distortions* into the economy. These result in the composition of output being suboptimal even if the output is produced and allocated efficiently. Since equality between the marginal rate of substitution and the price ratio is assumed to be satisfied more easily than the other conditions, distortions are chiefly due to inequality between the marginal rate of transformation and the price ratio.

Although we have already discussed monopoly as compared with competition (Section 6.8), it is important to realize that, in a general equilibrium setting, the effect of imperfect competition is essentially that of a distortion.

If industry A is a monopoly, it will produce the output for which marginal revenue is equal to marginal cost. But marginal revenue is *less* than price, so that

$$MC_A < p_A.$$

Thus if B is perfectly competitive we will have $MC_B = p_B$, so the marginal rate of transformation will be given by:

$$MRT = \frac{MC_B}{MC_A}$$

$$> \frac{p_B}{p_A}.$$

This results in the distortion.

It has sometimes been argued that no distortions occur if all firms are monopolies with the same *degree of monopoly* (measured as the ratio MC/p). But the optimal composition between goods and leisure requires that

$$MRT_{CL} = w/p_C.$$

This will be true only if $MC_C = p_C$, thus requiring perfect competition for at least one industry and, by linkage through the marginal rates of transformation between all pairs of goods, perfect competition everywhere.

The government can, and often does, introduce distortions. The most straightforward case is that of *selective sales or excise taxes*. Suppose the government raises revenue by a 10 per cent sales tax on A, but no tax on B. If p_A, p_B are the prices received by producers, the prices paid by consumers will be $1.1\,p_A$, p_B. The marginal rate of substitution will be equated (under perfect competition) to the ratio of the latter, $1.1 p_A/p_B$, while the marginal rate of transformation will be equated to the ratio of the former, p_A/p_B, so the rates will not be equal.

Most other forms of taxation can be shown to introduce some distortions. A general sales tax (on *everything*) or an income tax distort the labor-leisure relationship, for example, by making the effective ratio of goods prices to wages different to the consumer than to the producer.

It is possible to conceive of policies (called *second best* policies) in which the government introduces distortions designed to partly counteract other distortions which it does not choose to (or cannot) eliminate. With monopoly, prices in the monopoly sector are too high, and those in the competitive sector too low, compared with those for the optimum. The government might place sales taxes on *competitively* produced products to partly redress the balance.

The actual sales tax structure in the United States is actually opposite to this—taxing monopolistically produced products (manufactured goods) and exempting competitively produced goods (agricultural products). Thus it probably *increases* the distortions.

10.5 Interpretation and Policy Implications

Before interpreting the Pareto optimum, we should be careful to remember what was pointed out in Section 10.1, that the use of the Pareto analysis has been in cases in which we assume no *externalities*. If one individual's welfare is affected by the welfare of others, it is no longer necessarily true that we can consider a configuration better because one individual has more *goods* and no others have less. If the rich Prince becomes richer, with the peasants' physical consumption unchanged, the peasants may nevertheless feel worse off (envy), and the fundamental Pareto criterion is not satisfied. The fact that the peasants are worse off from envy does not matter—Paretian welfare is based on whether or not a consumer is *in fact* better off, not on any moral judgments as to whether we think he *ought* to feel better off or not.[7]

Corresponding difficulties arise with respect to other types of externality. In Section 5.1 it was pointed out that the costs (and benefits) of an action may not all fall to the decision maker. To the extent that there are external costs or benefits of an action over and above the private costs or benefits, the optimality conditions *I, II,* and *III* may give a false reading of the situation. Consumers may be "paying for" air pollution provided "free" by industry.

Assuming that externalities do not exist,[8] or can be taken into account by suitable modifications of the analysis, it is important to be clear as to exactly what is, and what is not, implied by Pareto-optimality.

In particular, Pareto-optimality is completely neutral as to initial distribution of wealth. For a given distribution, there is a Pareto-optimal configuration of the economy. If all the wealth was taken away from the rich and spread among the poor, there would be a different Pareto-optimal configuration. To move from the first configuration to the second necessarily involves making some better off and some worse off, and the Pareto criterion cannot rank the configurations at all.

---

[7] The distinction is more hazy in the intertemporal case. See Section 11.4.

[8] Some authors would argue that externalities are, in fact, of predominant importance and that much that is wrong with the United States is due to having neglected them. A point of view that can be interpreted to mean this is given in Galbraith, J. K., *The Affluent Society*. Galbraith speaks of "private wealth and public squalor." The existence, or nonexistence, of important externalities is a question of *fact*.

Let us imagine the United States was a perfectly competitive economy, with no externalities or indivisibilities, and in competitive equilibrium. Then the configuration would be Pareto-optimal. But this would not mean that all was perfect. We might decide, on special criteria not included in the Pareto criterion itself, that the distribution of income was far from desirable. If we redistributed wealth we should, however, be suboptimal if the Pareto conditions were not met *at the new wealth distribution.*

Another point of great importance is that the conditions for efficiency and optimal composition are *technical* conditions in terms of marginal rates of transformation and substitution and do not depend on *prices.* Perfect competition (which depends on prices) may, under the appropriate conditions, provide a *means* for ensuring that the conditions are met. Thus perfect competition is simply a means to an end, not an end. Nor is perfect competition the only means available—centralized control, or partial decentralization with appropriate shadow prices could achieve the same ends, and do this in the case (indivisibilities) in which perfect competition might not work, but with much greater administrative complexity.

There is nothing in the optimality conditions concerning the ownership of resources other than labor. The government could own all the capital and provided it rented this to *all* producers at the same price (not just to special producers operating government enterprises), it could distribute the income from capital as it pleased and the configuration of the economy could still be Pareto-optimal.

The optimality conditions, being simply technical requirements, contain no ideological implications. They apply equally to capitalism, socialism, or any other "ism."[9] *Whatever the political ideology of a country, it could make all its citizens better off by ensuring that production and allocation satisfied the optimality conditions.*

We shall see, however, in Section 11.4 that there may be a case for introducing distortions in certain relationships (not specifically dealt with here) which concern intertemporal behavior.

FURTHER READING

For discussion of some of the problems in welfare economics not covered here, see the early chapters in: Little, I. M. D., *A Critique of Welfare Economics,* Oxford University Press, 1960; and Rothenburg, Jerome, *The Measurement of Social Welfare,* Prentice-Hall, 1961.

---

[9] In fact, both *conservative* and *liberal socialist* economic philosophies have been based on the Pareto optimality conditions.

A nontechnical discussion of the optimality conditions is given in: Lerner, A. P., *The Economics of Control*, Macmillan, 1949; and an advanced discussion (the title notwithstanding) in: Quirk, J., and Saposnik, R., *Introduction to General Equilibrium Theory and Welfare Economics*, McGraw-Hill, 1968.

There is also a survey article on welfare economics by E. J. Mishan in: American Economic Association and Royal Economic Society, *Surveys of Economic Theory* (3 vols), St. Martin's Press, 1966.

Chapter 11 touches on many matters about which economists are not yet fully in agreement, and in which there remains very much work to be done.

CONTENTS

11.1 Limitations of Static Models 279

11.2 Consumers' Intertemporal Decisions 281

11.3 Intertemporal Decisions by Firms 288

11.4 Intertemporal Welfare and Growth Policy 292

11.5 Money 295

CHAPTER 11

TIME, CHANGE,
AND UNCERTAINTY

11.1 Limitations of Static Models

Although time has been explicit or implicit in much of what has been discussed so far—the market period, short and long run, lags and adjustments, speculation, working and fixed capital—we have not discussed *intertemporal decisions,* that is, decisions involving *choice* over time.

Many decisions involve time, but are not intertemporal because no choice is involved. The movement of the firm from short to long run equilibrium involves no choice; the long run situation is necessarily optimal and the firm gives up nothing in the short run. Time is involved only in the sense that the firm finds it impossible to move *instantaneously* to the long run configuration, something it would do if it could. A consumer's decision to save part of his income now, lend it, and receive a higher consumption level at some future time, is an intertemporal decision, however. The consumer has exercised a choice between extra consumption now (the amount of his saving) and extra consumption in the future.

Thus our analysis has been *static* in the sense that we have considered only situations (and the equilibria associated with them) in which the resources, technology and general context have been taken as data for a period, the decisions being made from among alternatives available in that period alone.

This does not mean that the analysis we have given applies only to a changeless society. It is perfectly consistent with a static analysis that the

279

technology, resources, even preferences, change from period to period, provided the future changes play no role in present decisions.

The static analysis is entirely appropriate if changes are exogenous, not the result of decisions taken. We will obtain a static equilibrium for each period (if there is sufficient time for adjustment), but the equilibrium will change from period to period. The simplest example is in the analysis of the single market, where we obtain an equilibrium for each period which changes as supply and demand (exogenous to the particular market) change.

Even if changes are not exogenous, but the consequence of earlier decisions, we do not have an intertemporal system *unless future changes are actually taken into account in present decisions.* Many factors that we treat as exogenous to simplify the analysis, such as population and preferences, are undoubtedly determined by social factors that themselves have been determined or influenced by earlier economic decisions. The exact influence of present decisions on such factors is generally unknown, so they are not taken into account in decisions.

We can also have *intertemporal externalities* (probably more important than static externalities), so that the future consequences of some present decision may fall to someone other than the decision maker. Again, no intertemporal analysis is necessary in order to determine, for example, the competitive equilibrium. However, welfare assessment may call for intertemporal analysis.

In general, even individual decision makers (consumers, producers) do make intertemporal decisions, so that any attempt at a complete analysis of the working of the economy must go beyond the static model. A fully intertemporal model of the economy is highly complex and involves many problems of both analysis and fact. Economists have barely scratched the surface of this study, so the reader need not suppose that the brief outline given here is necessarily hiding a mass of well organized knowledge.

When we introduce decisions concerning the future, we must face more squarely the existence of *uncertainty* than is necessary in the static analysis. We use the term here in its widest sense, to mean that the exact outcome of an event is not fully determinate. (This includes what is often differentiated as *risk,* where the *probability* of each possible outcome is known.) The idea of uncertainty is important in relation to the analysis of the demand for money, and we shall introduce it at that point. For most of our analysis, however, we shall simplify by implicitly supposing that the future events are known with certainty.

Decisions over time may involve many future time periods, and we can expect decision makers to view different periods differently—10 years from now different from 5 years from now, different from next year.

However the analysis of multiperiod intertemporal decisions can easily become bogged down in arithmetical technicalities. Since it adds nothing to the fundamental understanding of the problems of intertemporal decisions to study the arithmetic of compound interest or related topics, we shall confine much of the analysis to a simplified two-period model even though we lose something by the simplification. These periods will be referred to as "today" and "tomorrow," "this year" and "next year," or "the present" and "the future." The names attached to the periods are not meant to be taken literally.

11.2 Consumers' Intertemporal Decisions

Time Preference. In the static theory of consumer behavior, we assumed that the consumer had definite preferences with respect to the collections of goods available to him. If we consider the same physical good at different times to be different goods, we can assume the consumer to have definite preferences among these collections as well. That is, instead of considering preferences among collections of food and clothing now, we can consider preferences among different collections of food now and food tomorrow, the preferences themselves being taken *as of now*.

At a high level of abstraction, economists sometimes would argue that such preferences are all that we need to investigate intertemporal choice. There are, however, some very important differences between intertemporal choice and static choice. One is the nature of the budget constraint: in the static case, we assume that the consumer is always able to reallocate his expenditure by spending $1 less on one good and $1 more on another. In the intertemporal case, the budget constraint may be more complex: the consumer may not always be able to spend $1 more today by spending less tomorrow, and rarely by spending only $1 less tomorrow.

The other difference between the static and intertemporal cases is that it is common to assume *more* about intertemporal preferences than about static preferences. Consider the following table which shows three different collections, each giving quantities of a good C ("consumption") in each of two time periods, "today" and "tomorrow." We assume that goods cannot be stored—they must be consumed in the period for which they are available.

Of the three collections given, we would usually assume that the typical consumer prefers the collections in the order X, Y, Z. That is, for collections representing the same two-day totals and not too greatly different in their distribution over time, we assume the consumer will prefer to have somewhat more today and less tomorrow, rather than somewhat less today and more tomorrow.

TABLE 11.1

| | Quantity of C | | |
Collection	Today	Tomorrow	Total
X	101	99	200
Y	100	100	200
Z	99	101	200

This assumption about consumer preference over time is often described as *impatience*. It is a strong assumption about preference, since it is easily seen that if the columns "today" and "tomorrow" were "Good *A*" and "Good *B*," and the analysis was static, we should not have any expectations concerning the order of preference of the collections.

Although we shall assume that *all* consumers are "impatient," the *degree* of impatience depends on the individual. An index of this can be ascertained by comparing collections between which the individual is indifferent. Suppose we had two consumers, *I* and *II*, and found the following to be true:

I indifferent between (a) 110 today + 100 tomorrow, and

(b) 100 today + 111 tomorrow.

II indifferent between (a) 110 today + 100 tomorrow, and

(c) 100 today + 112 tomorrow.

Our conclusion would be that *II* is "more" impatient than *I*, since commencing with collection (a) in both cases, *II* requires an additional 12 tomorrow to make up for the loss of 10 today, while *I* requires only 11 tomorrow to compensate for the loss of 10 today.

The *excess* of the compensation tomorrow over what is given up today in order to remain indifferent, expressed as a ratio to what is given up, is the consumer's *marginal rate of time preference* or *rate of discount of the future*. For consumer *II* in the example it is 20 per cent ($\frac{12 - 10}{10}$, converted to per cent), while for consumer *I* it is 10 per cent.

The rate of time preference is sometimes expressed by saying that, if the rate of time preference is 10 per cent, the consumer will be indifferent between 100 today and 110 tomorrow. This approach has been avoided, because there is some evidence that the rate of time preference depends also on the evenness with which consumption is distributed over time.

Consider the two collections set out in Table 11.2, which, unlike those in Table 11.1, are not almost identical in the time distribution.

In this case, we should not be surprised if a consumer preferred collection *V* to collection *U* simply because it is more evenly distributed over time. He may well prefer to consume 90 today and 90 tomorrow,

TABLE 11.2

| Collection | Quantity of C | | Total |
	Today	Tomorrow	
U	195	5	200
V	90	90	180

rather than have plenty today and starve tomorrow, although *U* has a higher two-day total and also caters to impatience. (Remember that we are still assuming that *C* cannot be held over from today to tomorrow—if it could, then *U* would certainly be preferred, since the consumer could have 100 today and 100 tomorrow.)

Consumption Loans. Now consider two consumers, *I* and *II*, who are to receive nonstorable goods over two periods, as follows:

	Today	Tomorrow
I	100	120
II	120	100

We consider the possibility that both consumers can gain by some kind of trade. Goods cannot be traded from one period to the next in aggregate, but one consumer may give up some of today's goods to the other, in return for which the other will give him some of tomorrow's goods when tomorrow comes.

If the time preference of the consumers are motivated both by impatience and by a desire to even out consumption, then the latter could be achieved by a direct swap. *II* would give 10 units to *I* today, then receive 10 units from *I* tomorrow, so that both would consume 110 units in each period. But, because of impatience, *II* will not be willing to give up 10 today for only 10 tomorrow—he will want, say, 11 units tomorrow. If *I*'s rate of time preference is such that he is at least indifferent between 10 units now and 11 tomorrow, he would be willing to trade on this basis. Thus a possible equilibrium might be reached, with consumption patterns as follows:

	Today	Tomorrow
I	110	109
II	110	111
Transfer II to I	+10	−11

This trade can be described as either

(a) *II* makes a *consumption loan* to *I* today, to be repaid with an additional unit tomorrow.

(b) *II* trades *present goods* for *future goods.*

Looking at the transaction from the view point (b), we can see that 10 units of present goods have been traded for 11 units of future goods. That is, 1.1 units of future goods must be given up per unit of present goods, so that 1.1 is the *price* of present goods *in terms of future goods,* just as a money price of $1 per ton means that $1 must be given up in order to obtain one ton.

If we look at the transaction from viewpoint (a), *II* has lent 10 units and will receive back those 10 units plus an additional unit (because of time preference). This additional unit is *interest,* and its ratio to the original loan is the *rate of interest,* 10 per cent per "day" in this case.

There is a direct relationship between these two ways of looking at the trade:

If i *is the rate of interest and* p′ *the price of present goods in terms of future goods, then* i = p′ − 1 (× 100 *if* i *is given as a percentage*). *For a multiperiod context, an analogous relationship can be given.*

Since the trade will only take place if *II* (the lender) considers 11 tomorrow no worse than 10 today, and if *I* (the borrower) considers 10 today no worse than 11 tomorrow, a loan transaction will take place at a given rate of interest only if:

(1) The rate of interest is not less than the lender's rate of time preference, and

(2) the rate of interest is not more than the borrower's rate of time preference.

Savings. In a complex economy, consumers do not receive physical quantities of goods in different periods, they receive money payments *(incomes)* which may vary over time. Typically, any adjustments between incomes and expenditure on current goods *(consumption)* will be made by transactions in money terms. Actual choice of particular collections to be purchased from consumption expenditure can be made in the relevant period.

Thus the market for consumption loans will be in terms of money payments. A consumer who is due to receive a large income today and a smaller income tomorrow may trade a payment now for a receipt tomorrow, in order to even out his consumption. He will, in general, only be willing to do this if tomorrow's receipt exceeds today's payment by an excess determined by his rate of time preference. That is, he will lend some of his income now for repayment tomorrow only if he receives some interest. A consumer who is to receive a small income today and a large income tomorrow will trade a receipt now for a payment tomorrow, and will be willing to pay some interest on the loan.

Lending involves trading present payments for future receipts, and borrowing involves trading present receipts for future payments. We can also regard the lender as *buying a promise for future payment* (and the borrower as selling such a promise). In a complex society, such a promise will be institutionalized and embodied in a contract or *security*. Thus we can consider a loan as the purchase of a security from the lender's point of view, and the sale of a security from the borrower's point of view, so the market for *loans* and the market for *securities* are two aspects of the same thing.[1]

We also note that a consumer who lends from his current income is making his *current consumption less than his current income*. We refer to the difference as *saving*—the borrower is *dissaving*. When only consumption loans are involved, it is simply a matter of special emphasis whether we choose to regard the various transactions in terms of borrowing and lending, the purchase and sale of securities, or saving and dissaving.

From the discussion earlier in the section, we will expect a consumer to be more willing to trade between receipts in one period and payments in another, the greater the unevenness of his income between the periods. A consumer's expected average income is referred to as his *permanent income*,[2] the excess of actual income in a period above this being *windfall* or *transitory* income (this will be negative if actual income is below permanent income). Thus we will expect a consumer's saving behavior to be determined by

(1) The *rate of interest* (because of time preference).

(2) *Transitory income effects* (because of desire to smooth consumption).

(3) *Permanent income* (because saving, like other consumer decisions, is affected by income—it is usually accepted that savings can be expected to be higher when the consumer's permanent income is higher).

In the absence of unemployment, the most prominent irregularity in most consumers' expected future income streams arises from the prospect of ultimate retirement, and most of consumer savings associated with con-

---

[1] The market for loans is usually taken to mean the market for *new* loans. The securities market may include transactions in *existing* loans, when a creditor sells the right to receive the interest and repayment of the loan to someone else. In a competitive economy, it makes no difference whether the security is for a new loan or an old one, if other characteristics are the same.

[2] This concept is due to Friedman, who introduced the idea into a different setting.

sumption smoothing are related to retirement provisions. Such savings are frequently organized on a regular basis (perhaps with little option on the part of the consumer), through pension funds and social security. Savings of this kind are *contractual savings*.

The Loan Market. If we have a large number of consumers with diverse time patterns of income payments over time, we have the ingredients for a loan or securities market. Diversity of income patterns is necessary because if, for example, everyone was to receive income tomorrow and no one income today, the potential market would contain all borrowers and no lenders and could not operate. Since it is reasonable to assume that *aggregate* income will not vary so widely over time as individual incomes, there will usually be the appropriate diversity, with some consumers wanting to bring consumption forward and others wanting to defer some of their consumption.

For a given pattern of incomes over time, the number of consumers willing to lend will be higher at higher interest rates than at lower, while the number willing to borrow will be lower at lower interest rates than at higher. Thus if we consider the interest rate as playing the same kind of role as the *price* in an ordinary market, we will have upward sloping supply of loans and downward sloping demand for loans.

Thus, even with consumption loans only, we can expect that there will be a loan market with equilibrium at some *market rate of interest*[3] and some equilibrium level of loans. Later, as we consider investment in both human and fixed capital, we shall add any ensuing loan transactions into the consumption loan market, to obtain a general loan or capital market through which all loans will pass whatever their purpose.

Investment in Human Capital. Consumption loans represent an essentially passive adjustment by consumers to income receipts whose time pattern does not coincide with the preferred time pattern of consumption. But the consumer may make decisions over time that affect his income stream in a fundamental way. Or, to put it a little differently, the consumer may be in a position to choose between different income streams as well as between different consumption streams from a given income stream.

A good example of this kind of choice is the *career decision*. Let us consider a simple two-period model in which the consumer may choose between an unskilled career with relatively steady income over time, and a skilled career with no income during a training period but a later income exceeding that of the unskilled career. We assume no education costs other

---

[3] But see the discussion of the money market in Section 11.5.

than the foregone earning opportunities during the training period. The alternatives might look like this:

	Income	
	Present	Future
Unskilled career	100	500
Skilled career	0	650

Whether the consumer prefers the time pattern (in the absence of consumption loans) associated with the unskilled or the skilled career will depend on his time preference. The higher his rate of time preference (the more "impatient" he is), the more likely he will be to prefer the unskilled career. In the absence of consumption loans, his choice will depend only on his *personal time preference*.

If consumption loans are possible, however, he can make his consumption pattern different from his income pattern. In particular, he can borrow 100 now to make his present consumption with the skilled career equal to his present income with the unskilled career. Provided he does not have to repay more than 150 in the future, his future consumption will be no less with the skilled than the unskilled career. Thus, for a rate of interest sufficiently low, and the possibility of borrowing, the skilled career will be preferred *whatever the time preference*. With a well-organized loan market, therefore, the choice depends *only on the market rate of interest* and not on individual time preference.

Borrowing in this case differs from borrowing in the earlier consumption loan examples in that, as a result of borrowing, the consumer is able to *increase* his lifetime income—he becomes more "productive." The increase in his lifetime earnings is a *return* to education, and to the borrowing needed to finance it. If borrowing is possible, education will be worthwhile in the most direct sense (increased lifetime consumption) if the return to it is at least as great as the interest payments on the loan.

Since borrowing for education gives a return in terms of increased income, we consider it as an *investment*, as contrasted with a pure consumption loan which carries no external return, although it gives some "psychic" return to the borrower by enabling him to reach a more preferred situation.

Since an investment of this kind represents, in a sense, investment in an "improvement" to a human being, we refer to it as an investment in *human capital.*

Education is only one type of activity that can be viewed as investment in human capital.[4] Medical treatment can be regarded in a similar

---

[4] For applications of the concept of investment in human capital, see: Becker, G. S., *Human Capital.*

way. In treating these topics at more than the simplest level, we would take account of factors not discussed here. In particular, the simple financial costs and returns analysis needs to be modified to take account of the possibility of (a) "returns" to the individual additional to, or in place of, financial returns—personal enjoyment and social status from possession of a college degree, for example, and (b) externalities, which may give gains to society as a whole not reflected in income differentials and may require special policies.

11.3 Intertemporal Decisions by Firms

Although production processes take some finite time and thus involve intertemporal decisions in a restricted sense, we shall confine our analysis to decisions covering longer time horizons. For perfectly competitive firms, intertemporal decisions are confined to decisions concerning production and thus almost entirely to decisions concerning fixed capital.

Firms in monopoly or oligopoly situations, especially complex multiproduct firms, are necessarily involved in intertemporal decisions concerning the demand for their products. Selling at a high price now, even though it would maximize profits for the current period, may have effects on the demand schedule for the product in future periods. Definite choices may be involved between higher profits now with lower profits later or lower profits now with higher profits later, even though the firm's costs and production conditions are constant over time. These considerations are highly complex and no simple generalities can be established for the "typical" firm, so we shall not discuss them further.

We shall concern ourselves with decisions concerning fixed capital. As in earlier chapters (4, 5, and 6), we shall separate decisions concerning the purchase of capital services from decisions by the capital-owner, who may or may not be the user of its services. To simplify the analysis, we shall suppose there is a single type of fixed capital ("machines") whose services (machine-hours) can be freely bought and sold on a market. If the machine-owner uses his own machine services in production, we assume he can sell any surplus, or buy any deficit, of machine-hours. We shall also assume, again for simplicity, that

(i) the number of machine-hours per month or year, per machine, is technically fixed;

(ii) the machines do not wear out, so that depreciation can be omitted.

Relaxing these assumptions gives a more complex analysis, but not a more enlightening one.

In any period, if the total number of machines is fixed, so the supply of machine-hours is constant, the market price of machine-hours will be determined by demand. Thus the payment for machine-hours will be a *quasi-rent* to the machine owners. The use of existing capital, in our simple model, involves no intertemporal decisions.

Investment. Intertemporal considerations are involved, however, when the machine-owner decides whether or not to buy a *new* machine. The total purchase of new machines is *gross investment*. If the machines wear out, as we have assumed ours did not, some of the new machines are to replace others which have worn out. The *addition* to the total capital stock is *net investment*—it is equal to gross investment less replacement. In our simple analysis, net and gross investment are equal, but the difference can be considerable in fact. However, the decision, whether or not to buy a new machine, is the same whether the machine is a replacement or not, provided the economy is competitive. In other words:

All investment decisions are gross investment decisions in a competitive economy. If it is profitable to replace a wornout machine, it is profitable to purchase an additional machine, and if it is not profitable to purchase an additional machine, it is not profitable to replace it.

The profitability of investment is determined by a comparison of cost and revenue, but the comparison is intertemporal because the cost of the machine is incurred at the initial point of investment, while the revenues are generated over later periods. In the absence of a well-organized loan market, the decision would be based on some kind of time preference. We assume, however, an organized loan market (or *capital market* as it will usually be called when expanded beyond consumption loans), that enables the machine-owner to adjust his financial flows.

For our simple case, we can suppose the machine-owner borrows to pay for the machine and pays annual interest on the loan. Since the machine does not wear out, we can suppose the loan is for an indefinitely long period or else that it is for a year at a time, but this year's loan is repaid by taking a new loan next year, and so on.

In terms of the simple model, the number of machine-hours per year is constant. If machine rents are constant and expected to remain so, the annual return on the machine will be constant at some level R. If P is the price of the machine and i the rate of interest, the interest payment each year will be iP. Thus for each year we have:

Annual revenue　　R
Annual cost　　　　iP.
Investment will be profitable if and only if[5]

$$R \geq iP.$$

---

[5] As in the case of the profit maximizing output (Section 6.5) we assume that investment will occur when $R = iP$, that is, so long as it is *not unprofitable*.

Note that the profitability of investment depends on the relationship between *three* parameters: the price of the machine, the rate of interest and the annual rental value or return. Sometimes it is convenient to use the ratio R/P (the *rate of return*), and state the criterion for profitable investment in terms of the relationship between the rate of return and the rate of interest, as

$$R/P \geqq i.$$

The Level of Investment. The criterion given above as to whether it is profitable to invest or not gives no indication as to *how much* investment will take place.

It is not useful to draw a demand curve for capital *in the individual firm* in the way we can draw the short-term demand curve for labor (Section 6.10). While it makes sense to consider the firm to have capital fixed in the short run and to vary labor (thus giving the demand curve), varying capital with labor fixed is usually an irrelevant decision. A firm's investment decisions (assuming it wants to own its own machines) concern its *scale,* not its capital to labor ratio. The firm that expands its capital will expand its labor in proportion, to maintain the optimum input mix so long as input prices are unchanged.

For a perfectly competitive firm under constant returns to scale, size is indefinite. The firm will presumably expand by as much as it can borrow, and the size distribution of the firms will be determined by essentially random influences. An imperfectly competitive firm has an optimum size determined by its market—under constant returns to scale, it will expand to the point at which its profit maximizing output is just being produced with no capital limitation.

The *aggregate* level of investment is determinate, however. It is determined by the joint equilibrium of *three* separate markets:[6]

(1) The market for capital services, determining R.

(2) The market for new machines, determining P.

(3) The loan or capital market, determining i.

Given sufficient time, we can expect an equilibrium to be reached as a result of events in all three markets. Let us suppose that investment is the only thing changing in any of the markets and that initially $R > iP$ so that investment is definitely profitable. As investment takes place, this increases the demand for new capital, tending to increase P, and for loans, tending

---

[6] This is really a problem in general equilibrium. We are attempting to follow tradition here by using simple supply and demand analysis, which is essentially a partial equilibrium tool. We do this by using the market analysis in a rather impressionistic fashion, since there are, strictly speaking, no independent and constant demand and supply schedules.

to increase *i*. The additional capital will increase the supply of machine-hours, tending to decrease *R*, so that the investment will tend to bring *P* and *iP* closer together. When $R = iP$, investment will cease or become marginal and we will have equilibrium.[7] If machines wear out faster than replaced, the supply of machine-hours will fall, their price (and thus *R*) will rise to make it once more profitable to invest.

The dynamics of the trio of markets may not work as smoothly as the above description suggests. All the problems associated with market dynamics, especially those arising from lags, are compounded because of the three markets. There are lags between borrowing and building the capital —some types of capital such as buildings, transport equipment for heavy duty, heavy machinery, may take months or even years to construct. Then there are further lags between constructing the equipment and discovering its ultimate effects on production. It is quite possible that investment occurs until *iP* rises to the original level of *R* but, because of lags, the full effects resulting in the fall of *R* do not become apparent until the investment is complete. Ultimately we reach the disequilibrium situation with $R < iP$ (overinvestment).

Other Types of Investment. There are costs, other than those associated with fixed capital, which can be analyzed along the above lines because they involve intertemporal decisions. If some outlay *(entry cost)* is necessary to obtain information, attract initial customers, buy organization membership (as in a stock exchange), or otherwise do what is necessary to enter an industry, this should be viewed like an investment. It will be profitable to enter only if the anticipated rate of return exceeds the interest rate. This means, of course, the return net of ordinary costs—for an imperfectly competitive industry the return would be the monopoly profit. Note that *once the firm has actually entered,* any interest or other payments associated with the entry cost are fixed costs and are henceforward irrelevant to decision making, unless the right to entry can be sold to another firm.

A firm may invest in *research and development* if it can make *private* (by patents or secrecy) the return, or a sufficient part of the return, from consequent technological change. A firm may even invest in *human capital,* such as training programs for employees or prospective employees, if it expects to obtain some part of the return for itself.

---

[7] At equilibrium, in this sense, the stock of capital will remain stationary. *Dynamic models,* briefly discussed in Section 11.4, require something to maintain net investment at a positive level. This could be exogenous change in technology (leading perhaps to a steady fall in *P* relative to other prices), growth in the labor force (preventing *R* from falling as the capital stock grows).

11.4 Intertemporal Welfare and Growth Policy

Welfare. In a static setting, we can go far with the relatively simple and noncontroversial ideas that:

(a) the individual is the judge of his own welfare,

(b) the Pareto criterion is a suitable basis for policy, for those situations between which the criterion gives a ranking.

Unfortunately these ideas do not provide the same foundation for intertemporal welfare judgments. In the intertemporal case we are forced to question even (a), and ask whether the consumer is the best judge of his own intertemporal welfare.

The problem can be illustrated by a simple example. In Section 11.2 we assumed that a consumer offered the choice *today* between the consumption patterns

(A) 101 today, 99 tomorrow,

(B)   99 today, 101 tomorrow,

would prefer (A) because of *impatience.*

But suppose now that the consumer is given his choice (A), and then is asked *tomorrow* whether he did not wish he had chosen (B), we should not be surprised if his answer was, yes. In other words, *impatience* may lead to later *regret.*[8]

Taking a completely external view of the consumer, we observe that consumption patterns (A) and (B) both offer the consumer 99 in one period and 101 in the other. We are entitled to wonder whether his "overall" *welfare* (whatever it is) should be affected by the *order* in which the two periods occur when his own view changes between one period and the next. His consumption over the two-"day" period is precisely the same in both cases.

Another way of looking at the problem is to consider that the consumer tomorrow is, in effect, a *different* consumer from what he is today. Thus his allocation from one period to another can be regarded, in some sense, as making one consumer better off and the other worse off, and so cannot be considered to come under the Pareto criterion.

Whichever way we look at the problem, it seems that we cannot avoid reaching the unsatisfactory conclusion:

It is an open question whether the consumer's own allocation of

---

[8] Of course, any decision may come to be regretted. In the static model, however, we assume that the consumer faces basically similar choices over and over, so that a mistake in choosing his collection today will not be repeated tomorrow. In the intertemporal case, the consequences of yesterday's decisions remain today and the *range* of available choices today is already restricted by the choice made yesterday. In the static case, today's choice is unrestricted by yesterday's.

consumption over time should be accepted as optimal for his own welfare.

Economists have barely commenced to investigate the problems of intertemporal welfare, so the above neutral conclusion seems to be the best we can do in the present state of the art.

Growth Policy. The above considerations have important implications for policy concerning the growth of the competitive economy.

By growth we mean growth in *output per head*. This may increase as a result of technological change but we shall ignore the possibility here. We shall consider a simple two-factor (labor and capital) model with constant returns to scale. Since population is assumed to be directly proportional to labor, output per head cannot increase unless capital grows faster than labor (in the absence of technological change) since output per head is directly proportional to the *average product of labor*. If capital and labor grow at the same rate, the average product will remain constant, and growth in our sense will not take place.

There are many specific models of growth, but in almost all of them the rate of growth will be greater, the greater is the rate of growth in the stock of capital. The increase in the capital stock in a given period is the net investment in that period, so a high rate of growth will result from a high level of investment. This may well be true even if growth comes from technological change, since this change often represents change in the type of capital itself—we say the change is *embodied* in the capital. To obtain the advantage of embodied technological change, we need to replace the old capital by the new as fast as possible, again requiring a high level of investment.

In the perfectly competitive economy, the aggregate level of investment depends on the combined effect of decisions by individual firms. As shown in Section 11.3, this level depends on the equilibria established in the markets for capital services, capital equipment, and loans. In long-run competitive equilibrium, the return to capital (price of capital services) will be determined by the supply of labor and the production technology which give the equilibrium relationship:

$$\frac{r}{MPK} = \frac{w}{MPL}$$

in the production of all commodities. The price of new capital will be given by the standard equilibrium relationships for the competitive firm in the long run:

$$P_k = MC_k = \frac{r}{MPK_k}.$$

The rate of return, under these conditions, is thus equal to MPK_k, the marginal product of capital in the capital-producing industry.

Thus, of the three determinants of investment, R, P, i, the first two are determined by essentially *technical* factors (resources and technology). The only *behavioral* determinant of the level of investment will be supply of savings. The more that consumers are willing to save at a given rate of interest, the higher the level of investment at that rate of interest.

Assuming no transitory income effects, the supply of savings will be determined by the consumers' *time preferences* and *income levels*. Many growth models assume that savings increase as incomes increase—since the investment then increases incomes, we obtain the dynamic that keeps the growth process going.[9] Whatever the specific growth model we use, it will usually be true that the rate of growth will be increased if consumers save more *at a given income level and rate of interest*.

The level of savings at each rate of interest and income level is determined by *time preference* ("impatience"). The lower the rate of time preference, the more consumers will save at given interest rate and income.

Since the growth of the economy has the most profound effect on the future welfare of its present citizens and more so on the welfare of its future citizens, a growth rate of 3 per cent in output per head will enable the next generation to have *twice* the consumption level of the present generation. Given the neutral conclusion concerning consumers as judges of intertemporal welfare, many economists (not all, by any means) would argue that, although the equilibrium of the competitive economy is optimal in relation to *static* considerations, it may result in too low a rate of growth. The low rate of growth is due to a low level of savings, due in turn to a high rate of time preference ("impatience") which may lead to a future situation that the consumers may "regret."

The logic of such a point of view would lead to the support of government intervention in *intertemporal* decisions (perhaps compulsory savings) even though such intervention may be considered undesirable (if the economy is, in fact, perfectly competitive) in relation to *static* decisions.[10]

Some economists are even willing to support the present statically suboptimal structure of the United States economy because it is believed to lead to a higher growth rate than would be achieved under competitive conditions. It can be argued along these lines that corporations distribute only part of their profits—essentially monopoly profits—as dividends and save

---

[9] The best known simple model is the *Harrod–Domar* model, discussed in texts on macroeconomics and economic growth.

[10] The existence of *intertemporal externalities*, mentioned in Section 11.1, would provide another case for such intervention. It is very likely that investment in human capital, and in much research, as well as investment in things usually done by governments (roads, dams, bridges), is subject to intertemporal externalities of this kind.

the remainder (about three-quarters), whereas the consumers would save a smaller proportion if the profits were entirely distributed.

The idea of growth as a deliberate policy is relatively new in Western economies. The difference in the emphasis on growth as a *policy* target is probably more important a difference between, say, the Soviet Union and the United States than are the differences in the static operation of the two economies.

11.5 Money

In spite of the strong association of money and economics in the mind of the layman, many texts on microeconomics and price theory do not discuss money at all, and we have come around to it only in this, the last section of the book.

The reason is simple enough. The usefulness of money in the economy is entirely due to the very things that are, for simplicity, assumed nonexistent in the simple static model of the economy. Without intertemporal effects and uncertainty, there is no role for money in the system.

The Demand for Money. We take money to be something which is acceptable by everyone in exchange for anything, which cannot be itself consumed, and which is durable and storable. The fundamental problem in discussing money is to establish reasons why persons should be willing to *hold* it rather than exchange it immediately for some consumable good. When we refer to the "demand for money" we do not refer to the demand for money to spend (presumably without limit), but the demand for money to hold, or the demand for money *balances*.

A consumer who keeps $50 in his bureau drawer, or $1,000 in his checking account for an indefinite period is *foregoing consumption* since he could spend the money at any stage. On the other hand, since he is foregoing consumption in any case, he also has the option of *lending at interest*. We must view the demand for money balances in terms of the two options available, spending and lending. For consumers to be willing to hold money, there must be something about the role of money that makes the consumer willing to forego present consumption to hold a balance, and something that makes the consumer willing to forego interest to hold the balance specifically as money.

A primary motive for holding balances of some kind is the *timing of transactions,* closely related to the idea of the smoothing of consumption discussed in Section 11.2. A consumer may receive his income at intervals, but wish to consume at a steady rate over time. A consumer may receive wages of $70 every Friday, but wish to consume at a steady rate over the week. One possibility is that he converts his wages *immediately* into stocks of goods and consumes these over the week. For various reasons it is likely to be more convenient and economical for the consumer to hold stocks of money rather than goods, and spend these over the week. Thus the consumer may spend at a rate of $10 per day, running his money balance down from $70 each Friday to zero each Thursday following, giving an *average balance* of $35. A balance of this kind is a *transactions balance*.

Not only may the timing of transactions be irregular over time, there may also be some *uncertainty* about the level of transactions. The consumer may wish to be in a position to pay for, say, medical treatment which may or may not be necessary and so may maintain a *precautionary reserve*. Our consumer, therefore, may wish to hold an average balance of $50, including a precautionary $15.

We still have to explain why the consumer does not *lend* his balances and obtain interest. The explanation here lies in uncertainty of various kinds. If the timing of transactions were certain, the consumer could arrange loans such that $10 was repaid each day of the week so he would not need to hold money for transactions balances. The precautionary reserve, by its nature, would be held as money. Even the transactions balances, or part of them, would not be lent if the *timing* was itself uncertain and the consumer could not be sure that he would not need to spend $15 on Tuesday and $5 on Wednesday rather than have the expenditure the same on both days. With uncertain timing, a smooth cycle of loan repayments could not be organized. This uncertainty of timing and of the level of payments means that the lower the money balance, the greater the risk of being caught in an undesirable financial situation.

The immediate availability of money balances at face value, compared with loans whose repayments may not come at the appropriate time or which the borrower may have to be asked to repay before time (at some loss to the lender) makes money a *liquid* asset. If we have money and various securities of different types, we often speak of them differing in their degree of liquidity—money, by definition, has the highest degree of liquidity possible.

The Demand Curve for Money. We have established motives for the existence of a demand for money balances. Now we wish to consider how the level of balances will be influenced by the market parameters.

Since the *level* of a consumer's transactions will rise with his income, we can presume that his desired money balances will also rise with income. Since his holding of balances in money rather than securities represents a balancing of foregone interest against the risk of being caught in an undesirable financial situation (illiquid), we can expect that, if anything, the consumer will be less willing to hold balances as money when the interest rate is high than when it is low. In general, we shall expect that, if the rate of interest rises, the consumer will shift some of his balances from money into securities, but not all, until his new balance of risk against foregone interest is struck.

Thus we usually consider that the demand for money balances, aggregated over consumers,[11] will:

(a) increase when income increases,

(b) decrease when the rate of interest increases.

The Money Market. The supply of money depends on what acts as money in the economy. One of the great social inventions of the last two centuries or so has been that of banknotes and checks, which provide something that acts as money (acceptable for all transactions) but has virtually no production cost.[12] Thus the supply of money does not depend on the availability of physical resources but on the decisions of the monetary authority or central bank.

We can usually consider the supply of money to be arbitrarily determined by monetary policy (although a competitive model can be set up with no central authority).[13] We have already derived the demand conditions, so we have a *money market*.

The equilibrating variable in the money market, in terms of the analysis we have given, would seem to be the *rate of interest*. But this is also the equilibrating variable in the loan or securities market, so we cannot adopt a simple partial equilibrium approach.

One class of macroeconomic models avoids the potential dilemma by noting that both markets depend on two variables—the level of income and the rate of interest. In Keynesian models,[14] the demand for loans is influenced only by the level of investment, and the level of investment determines aggregate income (through the multiplier). Thus we can treat the markets as a pair, each depending on income and the rate of interest, and the two jointly determining the levels of both variables.[15]

---

[11] Although we have referred to the holders of money balances as "consumers," firms will also hold balances for similar reasons.

[12] Unlike gold or early monetary standards.

[13] In a competitive model with no monetary authority, money cannot be something with no cost of production, otherwise it will be manufactured without limit and cease to be acceptable. Obviously, money must be *scarce,* either from natural or artificial causes.

[14] Such models are discussed in all macroeconomics and principles texts.

[15] The best known analysis is probably the *"IS-LM"* curve analysis of Hicks. In this we draw the curve representing those combinations of income and the rate of interest that give equilibrium in the *money market* for a given money stock. This is the *"LM"* curve. The *"IS"* curve gives the income-interest combinations that equilibrate the loan market. The intersection of the curves gives the income and interest rate at which both markets are in equilibrium.

The demand for money depends, however, on a parameter we have so far neglected, as well as on income and the rate of interest. This parameter can be described as the "general level of prices," and we now turn to investigate its influence.

Real Balances. Suppose the consumer of our earlier example, with an income of $70 per week was in equilibrium with desired money balances of $50. Now suppose that, by some miracle, *all* prices and his money income were halved overnight. The consumer could still buy exactly the same collections of goods as before because, as we saw in Section 7.4, changing income and prices in the same proportion leaves real choice unchanged. Thus his real consumption level is unchanged. But would he still wish to maintain a money balance of $50?

In terms of the suggested motives for holding money balances, we would expect not. To maintain the steady flow of daily expenditure would now require an average balance of only $17.50 instead of $35. At the new prices he could cover exactly the same uncertain eventualities with a precautionary reserve of $7.50 as he could previously with $15. Thus a balance of $25 would now perform *precisely* the same functions as the previous balance of $50.

The desired money balances are related to a specific degree of command over real goods and services—the demand is a demand for a given level of *real balances*. If the price level (meaning *all* prices, but not interest rates which are already a ratio) were to double, balances would need to have double the money content to give the same real balance.

Thus the demand for money depends on the price level as well as (real) income and the rate of interest, and will increase when the price level increases.

Instead of considering the rate of interest as equilibrating the money market we can, therefore, consider the rate of interest to be determined in the loan market and the *price level* in the money market. This is the "classical" approach.

The Real Balance Effect.[16] In the case of the miracle we described above, the consumer would find that, at the new price level, he has $25 more than necessary to maintain exactly the same consumption pattern and real balances as before. This $25 represents a windfall to the consumer—he can be expected to spend or lend part or all of it, but we cannot predict exactly what he will do since this is a dynamic and disequilibrium situation. The

---

[16] The classic reference on this topic is: Patinkin, D., *Money Interest and Prices* (2nd ed.), Row, Peterson, 1965.

behavior which results from the existence of this windfall is called the *real balance effect*. If prices had doubled instead of halving, the consumer would have found his real balances to be too low, and would have had to forego some consumption (or sell some securities) to increase them.

Note that, in the case of our miracle, the consumer makes a *permanent* gain from the increase in real balances, provided prices do not increase afterward.[17] He could invest the extra $25 and have an interest payment over and above his regular income in every future period. One of the results of the permanent increase in his income is likely to be that he will hold higher real balances, so he may well choose to lend only $24, maintaining new money balances of $26 because of the increased income from lending the $24.

---

[17] In a general equilibrium setting, real wealth cannot rise if the quantity of goods is unchanged. Thus the real balance effect may *result* in bringing about price changes.

MATHEMATICAL NOTES

These notes are confined to matters in which a knowledge of elementary calculus, or a willingness to handle a little more elementary algebra, illuminate or simplify the analysis in the main text.

The section numbers in the notes refer to the appropriate section in the main text.

No attempt has been made to extend the material in the main text, or to use mathematical methods beyond those of elementary calculus. Nor have mathematical notes been given on matters to which the author believes they have little to add without using more advanced techniques.

The reader who is willing and able to attempt a more advanced mathematical approach to economics should consult the author's mathematical economics book, *Mathematical Economics*, Macmillan, 1968.

CHAPTER 2

Section 2.5

   Elasticity

   If $y(x)$ is *any* function of *any* single variable x, the *elasticity of* y *with respect to* x is defined as:

$$\eta = \frac{x}{y} \cdot \frac{dy}{dx} \; .$$

It is the limit of the ratio $\dfrac{\Delta y}{y} \Big/ \dfrac{\Delta x}{x}$ as $\Delta x \to 0$, and is a function of x, so defined at a point.

   A very useful relationship is the following:

$$\frac{d \,(\log y)}{d \,(\log x)} = \frac{d \,(\log y)}{dy} \cdot \frac{dy}{dx} \cdot \frac{dx}{d \,(\log x)}$$

$$= \frac{1}{y} \cdot \frac{dy}{dx} \cdot x$$

$$= \eta$$

so that the elasticity of y with respect to x is the derivative of log y with respect to log x.

Partial Elasticities

If $y(u, v)$ is a function of the two variables u, v, we have *partial elasticities* with respect to the two independent variables. These are defined in a manner analogous to the total elasticity, but with a partial derivative in place of the ordinary derivative. For example,

$$\eta_u = \frac{u}{y} \cdot \frac{\partial y}{\partial u}.$$

Since demand is a functional relationship between quantity and several variables, the various demand elasticities are partial elasticities. It is usual to ignore the partial notation if it is clear from the context that only one variable is being considered.

Typically, we may have a demand function of the form

$$x = x(p, I, P)$$

where p is the good's own price, I is income, P is some other relevant price. Then η_p is the *own price elasticity* (what is meant by the "elasticity of demand" if the term is used by itself), η_I is the *income elasticity* and η_P is a *cross-price elasticity*.

For the downward sloping demand curve, we will have $\eta_p < 0$. η_I could have any sign—if < 0, the good is said to be *inferior*, if > 0, to be *normal*. η_P could also have any sign—if > 0, we say the two goods are *gross substitutes*, if < 0, they are *gross complements*. If $\eta_P = 0$, the goods are said to be *unrelated*.

Constant-Elasticity Curves

If we take a relationship of the form

$$x = A p^\alpha I^\beta P^\gamma \qquad (A, \alpha, \beta, \gamma \text{ constants})$$

and take logarithms, we obtain

$$\log x = \log A + \alpha \log p + \beta \log I + \gamma \log P.$$

The partial derivatives are

$$\frac{\partial (\log x)}{\partial (\log p)} = \alpha \qquad \frac{\partial (\log x)}{\partial (\log I)} = \beta \qquad \frac{\partial (\log x)}{\partial (\log P)} = \gamma$$

so that α, β, γ correspond to the partial elasticities η_p, η_I, η_P, which are thus constant.

If I, P and held constant, the demand curve has the equation

$$\log x = \log B + \alpha \log p \quad (\text{with } B = A I^\beta P^\gamma)$$

or,

$$x = B p^\alpha.$$

A curve of this form is a *constant elasticity curve*. In econometric work, there are tremendous advantages in the statistical fitting of *linear* relationships to data. Since a constant-elasticity demand relationship can be converted into a relationship which is linear in logs, it is extremely common to fit a relationship of this kind.

The Straight Line

A downward sloping straight line demand curve will have an equation of the form:

$$x = B - bp \qquad \frac{B}{b} \geq p \geq 0$$

where B/b is the price at which the quantity demanded just becomes zero, and b is the slope (numerical value).

We have

$$\frac{dx}{dp} = -b$$

so that

$$\eta = \frac{p}{x}\frac{dx}{dp}$$

$$= -\frac{p}{(B/b) - p}.$$

Thus the elasticity varies along the curve, provided $b \neq 0$.

For $p = 0$, $(x = B)$, we have $\eta = 0$ (completely inelastic).

For $p = B/b$ $(x = 0)$, we have $\eta = -\infty$ (perfectly elastic).

For $p = \frac{1}{2}B/b$ $(x = \frac{1}{2}B)$, we have $\eta = -1$ (unit elasticity).

Note that the unit elasticity point always occurs at half the price at which the quantity becomes zero (and at half the maximum quantity), that is, at the mid-point of the demand curve.

We can analyze the upward sloping straight line supply curve, $x = A + ap$, in the same manner, to show that ϵ (the supply elasticity) is 1 when $A = 0$, for all p, and $\to 1$ as $p \to \infty$ for other values of A, provided $a \neq 0$. If $a = 0$, $x = A$ for all p, and the supply is *completely inelastic* ($\epsilon = 0$). If the supply curve is horizontal, supply is *perfectly elastic* ($\epsilon = \infty$).

Expenditure and Elasticity

Consider the case in which only the good's own price changes, so that we have a demand curve, $x = x(p)$. Then expenditure at any price is given by $E = p \cdot x(p)$.

Taking the derivative with respect to price, we obtain:

$$\frac{dE}{dp} = x + p\frac{dx}{dp}$$

$$= x\left[1 + \frac{p}{x}\frac{dx}{dp}\right]$$

$$= x\,(1 + \eta)$$

where η is the (own price) elasticity of demand.

Since $\eta < 0$, $1 + \eta > 0$ if $|\eta| < 1$ (inelastic demand), $1 + \eta = 0$ if $|\eta| = 1$ (unit elasticity), and $1 + \eta < 0$ if $|\eta| > 1$ (elastic). Thus we have the relationship described in the text:

$$\frac{dE}{dp} \underset{<}{\overset{>}{=}} 0 \quad \text{according as } |\eta| \underset{>}{\overset{<}{=}} 1.$$

CHAPTER 3
Section 3.3
Continuous Dynamic Adjustment

Denote by z the *excess demand* in the market, so that $z = 0$ at equilibrium, and $z < 0$ when there is excess supply. Let p be the *deviation* of price from the equilibrium, with $p > 0$ when the actual price is above the equilibrium price, $p < 0$ when the actual price is below the equilibrium price, while $p = 0$ at equilibrium.

Obviously z is a function of p, and we must have $z = 0$ when $p = 0$ (the equilibrium point). For simplicity we shall suppose the relationship is linear, or that we are taking a linear approximation near equilibrium, so that

$$z = ap.$$

Now let us suppose that the behavior of the market is such that, when excess demand is positive the price moves up towards equilibrium at a rate proportional to the amount of excess demand, and when excess demand is negative the price moves down towards equilibrium at a rate proportional to the amount of excess, giving a relationship of the form

$$\frac{dp}{dt} = kz \quad (k > 0).$$

Substituting for z, we have

$$\frac{dp}{dt} = kap.$$

This is a first order differential equation in p which can be integrated immediately after separating the variables:

$$\int \frac{dp}{p} = \int ka\,dt + c$$

to give

$$\log p = kat + c$$

or, $$p = Ce^{kat}$$

where c is an arbitrary constant of integration and $C = e^c$.

If $ka < 0$, e^{kat} *decreases* with time and $p \to 0$ as $t \to \infty$, so that equilibrium is steadily approached as time goes on and the market is *stable*. Since $k > 0$, $ka < 0$ if $a < 0$, that is, if excess demand occurs when price is *below* equilibrium ($p < 0$) and excess supply occurs ($z < 0$) when price is above equilibrium. This will certainly be true if the supply and demand curves have the normal slopes, giving the stability condition of the main text.

If $a > 0$, we will have p increasing with t, so the market will be *unstable*. This requires "perverse" curves.

Section 3.4
The Cobweb Model

Assume a straight-line demand curve of the form $x^D = B - bP$. Since we have a period-by-period model, we must date the variables to give:

$$x_n^D = B - bP_n \quad \text{for period } n.$$

The "supply curve" is also assumed to be linear, but here the quantity is that for *one period later* than the price. That is:

$$x_n^S = A + aP_{n-1}.$$

The behavior of price is determined in the following way. Given P_{n-1}, x_n^S is determined from the supply equation. P_n is then determined as the price at which $x_n^S = x_n^D$. That is:

$$B - bP_n = x_n^D = x_n^S = A + aP_{n-1}.$$

This gives:

$$P_n = -\frac{a}{b}P_{n-1} + \frac{1}{b}(B - A)$$

which is a first order *difference equation* (relating prices at two successive time periods). Such an equation can be solved by *iteration* since, given some initial price P_0, the above equation gives P_1. We then feed this value of P_1 into the right hand side, obtain P_2, and continue the process.

Such an equation has an *equilibrium solution* P^* such that $P_n = P_{n-1} = P^*$ for all n. We can easily find the value of P^* since it must satisfy

$$P^* = -\frac{a}{b}P^* + \frac{1}{b}(B - A)$$

and so we have

$$P^* = \frac{B - A}{b + a} \ .$$

P^* is also the equilibrium price in the static sense. In the expression for P^*, B is the quantity demanded at zero price and A is the quantity supplied at zero price. For an interior equilibrium we will have $B > A$ and so $P^* > 0$.

Now consider $p_n = P - P^*$, the *deviation* from equilibrium. Substituting in the price-determining equation:

$$p_n + P^* = -\frac{a}{b}(p_{n-1} + P^*) + \frac{1}{b}(B - A)$$

Thus
$$p_n = -\frac{a}{b}p_{n-1} - \left(\frac{b + a}{b}\right)P^* + \frac{1}{b}(B - A)$$

$$= -\frac{a}{b}p_{n-1} \quad \text{(substituting for } P^*).$$

Suppose the initial deviation is p_0. Then we have, in succession,

$$p_1 = -\frac{a}{b}p_0$$

$$p_2 = -\frac{a}{b}p_1 = \left(-\frac{a}{b}\right)^2 p_0$$

$$\cdots\cdots\cdots\cdots\cdots\cdots$$

$$p_n = \left(-\frac{a}{b}\right)^n p_0 \ .$$

The quantity $(-a/b)^n$ will be positive for even n, negative for odd n, giving an *alternation* of price above and below the equilibrium. The absolute value of the distance of the price from equilibrium will be given by $(a/b)^n$. This will decrease with n if $a < b$ and increase with n if $a > b$.

Thus the condition for stability (given that a, b are both positive) is that $a < b$, that is, that the numerical value of the slope of the supply curve be less than the numerical value of the slope of the demand curve, as pointed out in the main text.

CHAPTER 4
Section 4.5

Properties of Smooth Isoquants

A smoothly curved isoquant implies a continuous functional relationship between the amounts of labor and capital necessary to produce a given output. Taking capital (k) as the independent variable, and labor (l) as the dependent, the shape of the isoquant implies

$$\frac{dl}{dk} < 0 \text{ (downward sloping to the right)},$$

$$\frac{d^2l}{dk^2} > 0 \text{ (convex toward the origin, that is, downward)}.$$

It is more usual to consider the isoquant equation in the implicit form

$$F(l, k) = C$$

which is easily adapted to more than two inputs. F is the *production function*, which is discussed in the Mathematical Note on Section 4.7.

Taking derivatives through the implicit form and rearranging, the reader can satisfy himself that the following relationships hold:

$$\frac{dl}{dk} = -\frac{F_k}{F_l}$$

$$\frac{d^2l}{dk^2} = -\frac{1}{F_l}\left\{F_{kk} + \left[\frac{F_k}{F_l}\right]^2 F_{ll} - 2\left[\frac{F_k}{F_l}\right]F_{kl}\right\}$$

where F_k, F_l are the partial derivatives of F with respect to k, l and F_{kk}, F_{ll}, F_{kl} are the second order partial derivatives.

The condition that the isoquant be convex to the origin

$$\left(\frac{d^2l}{dk^2} > 0\right)$$

thus requires that

$$F_{kk} + r^2 F_{ll} - 2rF_{kl} < 0$$

where $r = F_k/F_l$ and is essentially positive. It is obviously *sufficient*, but not necessary, for this condition to be satisfied that F_{kk}, F_{ll} be negative and F_{kl} be positive. We shall return to this condition in the note on Section 4.9.

Section 4.6

Substitution

For the 2-input isoquant, the *marginal rate of substitution of labor for capital* is the derivative $\frac{dl}{dk}$.

The tradition of the verbal analysis is to consider how the marginal rate of substitution of labor for capital varies with *labor* rather than with capital. That is, we consider $\dfrac{d}{dl}\left(\dfrac{dl}{dk}\right)$ rather than the ordinary second

order derivative $\dfrac{d^2l}{dk^2} = \dfrac{d}{dk}\left(\dfrac{dl}{dk}\right)$.

We have $\dfrac{d}{dl}\left(\dfrac{dl}{dk}\right) = \dfrac{d^2l}{dk^2} \cdot \dfrac{dk}{dl} < 0$ since $\dfrac{d^2l}{dk^2} > 0, \dfrac{dl}{dk} < 0$.

It is the difference between the old verbal tradition and the most straightforward mathematical approach that creates the confusion concerning the appropriateness of the word "diminishing," as mentioned in the main text.

Section 4.7

The Production Function

If x is the *efficient* output produced by inputs l, k, the *production function* has the form

$$x = F(l, k) .$$

Choosing some particular output $\bar{x}$, we obtain the implicit form of the isoquant equation as a contour of the production function:

$$F(l, k) = \bar{x} = C .$$

The production function (whose definition can be extended to cover any number of inputs) is a convenient analytical device only if it has appropriate continuity, that is, for smooth isoquant cases.

The Cobb-Douglas Production Function

In one of the pioneer empirical investigations, Douglas fitted a loglinear function suggested by Cobb to data for the United States. The form of the function

$$\log x = \log A + \alpha \log l + \beta \log k$$

or

$$x = Al^\alpha k^\beta$$

is now universally called the *Cobb-Douglas production function*. (Sometimes the name is confined to the particular case in which $\alpha + \beta = 1$, a relationship whose significance is made clear in the note on Section 4.8).

The Cobb-Douglas function is the simplest function having all the essential properties of a production function. Putting $x = \bar{x}$ we have the isoquant $l = Ck^{-\beta/\alpha}$, where $C = (\bar{x}/A)^{1/\alpha}$. The derivatives are:

$$\frac{dl}{dk} = -\frac{\beta}{\alpha} Ck^{-\left(\frac{\beta}{\alpha}+1\right)} < 0$$

$$\frac{d^2l}{dk^2} = \frac{\beta}{\alpha}\left(\frac{\beta}{\alpha}+1\right) Ck^{-\left(\frac{\beta}{\alpha}+2\right)} > 0$$

so the isoquants have the appropriate properties.

In the form $x = Al^\alpha k^\beta = F(l, k)$, the partial derivatives of the Cobb-Douglas function are as follows:

$$F_l = \alpha Al^{\alpha-1}k^\beta = \alpha x/l$$
$$F_k = \beta x/k$$

and the second order partial derivatives are easily seen to be:

$$F_{ll} = \alpha(\alpha - 1)x/l^2 \quad F_{kk} = \beta(\beta - 1)x/k^2$$
$$F_{lk} = F_{kl} = \alpha\beta\, x/lk\,.$$

The Cobb-Douglas function is the simplest (by far) of a class of functions known as *constant elasticity of substitution* (or CES) production functions.

The elasticity of substitution is defined as $\dfrac{d\left(\dfrac{l}{k}\right)}{d\left(\dfrac{F_l}{F_k}\right)}$ and is equal to unity

for the Cobb-Douglas function.

Section 4.8

Returns to Scale

Let our production function be $x = F(l,k)$, and consider the effect of increasing l, k by the same factor b (> 0). We obtain a new value of x given by $F(bl, bk)$. For $b > 1$, we say F shows increasing, constant, or decreasing returns to scale according as $F(bl, bk) >, =,$ or $<, b.F(l, k)$.

F is *homogeneous of degree r* if $F(bl, bk) = b^r F(l, k)$. Obviously (since $b > 1$), we have increasing, constant, or decreasing returns to scale according as $r >, =, <, 1$. Homogeneity of degree one is exactly equivalent to constant returns to scale everywhere, but homogeneity of degree less than (greater than) one is a very special and regular form of decreasing (increasing) returns to scale.

The Cobb-Douglas Function

This form of the production function (see the note on Section 4.7) is homogeneous, since

$$F(bl, bk) = A(bl)^\alpha (bk)^\beta = Ab^{\alpha+\beta}\, l^\alpha k^\beta = b^{\alpha + \beta}F(l, k)\,.$$

The degree of homogeneity is the sum of the indices, $\alpha + \beta$. If $\alpha + \beta = 1$ we have constant returns to scale. This is the most common form in which the function appears, and is usually then written as

$$x = Al^\alpha k^{1-\alpha}\,.$$

Marginal Rate of Substitution for Homogeneous Functions

Consider initial inputs l, k and new inputs $L = bl$, $K = bk$. Obviously, the ratio L/K is the same as the ratio l/k. If the production function is homogeneous, we have

$$F(L, K) = b^r F(l, k) .$$

Taking partial derivatives of both sides with respect to l, k (using the relationships $L = bl$, $K = bk$), we obtain

$$F_L \cdot b = b^r F_l$$
$$F_K \cdot b = b^r F_k .$$

This gives $F_L/F_K = F_l/F_k$ for all changes in L, K which leave the ratio L/K equal to l/k. Thus the marginal rate of substitution remains constant for all outputs if the labor to capital ratio is constant. It also implies that, for constant returns to scale ($r = 1$), we have $F_L = F_l$ so that F_l is unchanged by equiproportionate increases in l, k and is thus homogeneous of degree zero.

Section 4.9

Returns to a Variable Input

For a production function of the form $x = F(l, k)$, the *marginal product of labor* is the partial derivative F_l. If capital is fixed and labor varied, the change in the marginal product with the change in labor is simply the second order partial derivative F_{ll}.

In general, the convexity of the isoquant does not imply, nor is it implied by, $F_{ll} < 0$. In terms of the partial derivatives, the convexity condition is (see the note on Section 4.5):

$$F_{kk} + r^2 F_{ll} - r F_{kl} < 0 .$$

Since $r > 0$, it is quite possible for this to be satisfied with $F_{ll} > 0$ (increasing marginal product of labor) if F_{kl} is large and positive.

If a function $F(x, y)$ is homogeneous of degree r, we have by definition

$$b^r F(x, y) = F(bx, by) .$$

Differentiating this identity with respect to b, we obtain

$$rb^{r-1} F = x F_x + y F_y .$$

Since this holds for all b, and all x, y, we can put $b = 1$ to obtain

$$rF = x F_x + y F_y .$$

This result is known as *Euler's Theorem for homogeneous functions* (Euler discovered other theorems).

If $F(l, k)$ is a constant returns to scale function, F_l is homogeneous of degree zero in l, k (see mathematical note on Section 4.8) so that, applying Euler's theorem for $r = 0$, we have:

$$l \cdot F_{ll} + k \cdot F_{lk} = 0.$$

This implies that F_{ll}, F_{lk} must have opposite signs. The same can be shown to be true for F_{kk}, F_{lk}. Thus the only sign for F_{ll} (and F_{kk}) which satisfies the convexity condition is negative. Thus we must have a diminishing marginal product of labor if there are constant returns to scale. An argument of a similar kind can be used to show that decreasing returns to scale also implies diminishing marginal products (F_{ll}, $F_{kk} < 0$).

To show that we can get *increasing* marginal product if there are increasing returns to scale, we need only look at the Cobb-Douglas function. From the note on Section 4.7, we have:

$$F_{ll} = \alpha\,(\alpha - 1)\,x/l^2 \quad \text{for the Cobb-Douglas case.}$$

If $\alpha > 1$, which necessarily implies $\alpha + \beta > 1$ (α, β both > 0) and thus increasing returns to scale, we will have $F_{ll} > 0$ and the "law" of diminishing returns will not hold.

CHAPTER 5
Section 5.4
Optimum Input Proportions

We have a production function of the form $x = F(l, k)$ and inputs l, k can be purchased at constant prices w, r, respectively. The inputs that can be purchased for some given outlay C are related by the *isocost line*

$$wl + rk = C.$$

Now suppose we fix the production level at $\bar{x}$, and consider the minimum cost method of production. We have an isoquant $F(l, k) = \bar{x}$ along with l, k are related by

$$\frac{dl}{dk} = -\frac{F_k}{F_l}.$$

We can minimize the outlay C with respect to k, using the above relationship between l and k, to obtain the standard condition for a stationary point:

$$\frac{dC}{dk} = w\frac{dl}{dk} + r = 0.$$

Substituting for $\dfrac{dl}{dk}$, this gives

$$-\frac{dl}{dk} = \frac{F_k}{F_l} = \frac{r}{w}.$$

This is the condition for the optimum input proportions that may be read as tangency between the isocost line and the isoquant or as equality of the (numerical value of) the marginal rate of substitution and the price ratio.

Input Substitution

Along the isoquant, l is determined by k. Noting this relationship, we can consider the relationship between the labor to capital ratio and the input price ratio, around a given isoquant, and with optimum input ratios for each price ratio. We have

$$\frac{d\left(\frac{l}{k}\right)}{d\left(\frac{w}{r}\right)} = \frac{d\left(\frac{l}{k}\right)}{dk} \bigg/ \frac{d\left(\frac{w}{r}\right)}{dk} .$$

Now $\qquad \dfrac{d\left(\frac{l}{k}\right)}{dk} = \dfrac{1}{k}\left(\dfrac{dl}{dk} - \dfrac{l}{k}\right) < 0$ since $\dfrac{dl}{dk} < 0$.

From the condition for optimal proportions, $\dfrac{w}{r} = -\dfrac{dk}{dl}$ so that

$$\frac{d\left(\frac{w}{r}\right)}{dk} = -\frac{d}{dk}\left(\frac{dk}{dl}\right) > 0 .$$

(See the note on Section 4.6.)

Thus the input ratio changes in the direction opposite to the input price ratio, with substitution of some of the input whose price has fallen relatively for the input whose price has risen relatively.

Section 5.5

Cost Curves

We shall confine ourselves to homogeneous functions (see note on Section 4.8) and consider variations of cost with output when inputs can be purchased without limit at fixed prices. The production function is assumed to have the form $x = F(l, k)$.

Since the least-cost method will be chosen, we will have $F_l/F_k = w/r$ for all l, k. Since w/r is constant, F_l/F_k will be constant implying, for a homogeneous function, that l/k is constant.

If l^*, k^* are the inputs used to produce some reference level x^* of output, all other optimal inputs will be given by $l = ul^*$, $k = uk^*$, where u is a variable related to the level of operation (number of "doses" in the main text).

The cost of producing output $x = F(ul^*, uk^*)$ will be a function of u given by

$$C(u) = wl + rk$$
$$= u(wl^* + rk^*)$$
$$= uC^* \quad \text{where } C^* \text{ is the cost of } x^*.$$

The level of output, x, will be given by

$$x(u) = u^r F(l^*, k^*)$$
$$= u^r x^*.$$

Eliminating u between the equations for c and x, we obtain:

$$C(x) = (C^*/x^{*1/r}) x^{1/r}$$
$$= a x^{1/r} \quad (a \text{ is constant}).$$

$C(x)$ is the equation of the *cost curve*. Writing C', C'' for the first and second derivatives of C, we have:

$$C' = \frac{1}{r} a x^{\left(\frac{1}{r} - 1\right)}$$

$$C'' = \frac{1}{r}\left(\frac{1}{r} - 1\right) a x^{\left(\frac{1}{r} - 2\right)}.$$

The curve thus has the following properties:
  (a) it passes through the origin and slopes upward $(C' > 0)$
  (b) for constant returns to scale $(r = 1)$ it is a straight line $(C'' = 0)$
  (c) for decreasing returns to scale $(r < 1)$ the slope increases with output $(C'' > 0)$, and for increasing returns to scale $(r > 1)$ the slope decreases with output $(C'' < 0)$.

Average Cost Curves

Average cost $A(x) = C(x)/x$. Thus we have:

$$A = a x^{\left(\frac{1}{r} - 1\right)}$$

$$A' = \left(\frac{1}{r} - 1\right) a x^{\left(\frac{1}{r} - 2\right)}$$

$$A'' = \left(\frac{1}{r} - 1\right)\left(\frac{1}{r} - 2\right) a x^{\left(\frac{1}{r} - 3\right)},$$

so that the average cost curve
  (a) is a horizontal straight line $(A' = A'' = 0)$ for constant returns to scale $(r = 1)$,
  (b) is rising $(A' > 0)$ for decreasing returns to scale $(r < 1)$ and falling $(A' < 0)$ for increasing returns to scale $(r > 1)$.

Section 5.6

  Marginal Cost

  If $C(x)$ is the cost function, then $C'\left(= \dfrac{dC}{dx}\right)$ is *marginal cost*. Denoting C' by $M(x)$, then the graph of $M(x)$ is the marginal cost curve. The slope of the curve is given by $M' = C''$.

  One Variable Factor

  Consider cost with k fixed, l variable, and a production function $x = F(l, k)$. The differentials of the cost and production functions are, in this case:

$$dC = w\,dl$$

$$dx = F_l dl$$

giving

$$M = C' = w/F_l \quad (MC = w/MPL \text{ in the text}).$$

  All Factors Variable

  If all inputs vary, but in optimal proportions, F_l/F_k will remain constant and equal to w/r. Taking differentials of the cost and production functions we have

$$dC = w\,dl + r\,dk$$

$$= w\,dl\left(1 + \frac{r}{w}\frac{dk}{dl}\right) = r\,dk\left(\frac{w}{r}\frac{dl}{dk} + 1\right)$$

$$dx = F_l dl + F_k dk$$

$$= F_l dl\left(1 + \frac{F_k}{F_l}\frac{dk}{dl}\right) = F_k dk\left(\frac{F_l}{F_k}\frac{dl}{dk} + 1\right).$$

  Since $F_k/F_l = r/w$, the equivalent bracketed expressions are identical in the equations for dC, dx, giving:

$$\frac{dC}{dx} = M = w/F_l = r/F_k$$

as shown in the main text.

  Rising Marginal Cost

  Returning to the case in which only one factor (l) is variable, we have:

$$M = w/F_l$$

$$M' = -\frac{w}{(F_l)^2}F_{ll}\frac{dl}{dx}$$

$$= -w\,F_{ll}/(F_l)^3 \quad \text{since } \frac{dx}{dl} = F_l \text{ when } k \text{ is constant}$$

$$> 0 \text{ if } F_{ll} < 0.$$

Marginal cost will be rising for fixed k if $F_{ii} < 0$, which will certainly be true for constant or decreasing returns to scale (see Note on Section 4.9) but may not be true for increasing returns to scale (Note on Section 4.9).

Section 5.8

Total Average and Marginal

If $y(x)$ is any function of x (y, x regarded as positive), we have

$$\text{total } y = y(x)$$

$$\text{marginal } y = y'(x) \quad \left(= \frac{dy}{dx} \right)$$

$$\text{average } y = y(x)/x.$$

The *marginal curve* plots y' against x, the *average curve* plots y/x against x. The slope of the average curve is given by

$$\frac{d}{dx} \left(\frac{y}{x} \right) = \frac{1}{x} \frac{dy}{dx} - \frac{y}{x^2}$$

$$= \frac{1}{x} \left(\frac{dy}{dx} - \frac{y}{x} \right)$$

$$\gtreqless 0 \text{ according as } \frac{dy}{dx} \gtreqless \frac{y}{x}.$$

Thus the average curve is rising at the point x, stationary, or falling, according as the marginal curve is above, intersecting, or below, the average curve at x.

CHAPTER 6

Section 6.2

The Revenue Function

Denote the revenue function by $R(x)$ or by $R(p)$, according to whether we wish to consider the independent variable as price or quantity. It is usual to deal with it in the form $R(x)$. If the firm sells to all consumers at the same price, we have

$$R(x) = p \cdot x.$$

Average revenue is $R(x)/x$, and is thus equal to p.

Marginal revenue is R' $\left(= \dfrac{dR}{dx} \right).$

Revenue and Elasticity

We have:
$$R = px$$

$$R' = p + x\frac{dp}{dx}$$

$$= p\left(1 + \frac{x}{p}\frac{dp}{dx}\right)$$

$$= p\left(1 + \frac{1}{\eta}\right)$$

where η is the elasticity of demand $\left(= \frac{p}{x}\frac{dx}{dp}\right)$. For the definition of elasticity see the note on Section 2.5.

For a horizontal demand curve, we have $\eta = -\infty$, so that $R' = p = R/x$. For inelastic demand ($|\eta| < 1$) we have $R' < 0$, so that marginal revenue is negative.

Average and Marginal Revenue

Assuming the regular slope of the demand curve, we have $\eta < 0$. Thus $R' < p$ ($=$ average revenue) unless the demand curve is horizontal. The *less* the numerical value ($|\eta|$) of the elasticity, the *greater* the distance by which the marginal revenue curve lies below the demand curve for a given value of p.

Straight-Line Demand

As shown in the note on Section 2.5, a demand curve of the form
$$x = B - bp \quad (0 \leqq x \leqq B)$$

has elasticity which varies from $-\infty$ at $p = B/b$, $x = 0$, through -1 at $p = \frac{1}{2}B/b$, $x = \frac{1}{2}B$, to 0 at $p = 0$, $x = B$. $R' = 0$ when $\eta = -1$, so that $R' = 0$ at $x = \frac{1}{2}B$ (as shown in the main text). The equation for the marginal revenue curve is easily derived. We have

$$R = px$$

$$= \frac{1}{b}(B - x)x$$

$$= \frac{1}{b}(Bx - x^2)$$

so that
$$R' = \frac{1}{b}(B - 2x).$$

This can be compared with the demand curve written in its inverse form:

$$p = \frac{1}{b}(B - x).$$

It is easily seen that the marginal revenue curve is a straight line which commences at the top point of the demand curve ($p = B/b, x = 0$) and which lies halfway between the demand curve and the vertical axis for $0 \leq x \leq \frac{1}{2}B$. It crosses the x-axis at $x = \frac{1}{2}B$, and is negative for values of x in the range $\frac{1}{2}B < x \leq B$.

The General Case

To illustrate the fact that marginal revenue, while less than price, need not be falling, the diagrams in the main text numbered 6.4 (a), (b), (c) are drawn from the following equations. The reader can check that the marginal and average revenue curves are properly related, although the marginal revenue curve is downward sloping everywhere only in diagram (a).

Figure 6.4 (a) $p = x^{-\frac{1}{2}}, R = x^{\frac{1}{2}}, R' = \frac{1}{2}x^{-\frac{1}{2}}$ ($\eta = -2$)

$$R'' = -\tfrac{1}{4}x^{-3/2} < 0 .$$

Figure 6.4 (b) $p = x^{-2}, R = x^{-1}, R' = -x^{-2}$ ($\eta = -\frac{1}{2}$)

$$R'' = 2x^{-3} > 0 .$$

Figure 6.4 (c) $p = \dfrac{4}{x} + \dfrac{x}{2} - \dfrac{x^2}{4}, R = 4 + \dfrac{x^2}{2} - \dfrac{x^3}{4}, R' = x - \dfrac{3}{4}x^2$

$$R'' = 1 - \frac{3}{2}x$$

$$> 0 \text{ for } 0 < x < \frac{2}{3}$$

$$< 0 \text{ for } x > \frac{2}{3}$$

$$\left(|\eta| \geq 1 \text{ for } x \text{ in the range } 0 \leq x \leq \frac{4}{3} \right) .$$

Section 6.5

The Profit Maximizing Output

If we have continuous cost and revenue functions, $C(x)$, $R(x)$, the profit function is:

$$\pi(x) = R(x) - C(x) .$$

The most profitable output will be at a stationary point of (x) in the general case, that is, where

$$\frac{d\pi}{dx} = R' - C' = 0 .$$

At this output, $R' = C'$ (marginal revenue equals marginal cost).

If the firm faces a horizontal revenue curve (perfect competition), we have $R' = p$ (see note on Section 6.2), so that $C' = p$ at the most profitable output.

Since $C' \geqq 0$ in all but very exceptional cases (if then), we cannot have a stationary point where $R' < 0$. We will have $R' < 0$ when $|\eta| < 1$ (see note on Section 6.2), so a firm will not have its most profitable output at a point of inelastic demand, except as a corner solution.

There may be no stationary point of $\pi(x)$, in which case we have a corner solution, discussed in the main text.

To ensure that a stationary point of $\pi(x)$ is a maximum and not a minimum, the second order condition needs to be satisfied. That is:

$$\frac{d^2\pi}{dx^2} = R'' - C'' < 0 \, .$$

Assuming that the marginal cost curve is flat or upward sloping, $C'' \geqq 0$, so the second order condition will be satisfied if $R'' \leqq 0$ (provided we do not have *both* $C'' = 0$ and $R'' = 0$), that is, if the marginal revenue curve is horizontal or downward sloping. It is also possible for the condition to be satisfied with an upward sloping marginal revenue curve provided $R'' < C''$ — that is, if the marginal revenue curve cuts the marginal cost curve *from above* at the intersection.

ANSWERS TO NUMERICAL
EXERCISES

CHAPTER 2
Ex(1) (i), *C;* (ii), *A;* (iii), *B;* (iv), *D*
Ex(2)

Price	20	21	22	23	24	25
Quantity	209	179	159	139	119	89

Equilibrium: 139 tons at $23/ton.
Ex(3) New schedule—89 tons at all prices. Elasticity is zero, equilibrium at 89 tons, $22/ton.

CHAPTER 4
Ex (1) (ii) P_2 is inefficient.
Ex (2) P_1-P_3, 0.75 man-hrs/machine-hr; P_3-P_4, 2.0; P_4-P_5, 6.0.
Ex (3) At 84 machine-hrs, 42 man-hrs, P_3 will be used at level 10.5. At 84 machine-hrs, 72 man-hrs, P_4 will be used at level 12. The increase in output is 1.5 tons, the marginal product of labor is $1.5/30 = 0.05$ tons/man-hour.

CHAPTER 5
Ex (1) Costs ($) for each process and prices:

Process	Prices			
	(a)	(b)	(c)	(d)
P_1	9.5	8.5	16	23.5
P_2	*9.0	7.0	12	17.0
P_3	9.75	*6.75	10.5	14.25
P_4	12.5	7.5	*10.0	12.5
P_5	24.0	12.0	12.0	*12.0

(i) See table above. (ii) * *indicates least cost process, average cost is 1/10 of cost in table.*

318

Ex (2)

Output	Total Cost	Average Cost
100	67.5	0.675
200	135	0.675
300	225	1.00
400	345	1.05
500	465	1.08

(Outputs above 300 tons obtained by using P_4 for first 300 tons, P_5 which needs no capital for additional output.)

Ex (3)

Output	Total Cost	Average Cost
100	90	0.90
200	195	0.975
300	375	1.250
400	615	1.538
500	855	1.710

(The important difference between this and (2) is that average cost starts rising at a lower output. This is because the least cost process here is P_2, rather than P_3 as in (2). Since P_2 has a higher capital/labor ratio, the capital limitation becomes apparent at a lower output.)

Ex (4)

Output	Average Cost			Marginal Cost
	(i)	(ii)	(iii)	same for (i) and (iii)
0				1
1	1	3	4	1
2	1	1.5	2.5	1
3	1	1	2.0	1
4	1	1	1.75	1
5	1	1	1.60	1.6
6	1.1	1.1	1.60	2.5
7	1.3	1.3	1.73	3.7
8	1.6	1.6	1.98	5.2
9	2.0	2.0	2.33	7.0
10	2.5	2.5	2.80	

CHAPTER 6

Ex 1) (a) The short-run supply curve is derived directly from the table by replacing the marginal cost heading by price, and multiplying the quantity figures by 1,000.

(b) Long-run supply is horizontal at price $1.

Ex (2)   Output 4,000; price 6; profit 16,000.

Ex (3)   Output 5,000; price 6; profit 20,000; more elastic.

Ex (4)   Monopolist's price will be $5.5. This is maximum small-firm cost
for competitive output to exceed monopoly output.

Ex (5)   (a) 343 (approx). (b) 360.

Ex (6)

(a)

Wage	Man-Hrs.
1	5
2	4
3	3
4	2

(b)

Price	Quantity
0.50	10
0.67	14
1.00	16
2.00	17

INDEX

Activity 61
Activity analysis 60n
Adjustment, speed of 247–248
Advertising 160n, 172n
Aggregate behavior 11n, 182n
All-or-nothing offer 234
Amortization 131
Arbitrage 49–51, 51–52
  as production 50n
Arrow, K. J. 242n, 260n
Attainment of equilibrium 247
Average
  cost 106–107, 114–129
  cost curve 106, 108, 114–129
  product 85
  revenue 140, 142–145
Average, total and marginal relations
  120–125, 314

Backup theorems 250–251
Balances, money 295–296
Balances, real 298
Bargaining 216–218, 233–235
Basic market model 40–42
Becker, G. S. 287n
Behavior line 201
Benefits 93
  external 95
  private 95
Black market 36
Boulding, K. E. 31
Budget constraint 191–196, 224
  intertemporal 281
Budget line 99, 191–192, 198–199,
  210–211

Capita¹ 60
  fixed 129–132, 288–290, 293
  goods 225n

Capital—*cont.*
  human 228, 286–288, 291
  as input 60
  -intensive 254
  inventory 130
  market 271, 289
  working 148
Career decision 286–288
Cartel 170
Centralized control 244
C.E.S. production function 308
Ceteris paribus 10
Chamberlin, E. H. 159n
Characteristics, of goods 183–185,
  205, 218–221, 229
Cobb-Douglas production function
  307–309
Cobweb market model 43–48, 304–
  305
Cohen, K. J. 178
Collapse and instability 248
Collusion 170
Comparative statics 17
Compensated price change 204
Compensation 262
Competition
  "cutthroat" 167
  and efficiency 270–276
  imperfect 141, 167
  market 41–42
  monopolistic 159n, 167n
  and monopoly 164–166
  non-price 172n
  oligopolistic 139, 139n, 166–172
  perfect 141, 153–159, 247–248
  pure 141n
Competitive economy 238
  efficiency of 273–276
  equilibrium in 242–243

Competitive economy—*cont.*
  growth rate of 293–295
  role of prices and markets in 243–246
  stability of 247–249
Competitive market 9
Complements 56
Composition of output 265–270
Compulsory marketing 36
Computerized economy 37–39, 244
Computers, traders as 39–40
Conservatism 276n
Consistent preferences 186
Consumers 181–185, 237, 281–288
Contract curve 216–218, 253, 254, 264
Convex set 69
Convexity
  of indifference curves 192–193
  of isoquants 69
Corner solution 27, 214
Corporation, giant 176–178
Costs and cost curves 93–132
  arbitrage 50–51
  average 106–108, 114–129
  explicit 94
  external 94–95
  fixed capital 129–132
  general 93–95, 145–148, 311–312
  implicit 94
  with limited input 109–113
  long-run 105–108
  with minimum outlay 114–119
  production 95–97
  selling 160n
Cournot, A. 168
Cross elasticity 25, 55, 301
Cyert, R. M. 178

Decentralized control 243–246
Decreasing cost 88
Demand 11
  consumer 206–210
  curve 11–14, 16
  elasticity of 22–23, 23–25, 25–26, 300–302
  excess 29–30
  for inputs 172–176
  for labor 172–176
  for money 296–297

Depreciation 131–132
Dictatorial welfare function 259
Differentiated goods 185, 218–221
Diminishing
  marginal product 82–83
  marginal rate of substitution 72, 204
  returns 83
Discount of future 282
Disposable income 224n
Distortions in economy 273–274
Distribution 223–224
  of income 224–226, 234–235, 255–256
  of wealth 226, 255n, 276
Dividends 177, 225, 294–295
Domar, E. D. 294n
Dorfman, R. 246n, 249n
Dual 246n
Duopoly 167–172
Duplication of production processes 89
Dynamics 17, 43–49, 291n, 302–307

Econometrics 6, 6n
Economies of scale 88–91, 127–129
Edgeworth, F. Y. 39, 40n, 214n
Edgeworth box diagram 214–218, 252–256, 264
Efficiency, economic 63–64, 262–265, 271–276
Efficiency, technical 62–64, 67, 69, 72, 127–128, 263
  in consumption 205, 220
Efficient allocation 262–265, 270
Efficient production, range of 88
Elasticity 20–23, 300–302
  cross- 25, 55, 301
  curve of constant 24–25, 301–302
  and expenditure 25, 302–303
  income- 25, 202–203, 301
  and revenue 141–142
  of straight lines 23–24, 302–303
Endogenous 10
Engel, E. 201n
Engel curve 13, 201–202
Engel's Law 203
Entry 138, 153, 162–163, 229
"Equation counting" 241, 241n
Equilibrium 42

Equilibrium—*cont.*
  attainment of 247
  boundary 26–27
  of competitive economy 242–243
  of consumer 195–196
  of firm 152–153, 288–291
  general 237–249, 251–256, 290n
  growth 293–295
  interior 27
  investment 289–291
  market 6–7, 39–43
  of money market 297–298
  of related markets 56
  stability of, *see* Stability
Essential good 202
Excess demand 29–30, 42–43, 49,
  303–304
Excess supply 9, 30–31, 42–43, 49,
  303–304
Exchange 214–217
Excise taxes 274–275
Exogenous 10
Externalities 94–95, 261–262, 275,
  280, 294n
Ezekiel, M. 43n

Factor 225, 237
  intensity 253–254
  of production 223
  reversal 254
  see also Input
Feedback, in dynamic process 42, 43
Financing of production 148–149,
  290
Firm 137–138
  costs of 145–148
  demand for inputs by 172–176
  financing of 148–149, 290
  impersonal nature of 137, 181–182
  and industry 156, 156n, 157–159
  intertemporal decisions of 288–291
  investment decisions of 289–291
  large 159–164, 176–178
  monopolistic 159–164
  oligopolistic 166–172
  perfectly competitive 153–159
  revenue of 139–149
  size of 146, 157n
  welfare status of 137, 182
Fixed capital 129–132, 288–290, 293

Fixed cost or outlay 93, 115
Fixed input, production with 80–88
Flow input 130
Free good 28
Friedman, M. 285n

Galbraith, J. K. 176n, 275n
Games, theory of 139, 139n
General equilibrium 237–249, 251–
  256, 290n
Giffen good 208, 208n
Global stability 248
Good(s)
  and "bad" 188, 188n
  characteristics analysis of 183–185,
    205, 218–221, 229
  and commodity 183
  differentiated 185
  essential 202, 203
  free 28
  Giffen 185
  inferior 200, 201, 203
  luxury 202, 203
  new 218–221
  normal 200, 203
  number of different 243n
Government, role of 238, 259, 261n
Growth 293–295

Harrod, R. F. 294n
Hicks, J. R. 297n
Homogeneity, of production function
  78–79, 308–309
Household 182–183

Impatience 282, 292
Imperfect competition 141, 159–178,
  242, 273–275
Income
  -consumption curve 200–201
  distribution of 224–226, 234–235,
    255–256
  effect 198–203, 208
  elasticity 202, 301
  as market circumstance 8, 11, 11n
  permanent 285
  real 199
  sources of 224–226
  transitory 285

Indifference   185
  curves   188–191, 192–194
  map   190–191
Indivisibilities   88–91, 127–129, 165–
    166, 273
Industry   156–159, 157n
Inferior good   200, 201, 203
Information   243–246
  prices as   245–246
Information theory   245n
Input(s)
  coefficients   250
  demand for   172–176
  efficient allocation of   263–265
  limitation   109–114
  optimum proportions of   101–102,
    310–311
  -output analysis   64n, 249–250
  return to variable   79–88
  substitution between   70–72
Interest, rate of   131–132, 284–285,
    289–291, 297–298
Intermediate good   130, 223, 224n,
    225n, 237
Intertemporal decisions   279–295
Inventory   130
Investment   129n, 228, 286–288, 289–
    292
Isocost curve   98–101
Iso-outlay line   99
Isoproduct curve   67–70, 73–75, 306–
    308
Isoquant   67–70, 73–75, 306–308
Iso-utility curve   196

Joint products   61

Keynesian models   297
Kibbutz   224
"Kinked" demand curve   172n

Labor
  demand for   172–176
  income from   224–226
  -leisure choice   210–226
  marginal product of   79–88
  marginal revenue product of   173,
    174
  market   226–230, 232–235
  supply of   182, 212–214

Lancaster, K. J.   218n
Land, as primary factor   225, 230,
    231
Least cost presumption   96
Least cost process, choice of   96–98,
    101–105
Leontief, W. W.   64n, 249
Lerner, A. P.   276
L'Esperance, W. L.   8, 12n
Liberalism   276n
Linear programming   29n, 60n, 246n
Little, I. M. D.   276
Luxury good   202, 203

Macroeconomics   1–2, 230, 249
Macro-microeconomics   250–256
Maintenance costs   131–132
Marginal
  cost   110, 111–114, 313–314
  product of an input   81–88, 309–
    310
  rate of substitution   72, 194–195
  rate of time preference   282
  rate of transformation   267–268
  revenue   140, 142–145
  revenue product   173, 175
Market(s)   35–36
  basic model of   40–42
  circumstances   5, 8, 10
  cobweb model   43–48, 304–306
  competitive   11, 37–40, 156–157
  computerized   37–39
  dynamics of   43–49, 303–306
  equilibrium   6, 9 14–20, 37–40
  labor   226–230, 232–235
  models of   37–40
  money   297–298
  perfect   40
  period   7, 44
  related   55–56
  role in economy   224, 237–238,
    246
  stability of   42–49, 303–306
  watermelon example   7–16, 240,
    240n
Marshall, A.   156n
Minimum outlay, costs with   114–119
Minimum wage   229–230
Mishan, E. J.   277
Money   295–299

Monopolistic competition 159, 159n, 167n
Monopoly 159–166, 232, 274
and competition 164–166
degree of 274
profit 164
and welfare 273–276
Monopsony 232
Morgenstern, O. 139n, 197n

Negative feedback 42
Neumann, J. von 139n, 197n
Nonsatiation 187n
Normal good 200
Normal profit 231

Obsolescence 131
Offer curve 209
Oligopoly 139, 139n, 166–172
Oligopsony 232
Opportunity cost 94, 130, 132, 230

Pareto, V. 226, 261n
Pareto criterion 261
Pareto-optimal 261, 270, 273, 275–276
Pareto's Law 226n
Partial analysis 10, 240
Paternalistic welfare function 259
Patinkin, D. 298n
Perfect competition 141, 153–159, 247–248
Perfect market 40
Permanent income 285
Plans, of traders 5–6, 38–39
Point supply 28–31, 161, 234
Positive feedback 43
Predecision by traders 38
Preference, consumer 185–191
intertemporal 281–285
revealed 186
and welfare 187, 260
Price(s)
-consumption curve 209
determination in market 10, 37–43, 246
discrimination 161n
equilibrium 6
general level of 297–299
as information 245–246

Price(s)—*cont.*
intertemporal 284
relative 241–242
setter 161
shadow- 246, 246n, 273
taker 161
uniformity assumption 42
and welfare 270, 276
Private ownership economy 225
Product curves 86–88
Production 50n, 59–60
costs 95–98
efficient 61–64, 91, 263
function 72–73, 307–308
possibility curve 265
theory of 64–91, 306–310
Profit 138, 225, 231–232
-maximization 149–153, 316–317
Pure competition 141n

Qualitative information 20
Qualitative statements 20
Quantitative statements 20
Quasi-rent 231
Quirk, J. 277

Raw materials 64
Real balance effect 298–299
Real income 199
Real wage 210
Regret 292, 292n
Rent 230–232
Research and development 291
Resources 225, 237
efficient allocation of 263–265
Returns, diminishing 83
Returns to scale 65–77, 308
constant 77–79, 91, 106–107, 266
decreasing 79, 107–108, 266n
increasing 79, 89–91, 107–108, 266n
Returns to variable input 79–88, 309–310
Revealed preference 186
Revenue (of firm) 139–145, 314–316
Risk 280
Rothenburg, J. 276

Sales maximization 177–178

Sales taxes   274–275
Samuelson, P. A.   186n, 246n, 249n
Saposnik, R.   277
Satisficing   177
Saving   285–286
Scarce (economic definition)   28n
Second best policies   274
Selling costs   160n
Separated markets   161n
Shadow prices   246, 246n, 273
Short-run   109
Sign convention (elasticities)   22–23
Size (of firm)   146, 157n
Skill differential   227–229
Social welfare function   260, 260n
Socialist economies   224, 244, 276n
Solow, R.   246n, 249n
Soviet-type economies   29, 30–31,
    224, 244
Speculation   51–55
Stability
  of competitive equilibrium   247–
    249
  market   42–49, 303–307
  and speculation   53–54
State of nature inputs   76
Static models, limitations of   279-281
Stigler, G. J.   133
Stock market   36, 53
Straight line demand and supply   23–
    24, 143–144, 168–171, 302
Structural unemployment   230
Substitutes, gross   55
Substitution
  in consumption   203–206, 221
  effect   204
  efficiency-   205
  input-   61, 70–72, 102–105, 311
  marginal rate of   72, 194–195, 263
  output- or product-   61
  rate of   71
Suits, D. B.   8
Supply   11
  of competitive industry   155–159
  curve   13–14, 16, 155–156
  elasticity of   20–24
  of labor   212–214, 232–235
  of monopoly   161
  point-   28–31, 161, 234
  of savings   283–286

Tatonnement   40
Technical efficiency   62–64, 67, 69,
    72, 127–128, 263
Technological change   62, 293
Technology   61
Time   7, 60, 279
  arbitrage over   51–52
  consumer decisions over   281–288
  firms' decisions over   129–132,
    288–292
  welfare over   292–293
Time preference   281–285, 294
Traders   39–40, 48–49
Transfer income   225
Transformation curve   265–267
Transformation, marginal rate of
    267–268
Transitivity, of preferences   186
Transitory income   285
Transport problem   39n
Transport, as production   59

Uncertainty   280
Uncompensated price change   206,
    209
Unemployment   230, 243, 263
U-shaped cost curves   125–126, 146–
    148, 155
Utility   186–197

Variable cost   111, 115
Voluntary exchange requirement   35–
    37
Voting paradox   260n

Wages, determination of   226–230,
    255–256
Walras, L.   39, 39n, 40, 40n, 241, 241n
Wealth   226
  distribution of   226, 255n, 276
  effect   213
Welfare   36, 186–187, 259–262
  and efficiency   262
  individual as judge of   259–260,
    292–293
  interpersonal comparisons of   260
  intertemporal   292–295
  Pareto criterion for   261
Working capital   148